A Vintage Year

Helen S. Vandervort

PublishAmerica

Baltimore

First printing

ISBN: 1-59129-270-0
PUBLISHED BY PUBLISHAMERICA BOOK PUBLISHERS
www.publishamerica.com
Baltimore

Printed in the United States of America

To be crushed in the winepress of passion.
Gabriel Biel, 1425-1495

From wine what sudden friendship springs!
John Gay, 1688-1732

little about himself. She knew only he had a degree in Enology from the University of California at Davis and had worked for the Steiners the past three years as manager, grower and vintner of the small winery.

Hawk's map was accurate and easy to follow, although Selby had misgivings when she first looked at it scribbled on a scrap of paper. As per his instructions, she turned right at the Rickreall Junction, following the narrow county road to Zena Road, then Spring Valley and, finally, the second gravel road on the left. There was the LillyHill Winery sign, small but beautifully carved and touched with color, a spray of Lillies of the Valley in one corner.

Parking Old Blue by the side of the road, Selby read the sign twice again, her dry mouth making it difficult to swallow. Whatever fate or circumstance had in store for her, she'd find out today. She was always one to put her family first; perhaps now it was her turn. Selby told herself from now on she'd speak out, stand up for herself, and be more assertive. But for the moment, she needed to steady herself before seeing the vineyard that had been given her by a woman she barely knew. What had Lilly Steiner seen in Selby?

Taking a deep breath, she continued a strange journey that started two weeks ago when she was summoned to Mr. Levy's office for the reading of the will. The scene sprang to mind with all its surreal sights and sounds from Estelle Jacobs' verbal abuse of the attorney to the tears and whining of her five-year-old daughter Little Lilly. All who were gathered for the distribution of wealth were in shock when they heard that a stranger was to receive the bulk of the estate.

Selby shook her head to erase the outrage expressed by the relatives on hearing the bequests, and continued driving up the graveled lane, where she caught sight of a gray Victorian house nestled in a grove of oak trees high on a distant knoll. As the road dipped and curved around a low hill, she lost sight of the house, but came upon several metal-roofed buildings with loading docks and wide sliding doors gleaming in the emerging sunshine. Another LillyHill Winery sign over a narrow door was marked "Office." Parking next to a muddy jeep, Selby stepped out of Old Blue and looked at the acres of manicured earth; it was quietly, mysteriously beautiful.

In addition to the Jeep, a pick-up and a flatbed truck with stake sides were parked near the loading area. The office door was unlocked but no one was there; however, she could hear muffled voices and metallic sounds from an adjoining area. Carefully opening the interior door, she found Hawk and two other men struggling with a valve on a huge stainless-steel tank. Standing quietly, she admired Hawk's glistening bare torso. In spite of the cold, he was sweating, as well as being wet from the waist down. He wore a red baseball cap turned with the bill backwards. This handsome young man would be her partner in the vineyard if she accepted this strange and wonderful gift that was more than the vineyard, more than she could get her mind around at the moment.

By the rough language and the mess on the floor, Selby could tell this wasn't a good time to come calling, even though she had been invited. Hawk let out several expletives and turned the wrench one last time, saying, "There, you son-of-a-bitch!" The other men laughed, adding comments in Spanish to which Hawk responded in kind. It was then Hawk saw Selby standing in the doorway.

"Oh, I forgot," he said, wiping the sweat from his face with a muscular forearm. "That's okay. Come on while I get cleaned up; then we'll go up to the house." He pulled on a sweatshirt, saying to one of the men, "Call Fiona and tell her we'll be there in ten minutes."

Striding by Selby and out the door, he looked back to see if she was following. "We'll take the Jeep. I want to stop by my quarters and change." With that, he leaped gracefully into the vehicle, while Selby struggled with its high entry, hoisting her suit skirt up to mid-thigh for the climb. Hawk noticed and admired the exposed legs.

The Jeep jerked and bounced as he drove along a rutted alley in back of the warehouses. Beyond was a low red barn with living quarters over the tack room and garage at one end of the structure.

"You might as well come in and see where the hired hand lives if you're planning to own LillyHill," he said, sliding the Jeep to a stop and leaping out. "Come on. I won't bite."

Offended by his remark and attitude, Selby put on her 'mother face,' the one she used when one of her sons got out of line. Who does this kid think he is? This was hardly a good beginning for business partners, she thought.

Hawk bounded up a steep staircase built on the outside of the structure, waiting on the landing for her; he opened the door, motioning her inside. The apartment was about the size of her duplex unit, simply furnished and neat. It smelled pleasantly male with a hint of freshly ground coffee. Without inviting her to sit, he strode into the bedroom, leaving the door ajar. The combination living-dining-kitchen area had windows on three sides. To the north she could see the gray house on the knoll; the south and west windows overlooked the winery and some of the vineyards. She could hear dresser drawers opening and closet doors slamming; then she heard the shower. Selby thought he was a rather rude young man. How old is he? Thirty-something? Not much older than her twin sons, now twenty-seven and gone from home for nearly ten years. Only her youngest son, nineteen- year-old Justin—a freshman at the community college—still lived with her.

She wandered around the room, admiring winery posters and photographs of wineries. One enlarged photo of an attractive brunette with two young children was signed, "Love, Tracy." Wife and kids? Ex-wife? Girlfriend? Relative? She perused his bookshelves and the pile of magazines on a battered pine chest that served as a coffee table. He had an eclectic taste in reading, from viticulture bulletins to a biography of a President and a current techo-thriller.

She was startled when he entered the room, smelling of cologne and buckling his belt. He grabbed a faded denim jacket off the back of a chair, saying, "Ready for lunch? We'd better hurry. Fiona doesn't like to be kept waiting."

He was wearing a black turtleneck sweater that accentuated his broad shoulders; clean jeans clung to his slim hips and powerful thighs. His wet hair was pulled back into a small ponytail. Selby wondered why she was so interested in his appearance, but she continued her examination, noting that his gray reptile riding boots had pointed toes and doggin' heels. Whatever the reason, she felt particularly delicate and vulnerable next to this handsome, well-built young man. If he's trying to intimidate me, she thought, he's doing a great job. And that's silly; at forty-five, I shouldn't let anyone get the best of me.

The sun had done its work on the high, thin clouds, leaving the January sky a faded blue, the air softer now. Regardless, the open Jeep ride was cold and Selby clutched her thin coat with one hand as she held on to the frame of the doorless vehicle with the other. The narrow gravel lane curved up the hill to a grove of oaks that protected the house from summer heat and winter winds. Selby got her first close look at the residence as they pulled into a paved parking area in front of a triple garage. A covered porch wrapped the house; silver-gray shingles and white gingerbread trim gave the three-story home a classic Victorian look, even though it was only ten years old. Selby stared at the house, in awe of its size and design. Hawk touched her arm, steering her around to the front verandah, where Fiona McDermott waited at the door.

"Welcome to LillyHill," Fiona said with a stiff smile. "Please come in, Mrs. Browning. Paul. Lunch is ready. We'll tour the house after you eat. Perhaps you'd like to freshen up after your trip," she said. The housekeeper turned briskly on the heel of her sturdy shoe, her Black Watch pleated plaid skirt flaring slightly; a navy blue Shetland cardigan sweater over a prim white blouse completed her outfit. She was every inch the English housekeeper Lilly Steiner had called friend and companion. Selby followed her to the powder room door.

"Thank you," Selby said nervously. "I appreciate the opportunity to…ah, we didn't get the chance at the attorney's office, ah, Mr. Levy's office…to get acquainted." Selby felt like a complete idiot; the words tumbling out were making little sense. The housekeeper stared at Selby through thick, rimless glasses, then turned away, leaving Selby at the door of the elegantly appointed powder room.

CHAPTER TWO

While smoothing down her wind-blown pixie cut and touching up her lipstick, Selby wondered whether Fiona would stay on at LillyHill as noted in the Trust. How strange it must be for the housekeeper to accept a new owner. Then there was the issue of what to call her new partner—Paul or Hawk? It seemed as if the people she'd met couldn't agree on what to call him. She'd have to ask which he preferred, but his dark good looks and arched nose seemed appropriate for the nickname. She wondered if she looked like a bird? A sparrow? "I hope not," she said to her reflection. "I'd like to be a Bird of Paradise; well, who knows?"

Feeling tidy again, Selby returned to the spacious living room. Hawk was saying something about a broken valve on a fermenting tank that they had just washed and how he had to crawl around on the wet floor to find something that had blown off. That certainly explained his disheveled appearance this morning. Fiona seemed to be enjoying the story, laughing and tossing her head in a flirtatious manner, but stopped when Selby appeared in the archway to the living room.

Fiona said, "Ah. You're here. I've set luncheon in the dining room. Lilly did not like meals to be informal. Please follow me and I'll serve." Selby noted Fiona's stiff back and tightly permed gray hair, the finishing touches to this 60-ish woman. What bird is she, Selby wondered. Buzzard? No, that's unkind. Owl? No. A Shrike? Yes.

Two places were set across from each other at the large linen-covered table. Hawk held a chair for Selby, and then took the other one. "Isn't Fiona going to eat with us?" Selby whispered.

"Ask her; she probably will," Hawk said, flipping open the white linen napkin. Fiona returned with a tray holding individual homemade chicken pot pies, fruit salad and rolls.

"Please join us, Fiona," Selby said. "I'd like to get acquainted."

Pausing, as if to think it over, Fiona agreed and quickly set herself a place at the head of the table. Conversation was slow to come and quite formal.

Selby complimented Fiona on the lunch and thanked her for the opportunity to see the house. Hawk and Fiona reminisced about the nice things Frank and Lilly Steiner had done for them, little stories that gave Selby insight into the lives of two people she hardly knew, yet who entrusted Lilly Hill to her care.

Hawk seemed to know Selby felt left out of the conversation; he turned to her and said, "Tell us about your family, Selby."

"My youngest son, Justin, is a freshman at the community college, where I worked until last year until my position was eliminated," she explained. "My others two sons, Mike and Steve, are twins. Mike is in the Army, stationed in Germany, and Steve drives for Blue Line Freight." She paused and smiled at Hawk and Fiona, wondering if they were truly interested or just being polite. "Oh, and I have a two-year-old granddaughter, Amanda; she belongs to Mike and Rhonda. Steve isn't married." This all sounded so ordinary, so boring.

Fiona said, "Mr. Levy said you are a widow."

"Yes. For just over a year." Selby wasn't ready to share anything more personal than that at this time; it still hurt too much.

Again there was an uncomfortable pause. Clearing his throat, Hawk said, "Tell me again how you knew the Steiners."

Selby's first thought was that he hadn't been listening when she'd explained that a few days ago after the bizarre scene in the attorney's office. Then she realized he was again making an effort to ease this difficult meeting.

"I met Frank and Lilly when their son, Arthur, died," Selby explained, sipping from the crystal water goblet. "As you know, Arthur taught botany at the local community college; I worked in the Development Office. Arthur was a friendly, generous man; he kept all the secretaries in flowers from the greenhouse that served as a science lab for agriculture students. We often talked gardening; it's one of my passions."

Fiona solemnly nodded her head, saying, "Yes, he was a fine boy, very loving to Frank and Lilly. His illness was so troublesome; he just seemed to fade away."

The three luncheon guests were quiet, their thoughts going back to Arthur's strange illness. By the time the doctors made the correct diagnosis, it was too late. Arthur had been one of the first AIDS cases local doctors had seen; medications were few and untried at that time.

Selby broke the uncomfortable silence by continuing her story. "The Steiners called the college's Development Office after Arthur's funeral and asked to meet with the Director to set up an endowed scholarship in their son's name. Mr. Walling, the director, was away at the time, and, as his Administrative Assistant, I met with them. I believe they were in their late seventies then, and I didn't want to ask them to come back later."

"Yes," Fiona sighed. "He was their only son. Arthur's death nearly killed them."

"I had the same feeling." Selby said. "Anyway, working with the college's attorney, we set up an endowment for a half million dollars, the largest gift ever pledged to the institution. The Steiners agreed to give half the amount at that time and put the remaining amount in their Will. After that, I kept in touch with them through phone calls and personal notes over the intervening years—to keep them abreast of the endowment account. Then, when Mr. Steiner died, I made sure Lilly knew of remembrances in his honor that went into the endowment. Finally, when I lost my job, I wrote her a note saying that I would be leaving the college. However, she occasionally called me at home, just to talk. I think she was lonely."

Fiona said, begrudgingly Selby thought, "She felt you were a link to Arthur."

An uncomfortable silence followed. Finally, Selby made an effort to broach the issue of Lilly's state of mind. "Fiona, I feel very strange about the bequest; I need to make sure that it really is what Lilly wanted. I understand that you were more than a housekeeper for the Steiners, that you were a close friend, too. Could you tell me anything about Lilly's thoughts or state of mind during her last few months?" Selby said.

Fiona stared at Selby, analyzing the question. Putting down her fork, she said, "Lilly liked you. I'm sure she wouldn't have made the bequest if she didn't want it that way." She sounded defiant that anyone would question Lilly's faculties. "Her mind was perfectly fine until the last day or so when she slipped into a coma." Tears filled Fiona's eyes and she dabbed at them with the corner of her napkin. "Frank and Lilly talked about what should happen to Lilly Hill after..." Fiona paused to gather her emotions. She clenched her jaw and continued. "Lilly and Frank didn't like their relatives, especially Estelle; she's a greedy woman who never had the time of day for either of them. Just because their obnoxious child is named after Lilly, well, that cut no ice with the Steiners."

Selby recalled the tense scene with Estelle Jacobs, her husband, Alan, and the child in the attorney's office when the Trust was read. Estelle's indignant response, the poor child's tears, and the Jacobs' lawyers whispering in the background made for a very confusing and uncomfortable situation.

Fiona paused, quietly placing her coffee cup in its saucer, wondering if she were being too candid with this stranger who would soon own LillyHill. I don't want this woman here, but that's what Lilly wanted, she thought. There's nothing I can do about it—or is there?

"Please go on," Selby said, lightly touching Fiona's wrist. "I haven't agreed to accept the bequest yet. I need to understand all I can before I make a decision."

Fiona shook her head as if to say she couldn't talk about it any more. "If you are finished with lunch, I'll show you the house," she said, pushing her chair back. Hawk and Selby rose, too, exchanging glances.

"I've got some phone calls to make while you gals look at the house; I'll use the phone in the family room," Hawk said. "Great lunch, Fiona. You're my favorite cook!"

Fiona beamed at him, denying that it was anything special. She then led Selby through the antique-filled home. While the house looked like a classic Victorian, it had all the modern conveniences, wiring, and plumbing. Selby loved the covered porch that circled the house; a second-story sun deck protected the back entrance. Inside were three floors filled with livability in formal and informal areas.

"Frank had it built for Lilly as a retreat for their golden years and as an investment home for Arthur. But when Arthur died..." Fiona's throat closed up, stifling the sob that threatened. "This is...was...Frank and Lilly's room," she said, opening double doors to the master suite with its sitting room, sun deck, elegant bathroom, large dressing room with vanity and two walk-in closets. "I live upstairs. If you'll come this way."

On the third floor, Fiona had a bedroom, bath and separate sitting room. The views from the dormer windows were spectacular, overlooking the Coast Range to the west, the Cascade Mountains to the east and the rolling terrain of Lilly Hill Vineyard and surrounding farms to the north and south. "Oh, this is lovely," Selby said. "You must be very content here; I know I would be." Fiona nodded, but did not reply.

The tour finished in the family room where Hawk was talking heatedly on the phone with someone about parts and labor costs. Hanging up, he said to Selby, "I'll show you what's in the garage, and then we'll tour the winery."

What were in the garage were a silver Mercedes sedan and a white Ford Explorer. "Oh, my," was all Selby could say. The chauffeur's quarters over the garage would be perfect for Justin, if they moved here.

As they toured the winery, Hawk kept up a one-sided dialogue about making wine. "It's been said that the winemaker is a warrior; he's in a continual fight with nature—the weather, insects, disease, rot, bad luck. Winemaking relies heavily on the instruments of the chemist and the whims of nature."

He showed her the stainless-steel tanks and French oak barrels used for aging the wine, the crusher-stemmer, and the punching-down tool needed to stir under the solid cap of fermenting grapes. He bombarded her with statistics: the number of gallons in each of the huge stainless steel tanks, degree-days as the standard measurement of climatic heat, the tons of grapes grown per acre. "Enough!" Selby laughed. "I hope there isn't going to be a test after the tour. Oh, by the way, who were the men working with you this morning?"

"Robert Aznar and his son, Rio. Robert works full-time for us and Rio part-time. Rio had a head injury when he was young, so he's a bit slow mentally, but strong as an ox and a willing worker. Robert gives him things to do within his ability. Rio's a nice guy and very good at some things."

"How old is Rio?"

"Around 20, I think. The accident happened about ten years ago at a Little League game. As I recall, Robert said Rio was catching that afternoon and the batter threw the bat after hitting a pitch. Rio's had headaches and short-term memory problems ever since."

"He's fortunate to have a caring family. Where do they live?"

"About two miles from here on a little farm. Adelina, Robert's wife, is a great cook. She worked for the Steiners sometimes."

Selby nodded as she assimilated the information, saying, "I guess I'm going to have to do some reading about the wine industry if you and I are to be working partners. I hope you'll recommend some books."

"Does that mean you're going to become Mistress of Lilly Hill?" He seemed to have a smirk on his face; Selby was unimpressed with this rude young man.

"Never Mistress of Lilly Hill. Perhaps owner-in-residence. I'll let you know when I decide," she said firmly, finally feeling that she was back in control of herself and this unusual situation. "I do have one last question: Why are you called Hawk?"

He smiled and shook his head, as if it were a very silly question. "It was a name given to me in college—not a very original nickname, but it stuck. A Kestrel is a swallow-like falcon; technically, it's not a hawk. It's a small bird that hovers over its prey with rapid wing beats."

"And are you a bird of prey?" Selby asked with a smile, but he did not reply.

He walked Selby to her car, noting her gesture of smoothing down her skirt when she was nervous, of brushing a lock of hair off her forehead, of looking directly into his eyes when he spoke to her. She was an interesting woman. What kind of business partner would she be? She barely came up to his shoulder. He could pick her up with one arm. What would she be like in bed? Out of bounds, Hawk, he thought. This is strictly business.

CHAPTER THREE

Fiona was talking to herself. The habit had become more pronounced since Lilly's death. After all, they had been together for nearly 50 years. Fiona had come to work for the Steiners when they were newlyweds living in New York. Now she was all that was left. She hadn't done heavy cleaning for years, but was more of a lady's maid to Lilly. As the three of them—Frank, Lilly and Fiona—had grown older together; companionship, light housework and fixing simple meals became Fiona's role.

Clearing the luncheon dishes from the table, Fiona muttered a one-sided conversation with her dead employer. "Lilly, you've made a mistake giving LillyHill to a stranger. I know you like her. I know you think I'm too old and not educated enough to own the winery, but why a stranger? Why didn't you give it to Paul? Of course I'm glad you didn't give it to that nasty Estelle. Greedy bitch, that's what she is. And that nasty child of hers. Little Lilly, my foot! Whining and sucking her fingers. She'd have dirty fingerprints all over your beautiful house; she'd break things, too.

"I don't want the winery; I want the house. It should be mine. I've cared for it, cleaned it, polished the antiques, washed the crystal. Oh, Lilly! Terrible things are going to happen now."

Shaking her head, she set the dishwasher to rinse and hold, then climbed slowly to her suite of rooms on the third floor. This was her private space where she kept her treasurers. Her bedroom had glass shelves for her collection of thimbles—gifts from Lilly and Frank from their travels when they were younger. Fiona touched her favorites—the hand-painted porcelain one from Paris, an etched gold thimble from South Africa, an antique sterling one from England. Assuring herself that the collection was dust-free and properly placed, she wandered into the sitting room with its television, built-in bookshelves and view of the Coast Range. Her special chair, lamp and a small table were placed in a cozy corner; this was her sanctuary.

Fiona continued her muttering. "That Mrs. Browning—what was her name? Selby. With a name like that, she must have airs about her. Trying to weasel her way into my good graces by asking me to have lunch with them. I know that kind of game, Mrs. Selby Browning; you can't put anything over on me! I know your kind. You liked this room; you said you could be happy here. Are you planning to move me out? Lilly says I can stay here as long as I want, so don't you get fancy with me!"

Fiona sat down, lit a cigarette and picked up her needlework. Each day was the same: coffee, fruit and toast for breakfast, followed by housekeeping chores and the preparation of a nice luncheon; then needlework and soap operas, sometimes a nap in the afternoon. At five o'clock, she would fix tea with tiny sandwiches or soup; formal dinners were a thing of the past. Lilly and Frank ate lightly as they got older. Lilly didn't even want to eat after Frank died, but Fiona insisted. She fixed tempting little meals. Now, it was just herself to think about, except when Paul would come at her invitation for lunch or dinner. He was such a nice young man. She wished people wouldn't call him Hawk; that sounded so harsh.

It was good when that slut fiancée of his left. She was no good; I knew that the minute I saw her. Cheap thing with her skimpy shorts and tight T-shirts, her big boobs hanging out. No matter she had some fancy college degree. She said she was his research assistant. My foot! She just went out in the vineyard, leaning over the vines so the workers could see up her bottom. How could Paul take up with her kind? Well, she's gone now; I saw to that. Paul doesn't need that kind of distraction; LillyHill is enough. No wife or girlfriend is needed; he has the winery to think about.

She looked at her watch and reached for the television remote control. Fiona loved her soap operas; they were very informative, as far as she was concerned. The dramas were a slice of real life—those and her romance novels; she collected them, re-reading her favorites. She hadn't needed a man of her own; the one encounter she had when she was twelve years old had been enough. What had happened was wrong. Dirty. Painful. Secret.

She knew that some people had good marriages, like Frank and Lilly, although they did fight sometimes. That frightened her at first. But, as the years went by, she knew they would settle their differences and be friends again. And, as for children, she never did like them much—noisy, smelly, messy things when they were little, and a worry when they grew up. A nanny had taken care of Arthur when he was little. Of course if she could have had a son like Paul—handsome and charming, sweet to her. That would have been different.

Yes, the soaps were educational. She could spot a bitch or a slut by the way they dressed and walked. She could tell when a person was telling the truth or was lying. She had learned ways of getting even with bad people. She knew how to say things that could upset people, and they didn't even know she was doing it. Yes, she knew all about life. You didn't need a fancy college education for that.

Fiona's eyes became heavy and she put her needlework aside and stubbed out the cigarette in the delicate ashtray. Yes, she had been lucky. First, being sent to America from England when the Germans sent their V2 rockets over London. She had been ten years old and one of the many children sent to the English countryside, or to Canada. She had been sent to America to live with a cousin. As soon as she was fifteen years old, her cousin hired her out as a domestic. Again, she was lucky. Frank and Lilly Steiner had employed her, and, after fifty years of work, she had LillyHill.

Fiona dreamed fanciful dreams, dreams of walking in English gardens, being served tea by maids with frilly aprons, of butlers saying, "Dinner is served, Madam." She dreamed of explosions and fires burning buildings in London, of the wail of sirens and the running feet and dark cellars, of hands over her ears, of dead family. Of dead school chums who had played with her. She dreamed of rough hands on her young body, a hand over her mouth, something between her legs.

CHAPTER FOUR

Selby turned on her headlights in the mid-afternoon dusk as she drove back to the duplex from LillyHill. Her mind swirled with the images it had accumulated in the past four hours—vast fields of grapevines, huge steel tanks, oak barrels, a fantasy house, cars, broad shoulders, dark hair. No, he didn't really come with the bequest, yet he did. She had controlling interest in the winery stock, but he had 45 percent of the stock and was in charge of running the vineyard and the winery. If he weren't at LillyHill, there probably would be no winery; so, he comes with the deal, yet she had no control over him. Selby smiled wickedly at the thought of making him do her bidding. And it didn't have anything to do with the wine business. For the first time since her husband had been killed, Selby felt stirrings of desire, even if misplaced for the moment on a man twelve years younger than herself.

Selby also thought about her boys when they were young and about their father, Doug, returning from driving an eighteen-wheeler across the states. He told them stories of hauling freight over the majestic Rocky Mountains in snowstorms, of flaming sunsets as he drove west across Arizona, of herds of elk in Montana. The boys enjoyed hearing about huge bald eagles soaring above the crags, of ravens ripping apart road kill, or about the coyote that tried to race him in Idaho. For Doug, the flocks of geese in North Dakota, the egrets in Florida, and the wild horses in Nevada gave glamour to the tedious hours of sitting alone in the cab. As the boys got older, they wanted stories about the truck stops and the characters Doug encountered. His CB radio was magic to them; they spent hours trying to choose their own "handles." Doug was known as "Bald Eagle" in reference to his rapidly receding hairline.

Steve had followed in his father's footsteps, driving double trailers across the country for Blue Line Freight Systems. Mike rejected the loneliness of the long-haul trucker and joined the Army. Now Mike was somewhere in the Balkans. Married with one child, he and wife Rhonda happily moved wherever the Army sent them. Rhonda and two-year-old Amanda were in Germany at the moment, so Selby had to content herself with being a long-distance grandmother.

It was her youngest son, Justin, who wanted to put down roots, not only by settling in one place, but also by growing beautiful things. He was his mother's son in many other ways, too, unlike his older brothers, who worshipped their dad. Justin had a gentler nature and was less affected by the death of his father than the twins. Justin had his father's handsome blonde looks, but was tall and slim, a throwback from an earlier generation. His brothers were built like their father—stocky, solid—but with their mother's coloring—auburn hair, freckles, and gray eyes.

Selby and Doug married right after high school graduation—by necessity rather than choice—with fraternal twins Steve and Mike arriving that fall. The Sexual Revolution swept up Selby and Doug with inconvenient results. Abortion was never a consideration for them; small town values and conservative parents made them take the traditional route.

Doug had been the handsome, blonde football star at Crestfield High School. He was the defensive end who could stop a tank on the athletic field. Selby was the gamine-like cheerleader; the Valedictorian everyone said would go places because she was so smart. Doug's dream was to drive an eighteen-wheeler, eventually owning his own rig; Selby's dream was an MBA and her own accounting office. It never occurred to her that reaching Doug's dream would end in tragedy, and hers would begin with a whim of fate.

The rush-hour traffic slowed Selby's trip as she neared the suburbs of southwest Portland, requiring her to pay more attention to her driving. Thinking aloud, Selby decided that tonight she and Justin would have something special for dinner. She also made the decision that Justin had made last night—to accept the bequest. She knew she would sign the minute she saw the house. Still, no final decision could be made until a family council convened. That meant trying to locate Steve through the trucking company dispatcher and trying to get a phone call to Mike. Maybe the Army would send him home; it was a family emergency, of a sort.

Stopping at the grocery store, Selby bought two steaks that weren't in the budget, a loaf of French bread, and a bottle of sparkling apple juice that would substitute for the champagne the occasion deserved. The longer she could keep Justin away from alcohol, the better she'd like it. Doug used to drink too much; she'd often wondered if he had been drinking the night he was murdered. Well, that part of her life was over. She had LillyHill to think about today.

The phone was ringing as Selby struggled to unlock the door and hang on to the bag of groceries at the same time. "Yes!" she gasped into the receiver.

"Hi. It's me. Where have you been? I've called a dozen times this week."

"Elaine, my dear, dear friend. Have I got news for you!" Selby laughed.

"Lay it on me," Elaine laughed back.

"Not now; lunch tomorrow?"

"You can't make me wait! Lunch yes, but give me a synopsis. Are you okay?"

"Better than okay and you won't believe it."

"Try me."

"You know the appointment I had with the attorney, Levy?"

"Yeah."

"Well, I thought I was just invited to the reading of the Steiners' Will— you know, to accept the final gift to the college's endowment and they didn't know I no longer worked there."

"Yeah."

"Well…"

"Don't 'well' me! Tell me!"

"I was named in the Will, too."

"You're kidding! That's wonderful, or is it?"

"You'll just have to wait until tomorrow. But I'll need a ride; I'm going to let Justin take the car to school."

"Okay, but you have to buy lunch since you're an heiress and being cruel, making me wait for the rest of the story."

"Okay. Bye."

Justin was cold from riding his bicycle home, and, as usual, starved. He was a good kid. He needed a break and LillyHill might just be it. "Hi. Wash up; dinner's ready," Selby sang out from the kitchen. She lit a candle as a centerpiece and poured two tumblers of sparkling apple juice. When Justin saw the special dinner, he grabbed her, swinging her around and yelling, "You're going to do it! Yes! Take the money and run! Awesome, Mom!"

"Don't you think we need a full family council meeting to reach a decision?"

"Hell, no. Go for it. Steve and Mike won't care. They'll be happy for you."

Selby wondered. Justin was the kind to be happy for someone else, but she wasn't that sure of her older sons. They were too much like their father at times.

"I'll make you a deal. You can take the car to school tomorrow if you'll pick me up after your last class. We'll go downtown and sign the papers. I'll make an appointment with the attorney."

"Great! You know, you haven't told me a thing about the place. Is it cool?"

"Cool doesn't begin to describe it. Let me tell you…"

That night, when Selby retired to the bedroom and Justin crashed in his clothes on the unopened hide-a-bed in the living room, doubts and questions marched in disorderly array through her mind. She mulled each issue over and over, trying to talk herself out of signing, yet knowing she would be foolish not to accept a gift given in good faith. Perhaps Lilly knew something about the future that Selby did not or could not know.

Being a compulsive list maker, she turned on the bedside lamp, propped a lined yellow pad on her knees and began to list everything she needed to do and questions to ask Mr. Levy: When could she and Justin move into the house? What about Fiona? The Trust stated that Fiona was to have a home at LillyHill for as long as she wanted. Would she stay or go? Would Fiona continue to be the housekeeper or would she just expect to live there as a guest? What about Lilly's niece Estelle and her family? Would they tie things up in court, leaving Selby in limbo? If that was the case, then Selby should take the job she interviewed for this morning, if it was offered to her. That meant starting to work next week.

Selby re-read the letter Lilly Steiner had left for her. Tears filled her eyes as she read of the Steiner's great respect for her and the warmth they felt. She was again surprised and amused at the Steiner's first impression of Arthur's relationship with herself.

"When Arthur first talked about you, we thought he might have found someone he could love. We urged him to bring you to dinner so that we could meet you. I'm afraid we were very disappointed when he told us you were happily married. He loved you, too, as we did. Your friendship with Arthur was very important to us."

It was funny the way people jumped to conclusions, formed unsubstantiated options and built fantasies on the simplest acts of kindness or spoken words. Selby blew her nose and continued reading.

"I should explain something about Fiona to you since we've asked you to allow her to continue living at LillyHill for as long as she wishes. She came to work for us when she was very young, first as a kitchen helper, then parlor maid, and later as my personal maid. As our older servants passed on and our lives became simpler, Fiona took over as housekeeper. Her loyalty was never questioned and, over the years, she became family. Even though her

education is limited, she is very good at what she does, but she can be a bit rigid at times. However, once you get to know her, I'm sure you will love her as we did."

Selby wondered what "a bit rigid" meant. Perhaps not being familiar with having servants would be an asset in this situation. Selby could think of Fiona as an old aunt who came with the house, yet it would be nice to have someone else be responsible for the day-to-day tasks of running a house. How nice it would be to have a home again, Selby thought, and with a housekeeper at that.

There were other questions, but who to ask? What about Paul "Hawk" Kestrel? Who was he, really? Was he like a son to the Steiners after Arthur died? Does Hawk have a wife or a significant other? Would he allow her to be a working partner or would he just expect her to shut up, pay the bills and stay out of his way? Would she be able to curb her physical interest in her young partner? Would he laugh if he knew he was sexually attractive to her?

Selby fell asleep with the light on, the note pad next to her pillow, and dreamed she was at LillyHill trying to get into the house. The doors were locked; as she circled the house trying to find another way in, Fiona appeared at each window, scowling and saying something, but Selby couldn't hear the words. At last, Selby sat down on a wine barrel, gasping for breath, crying silently, agonizingly. Then Doug drove up in his truck, its monstrous headlights blinding her.

She awakened enough to realize that she had fallen asleep with the bedside lamp on. After rousing herself to turn it off, she fell back to sleep and dreamed again. She was sitting at a huge desk that was polished to a satiny luster. As she reached for a pen, her hand was covered by a man's hand. Turning, she saw it was Hawk. Then she was lying on top of the desk but now it was a bed with black satin sheets and Hawk was hovering over her, teasing her, his naked body just inches from hers. She asked him over and over, "Are you a bird of prey?" He dropped his lips to hers....and the alarm buzzed.

Damn! It was just getting good. Well, you silly old lady, a dream is as close as you're going to get to the gorgeous hunk. It's all business. Besides, I'm not sure I like or understand him. Pushing away the covers, she wiggled her feet into pink floppy bedroom slippers and headed for the kitchen to make coffee and wake Justin. Today was the big day, the day to sign away her old life and embark on her new one, whatever it was.

26

CHAPTER FIVE

Meanwhile, Paul "Hawk" Kestrel—LillyHill grower, vintner and cellarmaster—locked up the winery, checking to see if the stake truck was locked, the security light on and the alarm system armed. Thieves and vandals could do a lot of damage to the fledgling business. An unauthorized visitor could steal wine or even worse, disturb the aging of a vintage. The '99 Pinot Noir was doing well so far, although it had an unstable development in the bottle. Hawk knew it took three to five years to develop its characteristic perfume and velvet texture. Wine was not a mechanical process; it was grown. It was the result of a winemaker's sense of smell, and taste, the feel of the grape in his hand and on his palate. Hawk loved the acres of vines, the delicate green tendrils in spring, the dark green leaves in summer, and the heavy clusters of fruit in the fall. No, he didn't want anything to happen to the wine because of carelessness.

He'd had a love affair with wine all his life. The son of the cellarmaster of one of California's largest commercial wineries, he had been raised to follow in his father's footsteps of blending wines. But Hawk wanted to become a viticulturist, the grower of great vines. He went to school to study Enology at UC Davis, the Harvard of winemaking. His dream was to own a small winery that made exceptional wines. Before he could attain his goal, he had to have experience. A clash between father and son over a divorce and methods of winemaking sent Hawk to LillyHill after answering an ad to be "all things" to an emerging winery in Oregon's lush Willamette Valley. It was the type of challenge and experience Hawk needed to complete his education. Frank and Lilly Steiner told him of their dream, of how they had nearly lost it when their son died, and how they decided to continue in honor of their son. So Hawk moved to Oregon.

The Willamette Valley is at the same latitude—forty-five degrees north—as the Bordeaux region of France. It, too, has long hours of sunshine and degree days, micro climates that require specific kinds of grapes, and rolling hills that lift the vineyard out of the frost zone and allow the fruit to catch every bit of sugar-making sun.

For the past year, Hawk's concentration was centered on the vines and the wines, the aging, the blending, and bottling. When his fiancée, Adrianna, came with him to finish her research paper at LillyHill, his world seemed complete. But she left after six months with no explanation. Oh, he knew she hated the rain, the perceived lack of culture; she missed the parties in the Napa Valley and San Francisco, but there was something more that he could never put his finger on.

Perhaps it was just as well, he told himself. One brief, bad marriage, which could be blamed on him for being such a workaholic, was enough. He and Catherine were ill-suited to begin with, even if his father didn't think so.

Since Adrianna had been gone, he occasionally drove into Portland for a relaxing weekend with several flight attendants he knew, but winemaking was his mistress. Women got bored with his mini- lectures on viticulture and Enology long before he was through sharing his mountain of knowledge with them. At least Selby had seemed interested, had asked good questions, wanted a reading list. There was much more to tell; he'd see how quickly she got bored.

Hawk fixed himself a simple dinner of fresh pasta with olive oil, herbs and shrimp, sat down at the table and opened a copy of *The Oregon Grapevine*. He had always enjoyed reading while eating—the newspaper with breakfast and a novel or this bi-monthly Winegrowers Association newsletter for dinner. His former wife, Catherine, hated the habit. Hawk had to admit that it was rude, but he was alone now, so what difference did it make?

Sampling a competitor's Pinot Gris, Hawk analyzed it, making notes on a pad as to its acidity, texture, and bouquet. He drank a glass as he cooked and one with his meal, again jotting down notes on how it went with food. Yes, he could do as well or better, once his Pinot Gris grapes began producing under the LillyHill label.

Taking his supper dishes to the sink, he washed them quickly and poured another glass of the Pinot Gris to sip while he finished reading an article on Grape Phylloxera, an aphid-like insect that feeds on grapevine roots. However, his mind kept returning to the freckles that dusted the bridge of Selby's nose, her unruly hair with bronze highlights from the afternoon sun. Hawk had always liked long-legged blondes with full breasts. Then this petite widow, mother of three comes into his life. She was delicate in build, yet strong willed, with trim legs and small breasts—not much more than a mouthful. Come on, Hawk, get your mind back on the article, mentally chastising himself. She wouldn't be interested in messing around. Business is her top priority. But that mouth, that little bit of an overbite...now that's sexy.

The next morning Hawk wakened with a headache from too much wine. He rarely drank more than a glass or two, but last night he had let himself relax, his mind following an erotic path that ended with Selby in bed, her delicate arms around his neck, her legs around his waist. Plunging into the shower, letting the room fill with steam, he finished with an icy blast of water. Breakfast and two aspirin will fix this, he thought.

Taking a thermal coffee cup with him, he ran down the steps to his Jeep and bounced over the muddy lane to the winery office. Checking his calendar for the day, he saw that he had a meeting with the local growers group that gathered informally the first Tuesday of each month. It was a friendly gathering, a time to buy or sell used equipment, to gossip, to share information about grape clones or argue the pros and cons of sod versus no sod between rows of vines. He had something to share with the group this month: he was now part owner of LillyHill Vineyard. He wondered if or when Selby would move into LillyHill. Would her college-aged son come with her? How would she and Fiona get along? Would Selby get in his way running the winery? She had asked for a reading list. Well, he'd give her one that would keep her busy for the next three years!

CHAPTER SIX

Selby and the estate attorney Mica Levy sat at a large conference table working through piles of documents, financial reports, tax forms and annual reports. There was much more to inheriting $20 million in assets than to just "take the money and run" as Justin had suggested. Selby's learning curve went straight up and out of sight.

"Have you heard anything from the Jacobs?" Selby asked her attorney. "I need to know how things stand because I've been offered a position as manager of an insurance office. If the Jacobs are going to contest the Trust and tie things up for months, then I'll need to accept the position. My cash flow needs a transfusion."

Levy leaned back in his chair, removed his glasses and rubbed his eyes. She was a cautious lady; that was good, but she wouldn't need to have a job once all the legal details were settled. He said, "If you can hang on for a couple of weeks, all this should be settled. I hate to see you take a new job. Surely, you realize that you won't need to work—in fact, you won't have time to work. You're going to be a very busy woman handling your own businesses when everything is transferred to you."

"I know. It wouldn't be fair to the employer. But it's a great job. I might not find another one as good, if the relatives hold the bequest up in court for months or even years. I gambled once and lost, but I suppose this would be as good a time as any to try again." Selby gazed out the window, considering her options, the ramifications of waiting.

Levy said, "It's doubtful if they can break the Trust. It was set up long before your financial difficulties and we have depositions from Lilly's doctors as to her state of mind. The Jacobs will make some noise, but that's all it will amount to."

Selby sighed. "Okay, I won't take the job, but you've got to level with me, keep me informed. I don't like financial surprises; I've had enough of them in my life."

Levy was pleased at her quick mind and her ability to look to the future.

According to her, she had always done the family's tax returns and kept the books for the college Foundation, so she had a good grasp of some financial matters; however, it took a team of CPAs to handle federal and state income and property taxes on $20 million in holdings.

"You'll need to go to San Francisco and meet the Board members of Reed-Steiner & Company. Other than LillyHill Winery, the California real estate holdings are run by a Board of Directors. You'll serve on the Board; it meets quarterly or more often as needed," Levy said.

"Well, I can see why I won't have time to have a *real* job," Selby laughed. "Give me my homework and I'll get out of your way for today. Oh, by the way, I'd like to live at LillyHill. How soon could I move there?"

"Let's shoot for late February. We should be able to close everything in the next few weeks. Can you manage until then?"

Selby frowned as she gathered up the copies of documents Levy said she needed to read and understand. "I'll figure out a way. Maybe keep working as a temporary secretary—be a Kelly Girl, a very *old* Kelly Girl."

During the weeks of waiting, the reams of legal arguments, the depositions she gave and the prying into her life by the Jacobs' representatives, Selby kept her equilibrium by making more lists, by sorting her family's things into boxes marked for each son. She included childhood memorabilia—their Tommy-Tippy cups, high school yearbooks, athletic ribbons and trophies. Justin chose furnishings he wanted for the living quarters over the garage; it would be his home when he wasn't in college. Selby loved the idea that he was "home" but not underfoot. He was old enough to be on his own, yet she still wanted him near.

She was in a quandary what to take to LillyHill other than her personal items. The house was completely furnished and none of her things were nice enough to add to the beautifully decorated rooms. She made up several boxes of her favorite cooking utensils and the small set of tools Doug had given her for Christmas one year. Insulted at first by the gift, she quickly learned the joy of fixing a faucet or installing a new light switch. Family photographs, special weddings presents, bits and pieces of a long marriage were lovingly packed for the move. Everything else would be stored until the older boys came home to claim their heritage.

Selby felt guilty about not being completely open with the twins about the bequest. First, she left a message with Blue Line Freight to have Steve call her, as she had no idea where he was living or his hauling schedule. Three days after she left the message, he called.

"Hi, Selby. What's the matter now?"

"Hello, Steve. How about 'Hi, Mom, how are you?'"

There was a pause. Selby could hear country western music in the background. Steve must be at a truck stop or a tavern.

"Hi, *Mom*. How are you?"

"Fine, thank you, and how are you, dear?"

"What?" Obviously, he had not bothered to find a quiet phone. The laughter and loud music drowned out what she had said.

"Hey. Let me find another phone and I'll call you right back." With that, he hung up. Selby waited by the phone. Twenty minutes later it rang.

"Hi, Steve. Are you okay?"

"Yeah, sure. What do you need?"

Selby wanted to hang up on him. Well, fine, Steve, she thought in disgust. She had never asked him for any help this past year. Once he had sent her $100, probably because Justin had told him more about their financial situation than she had. The money had truly been welcomed and used for groceries.

"I just wanted to see if you were okay and tell you that Justin and I may be moving in a few weeks. As soon as we know for sure, I'll leave our new address and phone number with your dispatcher."

"Okay. Have you heard from Mike or Rhonda lately?"

"I had a letter from Rhonda last week. Everything seems to be fine. Amanda is talking a blue streak in German, too."

"Cool. Tell Justin 'hello' for me. I gotta go. Someone's waiting for me. Good talking with you. Bye."

Selby sat holding the receiver, the dial tone whining, telling her that her oldest son had no need for her anymore. In truth, he hadn't for the last eight or nine years. She wondered if he would change his mind once he found out about the bequest. Well, dear heart, you can just wait.

Selby's call to her daughter-in-law, Rhonda, in Frankfurt, Germany, had been much more civilized. Yet she held back most of the details and simply told her that she had inherited a house on some rural property southwest of Portland. The women talked mostly about Amanda—how Selby would have loved to be closer to her grandchild, to have seen her first steps, hear her first words. One day, we'll get acquainted, she thought. In the meantime, perhaps she could do something special for Mike and Rhonda now that she'd have some resources. Maybe she'd send them money for a computer and modem; they could use e-mail to stay in touch. Then it dawned on her: she could afford to fly to Germany! The thought made her shiver with excitement.

CHAPTER SEVEN

March came in like the proverbial lion the day the final papers were signed. Adding to the storm outside, Estelle added her thunder and rain—shouting and tears—in Levy's office. It was a scene that Selby had hoped to avoid, but that was not to be. Estelle just barged in without an appointment.

"I don't have anything to say to you, Mrs. Browning," Estelle said, tossing her handbag and mink coat on the conference table. "I still think there is something very wrong with the Trust."

There was no possible reply, so Selby kept quiet, rising from her seat at the table where she and Levy had been working. Estelle had come for the jewel case and Lilly's letter to her; there was also one for five-year-old Little Lilly to be opened when she had graduated from high school. Ripping open her own letter, Estelle skimmed the contents, snorted and shoved it into her purse. Tears of anger and frustration filled her eyes.

"I don't know why Lilly did this to me. You'd think blood would be more important. At least she says that we can use some of Little Lilly's trust for private school as soon as she is old enough."

Levy said, "Yes. Just give me the information on tuition and other costs that she may incur such as uniforms, books and special fees. I'm sure piano or ballet lessons are part of what Lilly had in mind for her great grand-niece, too."

That seemed to mollify Estelle. And, as she opened the jewel case to inventory the contents, she sighed and purred, touching each of the pieces, holding several up to the light. She shot smug glances at Selby.

Selby excused herself so Estelle and Levy could finish their business in private. She stood looking out the east window toward the Willamette River with its many elegant bridges. Today they were blurred with rain and low clouds. She hoped the weather wasn't an omen of things to come. In the last weeks she'd taken several trips to the vineyard, reassuring herself that it was, indeed, real. She also wanted to make friends with Fiona, but there was a wall that she could not break; it was an uncomfortable situation for both women.

What she really looked forward to was seeing Hawk and talking to him about his vision for LillyHill. Every time she visited, she learned more about winegrape growing, crushing, fermenting, bottling and aging the wines. She was so caught up in learning the business that she seldom thought about how to tell Steve and Mike the enormity of the inheritance.

The weekend of the move to LillyHill was cold; a mixture of rain and snow made everything a bit more difficult. However, Hawk had offered to help her move. The use of the large stake truck and an extra set of muscles was definitely an asset. Hawk and Justin loaded the pieces of furniture Justin wanted for the chauffeur's quarters where he would stay when he wasn't in school, then packed Selby's boxes of personal belongings on the truck, covering the load with a heavy plastic tarp. Her smaller personal items were loaded into Old Blue. Justin rode with Hawk; Selby was pleased that they seemed to enjoy each other's company. She followed the truck in Old Blue, which would be Justin's now. She couldn't imagine herself driving a Mercedes; the Ford Explorer was more her style, but, who knew, maybe one day she would grow into having elegant things.

Hawk backed the truck into the empty garage stall. He and Justin quickly carried the furniture and boxes up to the room above the garage. Selby went to find Fiona to see if they could have a cup of coffee.

"I usually have tea in the afternoon," Fiona responded to Selby's suggestion that a cup of coffee would be welcomed.

"Well, that would be fine, too," Selby said, sensing that Fiona was not taking this incursion into her territory with equanimity. Just wait until Hawk and Justin bring in my suitcase and boxes, she thought. Guess I need to use a little psychology on Fiona. "I know Hawk is hungry; he's worked so hard today. Would you know what kind of sandwiches he'd like? I'd be glad to make them."

At the mention of Hawk's need, Fiona brightened and said she would make coffee and a light meal. Yes, she had some things in the refrigerator that would satisfy him.

Well, Selby thought, that's one way to get things done around here. Wonder how often I'll have to use that strategy?

They gathered around the kitchen table and devoured a pan of lasagna that Fiona just "happened" to find in the freezer, along with applesauce, cookies, milk and coffee. Justin turned his innocent charm on Fiona, telling her she was a great cook and that he would have starved if she hadn't saved the day. She seemed pleased at all the attention, but when it was time to haul Selby's things upstairs, the coolness descended again.

"You know, Fiona, I think I'd prefer to stay in one of the guest rooms rather than the master suite," Selby said. "I just wouldn't feel right about using it until you've had time to take the items Lilly wanted you to have. Which bedroom would you suggest?"

Fiona seemed to approve of this suggestion and indicated the larger of the two bedrooms for Selby. Fiona referred to the other bedroom as Arthur's; it had been kept exactly as it had been when he was alive. That was creepy as far as Selby was concerned. Changes would have to be made. The blue guest room would be fine for a few days, Selby thought. I still don't know Fiona's intentions and I sure can't rush her.

Justin could hardly wait to get to his new "digs" and put things where he wanted them. He was almost on his own now and the urgency of getting settled was powerful. Fiona excused herself after cleaning up the meal, leaving Hawk and Selby alone for the first time in weeks. Exhausted and disheveled, Selby began to have misgivings about the move. It would have been perfect if Fiona weren't there, but after all, Selby was the intruder. "Hawk, thank you so much for your help today. Justin and I couldn't have done it without you," she said.

Hawk looked down on the petite woman who was smiling up at him, hair tousled, lipstick gone, faint tired smudges under her solemn gray eyes. She looked young and vulnerable at this moment, but he knew she had intelligence and a steel core.

"My pleasure. I enjoyed getting to know Justin. I remember when I had my first apartment. It's heady stuff for a kid. You don't look so sure about the move."

"I think you're aware of my problem. What can I do about Fiona? There's no reason why the two of us shouldn't get along just fine; the house is certainly big enough so that we wouldn't be stepping on each other. I do understand how she must feel with a stranger moving in. But surely she must realize that this is my home now, not Lilly's or hers. I'm afraid Lilly didn't think this aspect out very well."

Hawk put his arm lightly across her shoulders and gave her a tentative hug. "You gals work it out. Call me if things get too tense. Fiona and I get along pretty well; maybe I can help." With that he left through the door to the garage, and Selby heard the truck pull away. She pushed the electronic door closer to the garage and returned to the kitchen. My kitchen now. I hope it's not true that two women can't live in the same house. Quietly walking through the other rooms on the first floor, checking the locks on doors and windows, Selby tried to picture herself living in a house she did not choose. Yes, it'll work, she thought. I like it. Slowly she climbed the stairs to her new room and her new life. She could hear the faint sound of Fiona's television. A long, hot bath and sleep is what I need; tomorrow we can start with a clean slate.

As Fiona started down the stairs the next morning, she could smell bacon and coffee. Soft laughter and conversation drifted up the stairwell. This isn't the way it is supposed to be. I always have a quiet breakfast first and then take Lilly hers on a tray to the master suite. It's all changed now. Laughter disrupted her morning. Why should she have to change her routine? Well, she'd just have to tell this Selby person how things were done at LillyHill, thought Fiona, gritting her teeth.

As Fiona entered the kitchen, Selby smiled and said, "Sit right down. I'll bring you some coffee and you can tell me what you'd like for breakfast. Since you fixed supper for us last night, it's only fair that I cook for you this morning."

"Good Morning, Miss Dermot," Justin said, mopping the last of his fried egg with a piece of toast.

Fiona shuddered at the sight. He's so big...so active. I'm not used to having a boy in the house again. Selby put a mug of coffee in front of Fiona, chattering about how difficult it was to function in a strange kitchen, not knowing where things are.

Fiona responded by putting on a pleasant face and saying that she'd like some canned peaches—there were some in the refrigerator—and a piece of whole wheat toast, dry.

Selby quickly served Fiona's breakfast, but it was all wrong. She didn't use the correct dishes. The everyday Lennox was to be used; the Spode was for dinner. Where did these mugs with writing on them come from? *DB Transport, Inc.* Must be junk from the Browning family. Fiona never drank from a mug. The dish of fruit was too generous, the toast not quite brown enough. She resented the fact that it was this woman's house now, but Fiona could stay as long as she liked; no one was going to run her out by serving food badly.

"What do you do all day, Miss Dermot?" Justin asked.

"Justin, don't be rude," Selby said with a laugh. "Fiona doesn't have to account to us."

"No, I didn't mean that; I just wanted to know how things are supposed to go around here. You see," he said draining a large glass of milk, "I'm transferring to the University of Oregon spring term, so I won't get to really experience LillyHill until summer when I'm home."

Selby felt uneasy at Justin's openness, yet she hoped that the innocence of youth would open the door to Fiona's heart and mind. Perhaps she'd reveal her plans for the future. Houseguest or a housekeeper? Traveler or lady-of-leisure?

"Well, I usually have a quiet breakfast and then do whatever needs to be done around the house in the morning like dusting or watering the plants or making a grocery list. Once a week a girl comes in to do the laundry and the heavy cleaning, usually Thursdays."

"I didn't know that," Selby said, clearing the table and loading the dishwasher. "Is she good? Responsible? Perhaps you and I can talk with her about continuing her services."

"Yes. She does an acceptable job, but I have to watch to see that she doesn't break things." Fiona paused and then in a tentative voice said, "Lilly let me drive the Mercedes to grocery shop on Mondays and to get my hair done on Thursdays. I always drove her to the doctor and the beauty salon after Frank died."

"I don't see any reason to change that arrangement with so many cars here. Anyway, I'm more the Ford Explorer type," Selby said.

"Aw, Mom. I thought you'd want the Mercedes and I could have the Explorer," Justin said, half- kidding, half-serious.

"In your dreams, kid. You can take Old Blue to college," Selby said ruffling his hair.

"If you wish, Fiona, I'll help you sort out any of Lilly's things that she wanted you to have, if you haven't done that already," Selby said. "I want to inventory the kitchen and the pantry so that I can function better at meal time. As long as Justin is here, we'll be eating heartier than I usually do. Be sure to let me know if there are things that you prefer."

There she goes again...trying to worm her way into my good graces, Fiona thought. Well, I'll just stay out of your way. I can't bear to see what you'll do to Lilly's home.

After lunch, Selby walked down the long drive to the winery. She wanted to catch the rhythm of the winery and the vineyard. She also wanted to see

Hawk and thank him again for his help, but his Jeep was gone, the door to the office locked. Strolling back up the hill, Selby examined the house as she came slowly upon it on foot rather than driving up to it. It was a lovely house, classic and elegant. The daffodils had bloomed, but other early flowers confirmed that spring had come. In a week or two, the harsh lines of winter would be gone as leaves unfurled and more bulbs burst into bloom. Selby wandered to the back of the house where the rock garden gathered itself for an explosion of spring colors. The man-made waterfalls would be turned on as soon as the risk of freezing weather was past.

That evening, Hawk called to ask if everyone was settled in and how Fiona and Selby were getting along. It was agreed that he should come to brunch on the Sunday before Justin left for the University.

CHAPTER EIGHT

Selby had always liked the idea of brunch, although it didn't really fit into her former lifestyle with Doug. When he was home, he didn't care what he ate or when, as long as there was lots of it and served to him in front of the television set. There were always sports on TV—football, basketball, baseball, bowling, car racing. She'd tried several times to hold a Sunday brunch, but good conversation just didn't happen when there was a game on TV. With the men in front of the television, the women stood around in the kitchen and bitched about the men. It was not Selby's idea of an elegant party.

Perhaps her new life at LillyHill would include brunch as described in *Good Housekeeping* or *Bon Appetit*. Why not? She would try some new recipes and use Lilly's lovely dishes and linen. She'd invite her best friend Elaine and her husband Roy. Perhaps Justin would like to include some of his friends and she'd suggest that Hawk bring a friend. Did he have a lady to invite? she wondered. Perhaps he had other acquaintances he'd like to invite, too.

The idea of a small brunch mushroomed into a major production a few days later. The date was set, the invitations extended and the day of the brunch dawned clear and bright. In addition to two of his classmates, Justin invited his boss, Liam Walsh, the fifty-year-old widower who owned the nursery where Justin had worked for the past three summers and now on weekends. Liam had been particularly kind to Justin after Doug's death; he seemed to understand the loss of a loved one, as Liam's wife had died of cancer the preceding year. Rumor had it that his closely cropped curly hair had turned silver overnight. At first glance he looked quite ordinary—average height and build—but he had lively blue eyes behind steel-rimmed glasses. Selby thought his shy smile quite charming when she accepted his gift of a bonsai on his arrival for the brunch.

"Why, thank you. What a darling little tree," she said, examining the fully-formed pine, its tiny trunk twisted, its branches pruned to look as if it were growing on a windy coastal cliff.

"It's five years old," Liam said, peering closely at it and touching the soil to be sure that it was damp. "You'll need to water it often."

"I'm delighted you could come to brunch, Liam," Selby said. "You've been so kind to Justin. I know he enjoys working with you."

"He's a good boy—a hard worker. You should come to the nursery sometime and see what we have."

"Oh, I've been there—last Christmas when you had acres and acres of poinsettias in colors I've never seen before. They were gorgeous!" Liam nodded his pleasure at her enthusiastic response. She continued, "And I remember that you have lots of garden statuary. There was a darling little rabbit that caught my eye, but I didn't have a garden at that time."

Other guests began arriving, so Liam took the bonsai and stepped away to place it on a nearby end table. The living room was inviting with the glow of the fireplace and the view of the valley from the bay windows. Through the archway to the dining room, the table and sideboard were laden with food.

Although Hawk declined to bring a friend, leaving Selby no wiser as to his social life or significant other, he had suggested inviting some of the neighbors. Delighted at his suggestion, Selby sent invitations to the owners and managers of nearby wineries and vineyards. Owners from Strangeland, Witness Tree, Eola Hills and Bethel Heights wineries came. Representatives from Cristom and Flynn vineyards came, as did Orchard Heights and St. Innocent. They brought bottles of Chardonnay, Pinot Noir and Pinot Gris that had been grown and bottled on their estates. There was much swirling of wine in glasses, cork sniffing and holding up the thin crystal glasses to the light, admiring the color and robe of each vintage.

Fiona didn't like brunch. It was too late for breakfast and too early for lunch. It was pretentious. She could see right now that this Selby woman was going to try to be one of those la-de-da rich women. Lilly was never like that. True, Lilly was of another generation and had been born to wealth, married wealth, and was never very impressed with wealth. You can always tell the newly rich, Fiona thought.

But Fiona's attitude changed as she sipped a Mimosa. Champagne and orange juice were quite nice together, she decided. It was the first Mimosa Fiona had tasted, and she took to it immediately. After her second one, she relaxed and became flirtatious with Hawk, much to his amusement. She replenished the platters and bowls of food as guests returned again and again to the dining room to fill their plates with thinly sliced apples and Tillamook cheese, a Marionberry cream cheese torta to spread on bagels, a spinach and mushroom frittata with a light garnish of hollandaise sauce, baked ham with beaten biscuits, an herbed celery and walnut salad, assorted muffins and fruit tarts. The sideboard held a large coffee urn and Lilly's silver tea service. The guests complained of eating too much, yet returned for just one more tart or bit of cheese.

"Selby, your new home is fabulous!" Elaine exclaimed after the guided tour. "I'm dying to know more about the people you inherited," she said, tipping her head toward Hawk, who was talking with Roy. "Let's have lunch next week and you can fill me in."

"Great! I'll also tell you about the Housekeeper from Hell," Selby whispered. Selby had first met Elaine when she'd applied for a position at Willamette Community College where Elaine was the Director of Human Resources. They had the same off-beat sense of humor and dedication to their careers. Elaine's husband, Roy, was a druggist. They had two girls in college. Elaine had been the only person Selby could confide in when things got really tough after Doug's death.

The friends strolled into the dining room for more coffee. Outside in the yard, Justin and Liam were on their hands and knees, shirt sleeves rolled up, shoulder-deep in the irrigation system of the rockery.

"What in the world are they doing?" Elaine laughed. "Do you make your guests work off their brunch?"

Selby replied, "Those two can never seem to get enough landscaping, whether it's talking about it or doing it. Liam has been so good to Justin. And Justin talks about him constantly. I have a hunch that he's trying to play Cupid."

"Is Liam a prospect?"

"Hardly. We only met today. I've had too much on my mind this past year to even think about any type of relationship. And now, this inheritance has just given me more to handle. Of course it's much more interesting than being a bankrupt widow!"

"Interesting like a handsome business partner?"

"Don't I wish! But he's almost young enough to be my son. My guess is that he has someone. I saw a photograph in his apartment signed 'Love, Tracy.' She was beautiful and looked close to his age. She had two small children with her in the picture."

"Oh, well. Call me Monday and we'll set up a lunch date. This has been great. I'm so very happy for you."

"I know you are. Good friends like you are hard to find." The women embraced, once again sealing their long-time friendship.

Fiona had disappeared after brunch; the Mimosas and the rich food being too much for her. And she had worked hard, keeping the food supply organized, picking up empty plates and glasses. By three o'clock the guests had gone and Justin was in his new "digs" over the garage packing for college. Hawk and Selby cleaned up the kitchen together.

"Your first party was a success," Hawk said. "I hope you'll continue the Steiners' annual barbecue for the workers. It's really fun and they appreciate it."

"Of course, I'd love to do that. You'll have to tell me what's been done in the past. When is it usually held?"

"Right before harvest and crushing. There's a brief period while we wait for the grapes to be at their peak. The crew is in the area and once the harvest and crushing begin, we are busy, tired, dirty and grumpy. Perhaps you'd like to help with the harvest."

"I wouldn't miss it! That's the only way I'll learn the business. Thanks for adding the neighboring vineyard owners to the guest list and helping to clean up. I guess Fiona enjoyed the brunch, or at least the Mimosas," Selby laughed.

Walking Hawk to the door, she felt at home for the first time. He stopped, put his hands on her shoulders and kissed her gently on the top of her head. It was a sweet, tender gesture and she had no idea how to interpret it.

"Welcome to LillyHill, Mistress Selby Browning," he said. "On the next sunny day, I'll take you on a tour of the property the proper way. Find yourself some riding boots and I'll introduce you to Zephyr and Tucker." With that he strode to his Jeep and, waving, drove down the hill to the winery and his quarters above the stables.

Selby felt as if she had just had another Mimosa. The giddiness lasted the rest of the afternoon as she curled up with the Sunday newspaper. Her mind kept wandering to the party, Hawk's help in the kitchen and his hands on her shoulders. She liked the feel of his hands and would have liked to have them move softly over her whole body. But that was silly. He was young and, no doubt, had all kinds of women at his beck and call. Or not. He could have brought a friend and then maybe Selby's fantasies would stop. Well, I can dream. As Justin had once told her, "Never dream small." Of course, Selby mused, lustful dreams were not what Justin had in mind for his mother.

*

Selby drove to the community college later in the week to meet Elaine for lunch. It was strange to be back on campus after being let go so unceremoniously. She hoped she wouldn't run into her old boss and wondered if he had heard about the bequest. He'd really be ticked off if he had. Selby chuckled at the thought.

The two friends took their lunch trays from the noisy cafeteria into the faculty lounge. Old acquaintances welcomed Selby with open arms; it seemed as if she and Elaine would never have a moment to themselves. Finally, the area cleared as classes resumed and daily duties called the staff.

"How does it feel to be back on campus?" Elaine asked.

"Not as bad as I thought it would be...nice, in fact. Although I'm glad I didn't have to see Walling."

"Does he know about the bequest? I'm sure he'd be bent out of shape if he did. In fact, I think I'll tell him!"

"You are a bad person," laughed Selby. "I'd really prefer that details of the inheritance be kept quiet. I'm still not comfortable with the whole thing."

"Well, tell me about this gorgeous Hawk person!"

"Not much to tell yet. We're still getting acquainted. It's strange to inherit wealth and even odder to inherit a business partner and a houseguest and/or housekeeper. We're all fumbling along. It's like being in a play without a script. Improv on the stage of life."

"And this Housekeeper from Hell?" Elaine asked.

"That was an unkind thing for me to say. She's rather pathetic right now— lost her friends and has to deal with me. She doesn't know how she fits in any more than I know how she fits in. I need to sit down with her and ask, but I haven't quite figured out the words. It has to be said better than 'Are you going to work here or just be a guest?'"

Picking at their institutional fare, the two friends exchanged news and gossip about mutual friends and vowed to see each other more often. After taking their trays back to the cafeteria, they strolled to the parking lot. Elaine said, "I'm here for you anytime. Be careful of your business partner. He has eyes for you. No, you can't deny it. I watched him watching you. I think you're attracted to him, too. Go slowly. He looks like a heartbreaker to me."

CHAPTER NINE

April's gentle rains washed the sky to a bright blue and stirred the vineyard, the oak trees and Lilly's garden to life. The tulips finished blooming, while the lilacs, azaleas and rhododendrons started showing color. Hawk had phoned the house at seven o'clock one morning, saying simply, "Get your boots on, lady. We're going on a picnic today. See you at noon."

Selby's nervousness about the ride expressed itself in the oddest ways. First, she dropped nearly everything she picked up—silverware while she was loading the dishwasher after breakfast, a cup of powdered detergent while doing a load of wash, and the back-up disk to her computer. She hadn't been on a horse since she was in high school and then only a slow old nag rented at the beach. Fiona said that Hawk had Tennessee Walkers, whatever they were. There was also the matter of seeing Hawk again. She hadn't seen him since he kissed the top of her head weeks ago. Thinking about it still made her a bit giddy. It had been a busy time and Selby was ready to do something fun since she had spent most of her time reading business files and documents related to the estate.

She had moved the family room furniture to form a small office corner. Then she'd purchased a computer station, PC, fax, printer and linked the phone system to the winery. She had set up e-mail so she could communicate with Justin at college and with her daughter-in-law, Rhonda, in Germany, as well as with the San Francisco office of Reed-Steiner & Co. She finally had her own office, at home, overlooking a lovely garden—in fact, acres and acres of growing things. Selby's dream had come true, quicker and larger than she had ever imagined. But Fiona's tight jaw and stiff back signaled Selby that the new family room furniture arrangement was not suitable. Well Fiona, just deal with it, thought Selby.

Hawk came riding up the hill on a chestnut gelding, leading a gray horse with darker gray mane and tail. The gelding was tossing his head, prancing sideways, causing the mare to jerk her head and dance along with him. It was the first time Selby had seen the horses. At the sight of them, she began to get cold feet about riding. She stepped out on the porch, lifting a hand in greeting, as Fiona peeked through the curtains in the living room.

Hawk dismounted, doffed his imaginary Stetson and said, "Howdy, Ma'am. Ready to see the lower-forty?"

"I hope you realize that I haven't been on a horse in thirty years. Be gentle with me, or at least tell that huge animal to behave."

"Zephyr is very gentle. Mount up and I'll check the cinch and see if the stirrups are the right length for you."

It took Selby two tries to get her left foot in the stirrup and swing her right leg over the saddle. A friendly boost on her bottom from Hawk finally gave her the leverage to sit astride the horse. She imagined that she could still feel warmth and pressure of his hand through the seat of her jeans. Silly old lady, she thought to herself.

Hawk showed her how to hold the reins and lay them along Zephyr's neck to turn the mare. He then leaped into the saddle of his impatient mount, Tucker, and headed east up the hill behind the house. Zephyr followed without any urging from Selby, who felt insecure at being astride hundreds of pounds of horse flesh. As they rode in silence, Selby began to feel the "rocking chair" gait Hawk had described to her. That's what Tennessee Walkers were famous for, an easy rhythm that made riding the breed such a pleasure.

As she relaxed, she was able to admire the acres of rolling hills, some planted in vines, some still in pasture. Some vines were about eighteen inches high, set in black plastic to keep down the weeds and warm the earth. Each field had a name: Clone 296, South Slope, Pinot One, North Bench. The end poles of each row on the mature fields were numbered from one to 30. It seemed as if Hawk knew each field, each row, and each vine personally. He told her when the areas had been planted, with what, and when they could expect a harvest.

The surrounding land was a patchwork of evergreen forests and fields with small farms tucked in corners or nestled on hillsides like LillyHill. Copses of alder trees just leafing out and hay and grass seed fields turning pale shades of green were stitched together by fences and county roads, forming a lovely natural quilt.

Riding beside her, Hawk pointed out her land—where it started and ended—telling her which field he'd plant next and with what kind of vines. Pinot Blanc grapes, that's what he wanted—a new strain. He told her there were only seventy acres of Pinot Blanc planted at this time in the whole state. He pointed to a red-tailed hawk circling overhead, looking for a careless mouse or rabbit. Puffy clouds formed and evaporated. Freckles bloomed on Selby's nose. The sun was warm, but a refreshing breeze cooled the perspiration on the back of her neck. A small grove of oaks in a ravine seemed to be their destination. Pulling up, Hawk slid off Tucker, looped the reins around the saddle horn and tied a halter rope to a sapling; then he held Zephyr's bridle so that Selby could dismount. Her legs felt stiff, shaky and bowed— just like a real cowboy, she thought. After Hawk had seen to the horses, he untied a small bundle from the back of his saddle, took Selby's arm and led her to a fallen tree where he set out the picnic—bread, cheese, sausage, fruit and wine.

"See that line of trees over there by the fence—near that tangle of blackberries? Well, that property is for sale and I'm negotiating with the owners. I've been talking with them for the last six months. Now that I have partial interest in LillyHill, it seems more important than ever to acquire the adjoining land."

"Would you have your own vineyard then?" Selby asked, trying to understand.

"That was the original plan—to work that acreage when LillyHill no longer needed me, but now, it could be an extension of LillyHill. What I mean is the grapes could be bottled under the LillyHill label—or my own label."

"How large is the parcel?

"It's seventy acres with frontage on Oak Hill Road. The elevation is from 580 feet down to 350 feet and has Nekia soils, one of the most sought-after grape-growing soils in the Willamette Valley. There's an existing farmhouse; it's not much, but habitable. They're asking close to a half-million dollars, but I think I can get them down to a reasonable price."

"I didn't realize land could be that expensive."

"Well, when the soil is good, it's worth it. LillyHill is about forty acres. If we could add that piece, we'd have plenty of room to expand."

Selby turned to look closely at Hawk, the phrase "we'd have room to expand" making her wonder what he meant. "We" as in business partners? Of course. What else would he mean? You're being silly again, old girl.

It was late afternoon when Hawk and Selby returned to the stable. Conversation and laughter had filled the hours as they learned about each other's childhood, high school broken hearts, politics and plans for the future. Both felt that LillyHill could be a success if they worked together to reach the Steiners' goal and Hawk's vision of the winery. Selby told him of her nervousness about meeting the Reed-Steiner Board of Directors, the company which handled the real estate portion of her inheritance. It was a pleasant afternoon filled with good conversation. But there was more. She'd caught him looking at her and he'd caught her looking at him. It seemed as if each wanted to study the other, but not be obvious about the examination. Their eyes would meet, then look away. For two adults, the getting-acquainted ritual was not all that different from two teenagers exploring a relationship.

One last chore faced them—to care for the horses. "If you're going to ride, you're going to have to care for Zephyr; however, I won't make you muck out the barn. Rio does that," Hawk said. "You'll feel more confident as you get used to Zephyr. Grooming her is one of the best ways."

Selby took this in stride even though she was exhausted from the day. When the horses were finally brushed, fed and watered, Hawk and Selby closed the barn doors.

"How about some coffee?" Hawk said.

"I'd kill for a cup," Selby laughed. They climbed the stairs to Hawk's quarters.

"The bathroom's there if you want to wash up," Hawk said. "I'll make the coffee."

Selby could hear the coffee mill as she lathered up her dirty hands and splashed water on her face. She hesitated for a moment, then used Hawk's comb on her wind-blown hair. Walking back through his bedroom, she noticed the unique headboard of his queen-sized bed. A distressed iron bar, with matching iron brackets and finials, formed the top of the headboard; the panel beneath the bar was made from planks of antique pine in a natural finish that matched the dresser. Hand-crafted iron drawer pulls accented the warm wood. The beige sheets complemented blankets in colors of the southwest. She didn't know what she expected him to sleep in, but this sense of style was wholly unexpected. Hawk had the coffee ready as she returned to the living room.

"Sit. Put your feet up. You look tired."

"I am. I'm sure I'll be so stiff and sore tomorrow that I won't be able to move. I think I'll try out Lilly's whirlpool tub tonight."

"You've got to stop calling everything Lilly's, Selby. Everything is yours now, no matter what Fiona says or does."

Selby nodded and sipped the coffee. It was a French roast, dark and strong. Seeing that Hawk had his booted feet resting on the pine chest that served as a coffee table, Selby gently placed hers alongside of his. They sat in companionable silence, heads resting back on the couch, eyes closed.

She felt Hawk move off the couch, but kept her eyes closed, savoring the relaxed state of body and mind. When she felt him removing her boots, she helped by lifting her feet, one at a time. He began to rub her toes and arches. It felt wonderful.

"Cowboy boots can make your feet tired if you're not used to them," Hawk said. He peeled off her socks and continued to massage her feet. His hands felt strong, a bit rough from working on the vines. She opened her eyes and watched him watching her. He reached up and took her empty mug, placing it on the floor; then grasping her ankles, he gently pulled her into a half-reclining position on the couch. She watched and waited. He was on his knees now, sliding his arms around her, bending his face toward hers, his lips a fraction of an inch from her lips, waiting for her acquiescence or rejection.

In a soft, husky voice, Selby said, "Are you sure you want to do this?"

"I've wanted to do this from the time you moved in." His lips touched hers gently, testing her response, increasing the pressure, exploring her mouth as she responded by opening her lips to his tongue, and sliding her arms around his neck.

"Yes," he whispered softly, kissing her deeper, pulling up her shirt and cupping a breast with one hand. "Oh, yes."

His tongue was urgent and Selby responded in kind, her body warming, catching the excitement. Rising from his kneeling position, he sat on the couch beside her, leaning back, gently lifting and laying her body atop his. She could feel his warmth, his desire, and it increased hers. Things were moving quickly, heading for a situation she had not seriously considered.

Gently pushing back, Selby said, "I don't think I can handle this. Things are moving too fast."

"They certainly are," Hawk whispered in her ear, his breath sending shivers of delight down her spine. "I won't force you, you know."

"I know." But she didn't know; she just had to trust him. They lay very still. She was aware of him struggling for control over his erection. If she moved she knew she would go on auto-pilot and be lost to the sexual gratification that she needed and wanted.

Holding her shoulders, he sat her back up on the couch. "You are some sexy lady," he said.

Selby just smiled and shook her head. She said, "We need to consider the implications of...ah, er...

We're business partners. I have to think about adding another aspect to the relationship—even though it's...it's...very tempting. Sorry if I'm too practical, too analytical."

Wrapping her in his arms, he said, "I understand. Those considerations have crossed my mind, too." Then nuzzling her hair, he continued, "But the temptation was just too much today. Would you like me to drive you home?"

"No, I'd like to walk. It's not dark yet. Guess I need to clear my head."

She tucked in her shirt, pulled on her boots, turning to him once more at the door. "It was a lovely day. Thank you."

CHAPTER TEN

Selby took a deep breath as she began the quarter-mile trek up the gravel drive to the house. The warm giddiness of the afternoon seemed to make her light-footed, as well as light-headed. She smiled to herself all the way up the hill.

The windows of LillyHill were dark except for Fiona's top floor room. No welcoming porch light greeted Selby as she carefully made her way to the back patio that led to the sliding glass door of the family room. It was locked. The garage was also locked, as was the front door when Selby walked to the other side of the house and up the steps to the verandah. How strange for the doors to be locked. Well, I'll just have to ring the bell and hope Fiona hears it.

After a ten-minute wait and four tries on the doorbell, the hall light came on and then the verandah light. Fiona peeked out between the ornate etched glass in the front door. Slowly, she unlocked it and let Selby in. Selby swallowed her anger in hopes that Fiona would have a logical explanation.

"Hi, Fiona. What's with the locked doors?"

"I always lock up at dusk. You'll just have to carry a key if you are going to come in late."

"I hardly call six o'clock late, Fiona. At least you could have turned on a porch light."

Fiona turned without another word and climbed up the stairs. Bitch. I saw you come back from the ride a long time ago. I saw you go into Mr. Paul's apartment. Miss High-and-Mighty. Turn on your own lights.

Selby watched Fiona head back up the stairs. "Thank you, Fiona." Sarcasm wasn't very nice, but then, Fiona had not been very nice locking Selby out of her own house. Yes, she'd have a couple of extra keys made and keep one hidden outside to avoid another situation like this.

The incident put a cloud over the happy day. What in the world is Fiona's problem? Well, I guess it's time I asserted myself as far as she's concerned, Selby thought as she went into the kitchen for a glass of milk and some cookies to take to her room. In fact, I think I'll take a long hot bath in the whirlpool tub. And tomorrow, I'm moving into the master suite.

The next day dawned dark with threatening rain clouds moving over the Coast Range, bringing moisture from the sea—good for the vineyard, bad for Selby's mood and plan to take over the master suite. Bobbie Bassett, the cleaning woman, would come about nine o'clock. She could help Selby move furniture. Luxuriating in the bubbling bath the night before, Selby had mentally moved all the furniture in the master suite—Lilly's room—and made plans to buy a new bedroom set, all new linen and window coverings that reflected her taste. She'd shown enough respect for Lilly and had given Fiona more than enough time to get used to the idea of a new woman in the house.

Selby found Fiona in the kitchen having her usual dish of canned fruit and dry toast. The women exchanged polite greetings. Suddenly, Selby was starved. She wanted a huge breakfast, one that would stink up the kitchen with bacon and green onions and peppers and fried potatoes. One that called for fresh coffeecake loaded with cinnamon and walnuts. Yes. And freshly ground French roast coffee. She would take the next hour to mark her territory. It was that or pee in every corner of the house. As she began to assembly the ingredients and cookware she'd need for her feast, Fiona quietly left the kitchen.

Just as Selby was taking the coffeecake out of the oven, Hawk knocked at the back door and entered without an invitation. Selby's heart gave an extra kick to her chest as she struggled for an appropriate greeting. How should she behave towards him after yesterday? Were the deep kisses and exploring hands just adult playfulness or was there more to it?

"Mmmm. I could smell breakfast clear down at the office."

Forcing a laugh, Selby said, "Oh, you could not! What makes you think I'll share it with you?"

"All women have an instinct to feed men. Right?" Hawk asked, draping his arm across her shoulders. "Where's Fiona?"

"Upstairs, I think, I hope," she said, ducking out from under his playful embrace. "Guess what? I'm moving into the master suite today. Bobbie will help move furniture. I'm going to put all the lovely antique pieces in one of the guest rooms, restore it to a classic Victorian bedroom. Then I'll buy a new bedroom set, get new window coverings, linens, towels, everything that says 'me'."

"Let me know if I can help in the bedroom," Hawk smiled, wiggling his dark eyebrows and stroking an imaginary villain's mustache. "Oh, good morning, Fiona. How are you?"

"Good Morning, Paul. I'm fine, thank you. I've just come for a dustcloth, then I'll be out of your way."

Selby and Hawk looked at each other, mimicking the prim face that Fiona was wearing. When she left, Selby said, "This move is going to be tricky, but we'll deal with it. I promise to be nice, but firm. It's time for me to claim my space."

Turning her attention to making scrambled eggs, she cracked three more into the bowl, assuming that Hawk really did want breakfast. He watched her quietly, arms folded across his chest, ankles crossed as he leaned against the kitchen counter. She served two plates, placing an extra large piece of coffeecake on his. They ate in companionable silence, tired of forced banter and uncomfortable with references to yesterday's breach of business etiquette.

"Thanks for the breakfast. Oh, I really did have a reason for coming up. I want to attend a vineyard management conference in San Francisco the week of April 21. It'll cover pest control, grape diseases, sod culture—stuff like that. I've been invited to speak, to be part of a panel discussion. Thought you'd like to attend some of the sessions."

"That might work for me. I have to be in San Francisco that week to attend the quarterly Board meeting. I need to check out the condo in San Francisco, too. I'm wondering if we...I...really need it. If it could be sold, we might have more cash to put into LillyHill...to get some of the equipment you need for harvest. Plan to attend and I'll let you know what my schedule is that week."

"Thanks, boss-lady," Hawk grinned, lifting a hand to her as he headed out the door to his muddy Jeep.

Boss-lady! Well, I guess I am. Could he file a sexual harassment complaint if I put the move on him? Selby smiled at the thought and cleaned up the kitchen while she waited for Bobbie. She could hear Fiona puttering about in the living room and the dining room, dusting, watering plants, touching up a room that had not been used since the brunch. Selby's mind drifted back to Hawk's morning hug, the passionate kisses of the day before. Yes, she could easily get used to Hawk's attention. Was it possible to be kissing business partners? Fucking friends? Probably not. But right now, she felt powerful, energetic, and capable of running a multi-million-dollar business and having a lover. What she did not feel was confidence about handling Fiona. It was difficult to walk the fine line between meeting Lilly's wishes to give Fiona a home for life and having a life of her own. Her musing was interrupted as

Fiona returned to the kitchen.

"Fiona, I'm going to move into the master suite today. I'd like your advice on which antique pieces would look best in the blue guest room. I'd like to make it very traditional, showcasing Lilly's lovely things."

Fiona's first instinct was to tell Selby to go to hell. On second though, she could imagine making a sort of shrine to Lilly, placing things just so, arranging, touching.

"Well, if you think I could be of help..."

"Oh, I'm sure you will be, Fiona. Bobbie can help me move the larger pieces of furniture. Perhaps you will select the linens and accessory pieces. You know what would be best for the Steiners' twin beds. What would you think of putting the marble-topped table between the beds and..."

"Yes, with the Tiffany lamp on the table," Fiona said, brightening, rising to the occasion. "There are some lovely embroidered dresser scarves and sheets with heavy crocheted edges. And the gilt mirror should go in there..."

Selby sighed. Temporarily, a crisis had been avoided. But she knew that there would be others. She would have to re-read Lilly's letter. Wasn't there something about hoping that Fiona would take a trip to England? Yes. I'll read the letter again. Maybe I can encourage Fiona to travel; a month—or six—in England would be just the solution. With that happy thought, she began to draw a rough sketch as to where each piece of furniture should be placed so that she and Bobbie wouldn't waste a lot of time and energy. She could hear Fiona gathering up the small items off Lilly's dresser—the silver hairbrush and comb, the Spode dish for hairpins, the antique perfume bottles.

It took all day, but the blue room was finished, the Steiners' mahogany twin beds, dresser and armoire polished to a gleam, the old linens, feather pillows and lacy bedspreads lovingly attended to by Fiona. The bits of silver and glass were placed just so. Fiona had worked herself into exhaustion, but she was happy.

"I'll fix us some tea," she said, taking the cleaning basket with rags and bottles of polish down to the laundry room.

Bobbie and Selby carried, tugged and shoved the guest room furniture into some sense of order in the master suite, its size swallowing the double bed, small dresser and occasional chair. It was livable, but Selby knew that she would need professional help to decorate the suite. She had never had so much space that was just hers—space for a king-sized bed across from the fireplace, good reading lamps, and a small round table with chairs in the corner by the window. Her clothes didn't begin to fill even one of the two walk-in closets. The sitting room—well, she had never had a sitting room before. What did one do in a sitting room? And when would one sit in a sitting room? She had always been too busy holding a job, raising children, cooking, cleaning, washing and ironing. She had rarely had time to just sit, especially in a room made just for sitting. Maybe sitting rooms were for having a glass of sherry with your lover or lazy Sunday mornings with coffee and the newspaper. Maybe this is where she and Elaine would have tea and confide in each other. Maybe this is where Selby and granddaughter Amanda would become acquainted over cookies and milk. Perhaps it would be a better office space than the niche in the family room. The possibilities were endless!

In addition to Bobbie, who cleaned once a week, Adelina Aznar came once a month to cook and freeze several weeks worth of meals. There was lasagna, chicken pot pie, lamb stew, enchiladas, chocolate chip cookies and dinner rolls. This concept was completely foreign to Selby and she was torn between giving up the luxury of always finding something good in the freezer to "zap" in the microwave and going back to her cooking everything herself. It was hard for her to realize that she could afford services like this. But she wasn't convinced that it was a good use of money, no matter how wealthy. Yet it would keep Fiona out of the kitchen while providing good meals for Justin when he came home from college on the weekend. And she could always invite Hawk for dinner at the last minute. Get used to managing millions of dollars in assets and the perks that go with it, Selby. You are no longer a housewife-mother-secretary. You are a businesswoman who works out of her home.

CHAPTER ELEVEN

It had been ten days of hard study in preparation for her first meeting with the Board of Reed-Steiner & Company. Selby felt as ready as she ever would be. She'd read everything the attorneys and accountants had given her, called for clarification and requested additional materials on selected issues. She had asked for and received photographs of all the properties that Reed-Steiner held or managed. She wanted to make sure that she wasn't a slum-lord. Now there was nothing to do but fly to San Francisco and make the best impression she could on a group of men who were probably wondering about their new partner. What would they think of her? A gold digger? A bimbo? A dull, truck driver's wife?

Hawk had made the airline reservations so they could fly down together. Selby would go to the condo that came with the estate, while Hawk would stay at the Sheraton Hotel where the Vineyard Managers Conference was being held. They'd attend the conference banquet Saturday evening. It would give her the opportunity to meet other winery owners and managers, many of whom were old friends and acquaintances of Hawk.

But Selby had one other mission that was hers and hers alone: shopping for a whole new wardrobe. As she dressed for the early morning flight, she told her old blue suit that this was their last time together. It would stay in San Francisco for some needy person—it and anything else that Selby felt like leaving. She hummed to herself as she carried her suitcase to the garage and placed it in the Explorer. She would pick Hawk up at his quarters for the drive to Portland International Airport.

"I left my suit in San Francisco," she softly sang.

Several hours later, the jet lifted off into the early morning sun; Selby held her breath, helping the plane reach cruising altitude. Noticing this, Hawk said, "Does flying make you nervous?"

"Not really. I just haven't had the opportunity to fly very often and I still don't believe that something this big can get off the ground. I enjoy all the chaos that goes with flying though—the crowds, the excitement of going someplace, of having an adventure. I'm sure business people get tired of it, but it'll be a long time before I get to that point."

Hawk took her hand in his and held it until the stewards began to serve drinks and snacks. It felt good to have her hand held. He had a way of sliding his palm upon hers that was really quite sensual even though she was sure that he was just trying to make her feel more comfortable flying. She allowed him to gently massage her knuckles with his thumb.

"Let me read your palm," Hawk said turning her hand over, pressing it open. "Ah, you smile, Ms. Skeptic, but I am a trained palmist with ninety-nine percent accuracy." Selby giggled as he began to make soft noises over her hand, tsking and tut-tutting and humming. "Now this is your life line. It is long and strong. You will reach ninety or even one hundred, presiding over LillyHill with many grandchildren and great grandchildren named after you in hopes that they will inherit LillyHill. Let's see, there's Selby-Bob, Selby-Jane, Selby-Sam."

"I hope Mr. Levy will be still alive so that he can deal with the greedy relatives, "Selby laughed. "He does it so well. Go on, what else do you see?"

"Ah, this, dear lady, is your health line. There are three, no make that four breaks in it. You had the measles and three babies. That accounts for the times you've been sick."

"I'd hardly call having babies being sick. Anyway, Steve and Mark are twins, so I only had two pregnancies. You've used up your one percent error."

"Well, you had a day or two that you weren't as frisky as you usually are. Don't argue with the master. This is your wealth area. You are very prosperous—see, I told you I know this stuff. And this, this is your heart line. Oh, dear. Tsk, tsk. I wouldn't have thought that of you. I'm shocked!"

Selby pulled her hand away and folded her arms across her chest, hiding both hands. "I won't allow you to read about my love life." What if he could really see that she found him physically attractive? That she liked him to hold her hand? That she had erotic images of the two of them? How embarrassing! Don't get kittenish with him, Selby. You're too old for that.

"But don't you want to know what's foretold?"

"No, I'd rather be surprised," Selby laughed.

By the time the plane landed and they pushed their way through to the taxi stand, Selby wasn't so sure about the excitement and glamour of flying. Things were so easy at the Portland terminal, but San Francisco was a madhouse, at least on this particular morning. Sitting back in the cab, she took a deep breath and tried to soak up every bit of the scenery, no matter how dingy, how congested, how chaotic. She was doing the first fun, glamorous thing she had done in many years, if ever, and San Francisco was the perfect spot.

"Are you sure you'll be all right if I just drop you at the condo?" Hawk asked. "You don't know your way around the city and I'd hate to see you get into an area that isn't safe."

"I'll be fine. Levy told me the condo is located in a very nice area. I'm not going to do anything stupid. I'll just get settled in then catch a cab downtown. I have some shopping to do. I'll eat in tonight and then go to the Board meeting tomorrow at noon."

The Nob Hill area had many elegant structures, classically restored or elegantly refurbished. At each corner—Mason and Taylor, or California and Sacramento—another apartment building or condo caught Selby's breath. Surely, she couldn't own a Nob Hill condo in one of these buildings! But she did at 1170 Sacramento. She not only owned the condo, her company managed the whole building. No, she would not sell "her" condo.

"Okay, I'll pick you up at 6 o'clock tomorrow night. You've got my phone number if you need me before then," Hawk said, carrying her bag to the entrance.

"Stop worrying about me! I didn't just fall off a turnip truck; go do your own thing while I do mine."

It was strange to have a key to a home-away-from-home that she owned and had never seen before. The foyer light was on and it was obvious by the lemony smell that the condo had just been cleaned. Putting her suitcase down, she wandered through the rooms, noting the view from each window. One bedroom and the living room overlooked the bay; the kitchen overlooked the street. Selby unpacked in the bedroom with the bay view and prowled the kitchen for something to eat. The refrigerator had been stocked with milk, eggs, butter, cheese, juices, soft drinks, a split of champagne, designer water, fresh fruit, yogurt and a pasta salad. She found coffee and bagels. The freezer had a dozen different entrees and several flavors of Ben and Jerry's ice cream. How lovely to simply tell someone to "open the condo; I'll be there on Thursday." Money does make life easier.

After unpacking and enjoying a simple lunch, Selby called a cab for the short trip to the center of the city. Since she was not familiar with any particular dress shops, she went to Nordstrom, one of their many branches throughout the nation. She was comfortable shopping at the Portland Nordstrom store and knew which departments would have what she needed. Her one promise to herself was to avoid looking at any prices. She could afford anything she wished. First, she needed a knock-'em-dead power suit for the Board meeting. Next, she needed a wonderful dress for the banquet and, finally, shoes, lingerie and accessories.

It took all afternoon and she was exhausted by the time she hauled a dozen boxes and bags into the condo. She hung the purchases in the closet, considering each item as if she had not seen it before. The tailored suit was business-like without being stuffy; the cocktail dress was like nothing she had ever worn before. Oh, and the silk lingerie was pure indulgence, she thought, gently pulling the Oriental print nightgown across her bare arm. Lovely! She inhaled the leather scent of her new briefcase and tailored pumps as she removed them from the elegantly printed shopping bags. "Good job, Selby," she said aloud.

It would be good to stay in by herself, with no Fiona or anyone to disrupt her self-indulgent day and evening. After a hot shower, she wrapped herself in a new fluffy velour robe. She could eat when she wanted, what she wanted and how she wanted—even sitting on the floor in front of the TV. And that's what she did. Tomorrow she had one last thing scheduled before she faced the Board of Directors—a haircut and color at Chez Henri. She had been told that he was the best; at $150 a clip, he'd better be.

CHAPTER TWELVE

The new Selby Browning confidently walked out of Chez Henri and caught a cab to the Trans America building. She knew that she looked great in her silk and linen suit, its natural color accenting her auburn hair now glowing with professionally colored highlights. Of course Henri hadn't dirtied his hands tinting her hair; he had some minion do that, but he supervised the exact shade. Then, it was time for him to work his magic on her unruly waves. At last! A stylist who understood naturally curly hair. He didn't even ask her what style she wanted; he just began to cut. Now, her hair was shorter than she had ever worn it before with a slight asymmetrical shape. Carefully clipped tendrils clung to her neck or accented her forehead. Her ears felt exposed, but the clustered pearl earrings with the delicate drops would keep her from feeling naked. When he was finished, he insisted that she have her make-up redone and that she dump all her old cosmetics and use only the colors he chose. Why not? He was the professional in this area. And when the salon had finished with her and she had dressed in her new suit, she knew she could handle anything.

The four board members, the comptroller and the attorney had taken their usual places around the polished teak table in the boardroom high in the Trans-America Pyramid, one of the corporate buildings that gave San Francisco its unique skyline. They arrived early in anticipation of meeting Selby Browning. Only old Graham Reed was missing. Exactly on time, Selby was ushered into the boardroom. The men stood and introduced themselves one by one. Selby tried to read their response to her. Their eyes, their handshakes, their greetings told her nothing. Reed arrived in his wheelchair, which was pushed by his nurse-chauffeur. Reed's rheumy eyes seemed a strange pale blue behind the thick glasses. He sat scrunched down, his bald head nestled between bony shoulders. Thin knees poked up a plaid robe over his lap. Selby walked over to him and extended her hand. He held it with both hands, examining her carefully.

"Frank and Lilly spoke highly of you when Arthur died. Think you can handle big business?" he wheezed, chuckling, and then had a coughing spasm. His keeper, as Selby thought of him, quickly ministered to the old man, then pushed him to the head of the table. With that, senior partner Reed called the meeting to order.

In spite of Graham Reed's physical limitations, his mind was sharp. He watched her and listened carefully when she spoke. Even though it seemed as if some of her questions were brushed aside as frivolous, she stood her ground, whether asking for clarification on a particular line of the financial report spreadsheet or the reason why hazardous waste clean-up was taking so long on property No. 273. Her goal for the day was to be clear on all matters regarding the quarterly meeting. Learning about the overall business would take much more time. She felt that she had passed the first test, but knew she'd be on trial for the next year or so.

At the close of the meeting, luncheon was served in an adjoining private dining room with views across the city and to the bay. The table gleamed with crystal and silver under an ornate chandelier, the centerpiece of fresh flowers picking up accents of teal and mauve from the thick carpet. A first course—a thick, spicy mulligatawny soup filled with chicken, rice, eggplant, apples and curry—was followed by a salad of wild greens garnished with cold lobster and miso dressing. Assorted fruit and cheeses finished the meal. A California Chardonnay was served during the meal, with port and Ethiopian coffee to finish.

After a few polite questions to Selby about her family and the winery, the men slipped into their habit of talking local politics, which excluded Selby. She didn't mind; it gave her the opportunity to enjoy the surroundings and to catalog various impressions about each of the board members. Overall, her first impressions were positive. She suspected she had a strong ally in the ancient Mr. Reed. Occasionally, she caught him peering at her, giving a friendly nod and half smile. Yes, she would be sure to pay attention to business and ask his advice or clarification on matters.

At two o'clock the group pushed back their chairs, gathered their briefcases and headed for other appointments. Selby had no definite plans, as she wanted to make sure that she gave her full attention to the meeting. Now, she had several hours to herself before dressing for the banquet. It was pleasant to saunter down the street, stopping at an art gallery or boutique, gazing up at the skyscrapers and elegant hotels. F.A.O. Swartz lured her in with its extravagant window display of toys. A gift for her granddaughter from this prestigious and over-priced shop would be appropriate. Wandering the aisles, she was overwhelmed by the variety of ostentatious toys. Finally, she found the perfect gift: a telephone that would record her voice. Two-year-old Amanda had just learned what telephones were for and loved to say "Hi, Gamma" whenever Selby called Rhonda. Selby recorded her messages on the toy phone and had the gift shipped to Germany. It was so simple, so clever, she thought— push button No. 1 and the recording said, "Hello, Amanda. This is Gramma. How are you?" Push button No. 2 and Selby asked, "Do you want to play dolls?" Each telephone button had a separate message or question. By pushing the zero, Amanda would hear, "This is Gramma. I love you. Good-bye."

Back out into the street of dazzling shops, a pair of topaz earrings in the Fabulous Fake jewelry store caught her fancy. They would be perfect for the brown silk chiffon she'd wear tonight. Next she found a pair of gold kid sandals and a petite drawstring evening bag in brown satin. Her final purchase was a beige raincoat of some high-tech fabric that looked like sueded silk. Catching a cab, she returned to the condo for a long, self-indulgent bubble bath. Hawk was to pick her up at six o'clock. She wondered if he would wear a suit. She'd never seen him in anything but jeans. He'd even worn jeans to fly down to San Francisco. Well, if she looked as good in jeans as he does, she'd wear them all the time, too, Selby mused.

The three-way mirror in the condo bedroom filled the room with cloned, attractive women. Selby felt naked. Yet she was very properly dressed— appropriately covered from neck to wrist to knee. It was just that she had never gone without a bra in public, but the cut of the dress and the chiffon overlay did not allow for extra straps to show. The thigh-high sheer hose and brown satin bikini panties allowed the brown satin slip to touch parts of her body that usually were covered with a camisole and pantyhose. It was a delicious unfettered feeling. The brown chiffon dress floated down over the spaghetti-strapped slip, stopping just above her knees. Hmmm, shorter than she usually wore her clothes. Oh, well, this is San Francisco. Tiny snaps held the beaded cuffs around her wrists and the high band at her throat. The wrist and throat bands were heavily embroidered with gold and crystal beads; the two-tiered skirt fluttered as she walked. No, this woman did not look like Mrs. Doug Browning. She looked like Ms. Selby Browning, a woman of the 21st Century.

Just before six o'clock, Hawk called on the condo intercom to be admitted. Security was tight as well as constraining to residents and visitors not used to living in a large city. At his tap on her door, she flung it open with a smile and stopped, speechless. He was wearing a tuxedo. Selby was stunned at how handsome and elegant he looked. Hawk was speechless, too. The woman before him was not the insecure, mousy lady he'd met in Levy's office four months ago. Here was a gorgeous woman with a commanding presence and a sense of style that belied her background.

"You're beautiful," said Hawk as he kissed her lightly on the cheek. "You'll knock 'em dead tonight."

"So will you," said Selby touching his sleeve. "Come in. Do we have time for a glass of champagne? I found a split in the refrigerator."

"We'll take time," Hawk said. "You are absolutely stunning."

"Stop. You're embarrassing me. It was fun to reinvent myself. I'm glad you approve. We'll make great looking business partners."

"I'm not very comfortable dressed like this. I feel like a headwaiter or a pimp."

"Hardly," Selby laughed. "Maybe—let's see—I know, a gigolo taking a middle-aged widow out for a night on the town."

They laughed and touched their champagne flutes, proposing toasts. "To a pleasant and productive partnership," Selby said.

Hawk responded, "To reaching our goal for LillyHill Winery."

The cab ride took no more than ten minutes. Hawk held her hand and kept telling her how lovely she looked. Selby glowed from the compliments and the glass of champagne. This was the first party in years she was eager to attend. So often when she and Doug would go to a party—and of course they were never as elegant as this one—he would drink too much and Selby would have to drive home and fend off or put up with his drunken lovemaking. No, tonight would be different; she was feeling beautiful and in control.

From the lobby of the Sheraton Hotel, guests rode down two levels of escalators to reach the ballroom where the Vineyard Managers banquet was being held. Hosted wine bars from various California wineries encouraged guests to sample reserve and estate bottled wines. No-host bars and long tables of appetizers lined the opposite wall of the foyer. Balloons, wreaths of grapevines, huge clusters of imitation grapes in fantasy colors looped and hung from the high ceiling over the banquet tables. Tiers of colored candles on mirrored centerpieces highlighted the black tablecloths.

Selby hardly had time to take it all in before someone handed her a glass of wine and Hawk began to introduce her to old friends, colleagues, and other vineyard owners.

Amid the swirl of names and faces, Hawk managed to find her free hand. It was as if he had to touch her to be sure she was not just his imagination or to protect her from the mob of partygoers who were well into the festivities. By the time the guests found their tables, ate, heard the speeches and applauded the award recipients, Selby felt quite numb.

"I need a break from the noise and crowd," she said. "I'll be right back." She struggled through the revelers to the ladies room. The quiet space of the cubicle gave Selby a moment to let her head clear. The voices of two women caused her to pause before emerging when she heard Hawk's name. One was saying, "He can put his shoes under my bed anytime." Selby slipped out of the cubicle when the women, laughing and making other intimate remarks, went into empty stalls. Quickly she washed her hands and stepped into the mirrored lounge to touch up her lipstick and hair. As she was finishing, the two young women joined her at the mirror.

One said, "I hear he and some woman are partners in an Oregon vineyard. I wouldn't mind being his partner!" The other's reply was lost as Selby rushed out of the lounge, not wanting to hear their gossip. Hawk was deep in conversation with one of the vineyard owners when she returned to their table.

The man was saying, "...Half the original planting, about twenty-three acres, was planted to Pinot noir. We used several clones to enhance the complexity of the wines and we're getting an average of three tons of grapes per acre."

Hawk asked, "You get about 200 cases per acre?"

"Yes," the man said, noticing Selby and quickly rising to hold her chair as she sat down.

Hawk smiled and sought her hand under the table. "Glad you didn't get lost in this madhouse. It should settle down pretty soon. I'll ask you to dance as soon as they play something slower. Of course you dance with me at your own risk."

"Hawk, you're a lucky man to have such as attractive business partner. Mine is just plain ugly!" one of their dining companions said, turning to the man sitting next to him. Everyone laughed, turning their attention to the dancers on the floor. The band began to play some soft rock. Hawk stood and held out his hand to Selby, and they threaded their way to the crowded dance floor. They assumed the position, barely touching, each nervous about stepping on the other's toes. They danced slowly, properly apart as business associates might. However, as the dance floor became more crowded, their bodies were nudged closer and soon they were moving smoothly together, letting the music and the ambiance of the evening suppress their inhibitions. Selby's mind drifted back to the exploratory kisses in his apartment after their ride through the vineyard several weeks ago. She could almost taste him, feel his hands on her breasts. She closed her eyes and let the memory flood into her mind. Was he remembering, too?

When the tempo picked up, they returned to their table, talking viniculture, yield, press capacity and the skyrocketing price of French oak barrels that were nearing $800 each. Through all this, Hawk still touched Selby gently— on the hand, her shoulder, the small of her back, once on her knee. Her mind was becoming overloaded from the technical talk. She longed to drift on the slight buzz she had from the wine. Hawk had to speak to her twice before she heard him.

"Oh, yes, I'd love to dance again."

The band was catering to the older crowd now with big band tunes. "Just One of Those Things," "As Time Goes By," "I've Got You Under My Skin."

She slid into his arms, enjoying the feel of his body against hers, his hand riding even lower on her back now, his head closer to hers. They moved easily together, not talking, enjoying the intimate contact. Selby gave a wistful sigh.

Hawk leaned closer to hear her. "What?"

She looked up at him, studying his face, and said, "I want you."

He studied her face, took two quick pivots and said, "I've wanted you ever since our picnic." His voice was husky with emotion. Then half-kidding, half-serious, wondering if she were teasing him, he said, "Your place or mine?"

"Which is closer?"

After two more quick pivots and a slow dip and sway, he said, "Well, the condo is about a mile from here, but my room is upstairs on the eighth floor."

She hesitated, knowing it was not too late to change her mind, to say she was just kidding. Instead, she said, "Your place."

He gave her a broad smile and led her through the throng of dancers. They stopped by the cloakroom to retrieve their coats and walked business-like to the elevators. After all, what they were to embark upon was no one else's business. They rode quietly up with several other passengers, getting off at eight. They walked sedately down the hall to the door of his room. As he slipped the coded card into the lock, Selby asked, "Do you have protection?"

"As they say, don't leave home without some," he said with a smile.

CHAPTER THIRTEEN

Hawk took Selby's raincoat, hanging it in the closet while she strolled across the room and looked out the window at the city below, its lights shimmering, mirroring her emotions. She wanted—needed—what she had not had for so long. But she needed to be with a man she could trust. Was Hawk the one? Was this the time and the place?

The hotel room was typical—two queen-sized beds, small round table with two upholstered chairs, an armoire hiding a television, a long low dresser that also served as a desk. Hawk found a soft jazz station on the radio and watched Selby as she walked over to the mirror and slowly began to remove her earrings.

"I can't believe I'm doing this," she said, more to herself than Hawk. The mirror reflected Hawk as he threw back the covers on one of the beds, exposing crisp white sheets. As she struggled with the snaps at her wrists and at the high neck of her dress, she watched him watching her in the reflection of the mirror. He kicked off his shoes, removed cuff links and cummerbund, then came over to her. He lifted the silk chiffon dress over her head, tossing it onto the other bed where it floated gently down on his discarded dinner jacket. He was a man with patience, though his excitement was high. Gently he pushed the thin straps of the satin slip down over her shoulders, the garment dropping to the floor around her ankles like a pool of melted chocolate. Still standing behind her, he cupped her exposed breasts in his hands, nuzzling her neck, touching her shoulder with his lips.

She bent to remove her thigh-high hose, but Hawk said, "Let me."

Turning her around, he dropped to his knees and carefully removed the slip from around her ankles. Selby placed her hands on his shoulders for balance as he lifted first one foot and then the other to remove her delicate high-heeled gold sandals and sheer hose. Sliding her brown satin panties down, his hands lingered over her hips, his lips touching her here and there. As he buried his face in her delicate thatch of ginger fluff, she grasped his hair, pushing off the band that held his ponytail, the mass of silky hair falling against her thighs.

Rising, he began to fumble with his shirt studs. "Let me," she said, her nimble fingers quickly removing the small fasteners as his hands explored her body, uncorking a rush of emotion that accelerated her desire. Roughly pushing his shirt open, she buried her face in the dark silky pelt that covered his chest. She inhaled his scent, a complex meld of soap, shave lotion and raw maleness. Their excitement increased as she struggled to unhook and unzip his pants, exposing blue striped boxer shorts and his desire for her. Scooping her up in his arms, he carried her to the bed, placing her gently and gazing appreciatively at her nakedness as he stripped off his shorts. They reached for each other in a frenzied effort to make every inch of skin touch.

They came together quickly, frantic to let their raw sexuality sweep everything in its way. Later, they took their time, studying each other's fingers, faces, the curve of each rib. He nibbled on her hips; she ran her tongue along his most private parts. Hawk spoke softly, expressing his pleasure and asking her if she liked this or wanted more or less of that. His love-making vocabulary included words Selby had taught her boys not to say in public; now, they sounded appropriate, lovingly very '90's. She liked his running dialogue; it was so different from when she and Doug had made love. Hawk expressed himself eloquently even when using four-letter words. She found herself wanting to tell him she liked the way he fucked, too, but could not say it.

Resting side-by-side, giggling at their appetite for each other, Hawk told her to roll over. At Selby's sober stare, he laughed and said, "No, it's not what you think. I want to give you a backrub."

Carefully, Selby turned on her stomach, watching him over her shoulder, her hands ready to push away if she didn't like what he had in mind. He straddled the back of her thighs, his genitals bumping lightly against her as he began to massage her shoulders. "Relax. Trust me." He stroked her shoulders and worked his palms and thumbs down her spine, following the curve of each rib. His touch was firm but gentle. By the time he got to her lower back, both of them were ready for love again.

They dozed in each other's arms. "Well, I guess I'd better get back to the condo," Selby said, eventually sitting up and stretching.

"No, stay."

They teasingly argued the pros and cons of Selby's staying or going, still touching, inhaling the scent of love. At last, it was agreed that he would escort her back to the condo and stay overnight—what was left of it—where two bedrooms were available, the only way either one of them would get any sleep that night. Selby dressed in her chiffon while Hawk slipped into jeans and a polo shirt. He threw socks, sweater, shorts and shave kit into a small bag.

The condo almost seemed like home now to Selby as they walked in the door. They kissed goodnight and went into their separate rooms. Selby took a long hot shower and tumbled into bed naked, feeling physically, mentally and emotionally fulfilled. She had never felt as powerful as she had today—first in the boardroom and then in bed. Where the hell had this woman come from? she asked herself. She smiled sleepily, letting all the bad times slip away. Her new life promised to be one of fulfillment on many levels. She knew there would be surprises along the way but felt confident that she could handle anything.

CHAPTER FOURTEEN

Selby wakened to the sound of the shower in the guest suite. Hawk was up. It was time to get ready for the final day of the conference. Selby slipped into her robe, splashed water on her face and ran the brush through her hair. Coffee. Lots of coffee, that's what she needed. Padding bare-foot around the kitchen, she sliced bagels, found cream cheese and orange juice in the refrigerator. Good enough for breakfast after the huge dinner they had consumed last night. She put a jar of frozen strawberry jam into the microwave and set it to defrost. She couldn't believe how good she felt this morning. Usually big parties left her feeling tired and grumpy the next day from lack of sleep and too much food and drink. But not today. She softly hummed one of the tunes they had danced to—*Just one of those things, just one of those fabulous flings. A trip to the moon on gossamer wings, just one of those things...*

As she dropped the bagels into the toaster, she turned to find Hawk behind her, warm from his shower, with a towel around his waist. His damp hair fell to his shoulders. She breathed in his scent and took strength from the warmth of his body. He pushed the robe from her shoulders as she loosened his towel. No words were needed. Their mutual desire, playful, yet intense, set the tone for their first morning together.

Hawk pulled a kitchen chair away from the table, sat and pulled her down to straddle his muscular thighs. The coffee pot sighed, its pump sucking at the reservoir. The two bagel slices automatically lowered themselves on either side of the hot element. The microwave beeped urgently; the jam was defrosted. It seemed to urge them on. The coffee pot gave its last heaving, orgasmic gurgle as the toaster raised the bagels, now hot and crisp. The kitchen smelled of fresh coffee, warm toast, and sex.

"We fuck like minks, don't we?" laughed Hawk as he held her close.

Selby's answer was to sink her teeth into his bare shoulder, hard enough to leave marks. Retrieving the dropped robe and towel, they enjoyed a quick breakfast, laughing at their insatiable appetites.

*

The sun threatened to break through the fog and give them a glorious day, a day too nice to spend indoors at the conference. However, they had no choice for part of the morning; Hawk was one of four presenters on a panel discussion of Sod Management. Selby would attend a session on marketing. But after that, they were free to enjoy the city until their flight left that evening.

"Let's not fly back tonight," Hawk said as they walked to the conference hotel from the condo. "Have you seen the Napa Valley vineyards? We can rent a car and stay a night or two in St. Helena or Calistoga. I'd like to introduce you to a couple of people if we can find them. Whadya think?"

"I'd love it! But what about LillyHill?" Selby asked.

"I call Robert every day. Things are fine, although we seem to have an infestation of pocket gophers that needs attending to."

"A plague of pocket gophers! That sounds quite biblical," Selby said in mock severity. "And just what do you do about pocket gophers?"

"Traps. Poison bait if the acreage affected is large."

"Oh, poor things! They can't be that bad, can they?"

"They feed on the root system, destroying a vineyard in short order. And the little buggers can lay down 800 feet of tunnel per acre if they have a mind to. That can cause damage to machines—and crew—as well as the grapes. Yeah, gophers can be bad if they aren't stopped."

Selby quickly turned her thoughts from the distasteful idea of killing soft furry animals. Instead of questioning his methods of controlling pocket gophers, she said, "Let's do it—go the Valley."

"Great! After I'm finished with the panel, I'll rent a car and pick you up at the condo about 12:30. You'd better let Fiona know you won't be back tonight."

They went their separate ways at the hotel lobby. Selby had trouble concentrating in the marketing session. Her mind drifted to the pleasures of the evening before and the lascivious breakfast. She kept waiting for doubts or guilt to descend upon her, but there was nothing but a warm glow and a smile that appeared at inappropriate moments. At last, the session was over and she dashed out of the hotel and up the street to the Banana Republic where she bought khaki shorts, a tropical print blouse, a wide-brimmed hat and a cardigan sweater with a tiger's face woven into the back. Crazy clothes for a crazy couple of days in wine country.

Leaving a note for the invisible gnome who cared for the condo, Selby tried once again to call Fiona. Only the answering machine responded, so she left a message that she would fly home a day or two later. Fiona must be grocery shopping or having her hair done, Selby mused. She raided the condo kitchen for bread, cheese and fruit for a picnic in the car as they drove to the Valley. She packed a few things for overnight and slipped into her new shorts, blouse and sweater. When she saw that Hawk had rented a red Mustang convertible for the trip, she was glad she had succumbed to buying the hat. It was going to be a great day!

They headed northeast on Interstate 80, over the Oakland Bay Bridge, past the University of California at Berkeley and on to Highway 29, which snaked through small towns and vineyards to St. Helena and Calistoga. Stopping at one small vineyard about the size of LillyHill, they talked with the owners and tasted several of the estate wines. Selby extended an invitation for them to visit LillyHill if they were ever in the Willamette Valley. As they continued on their impromptu trip, the sun was full on the leafed-out vines that marched in orderly ranks over one rolling hill after another. Several miles further on Hawk pulled into the long driveway of the largest jug wine producer in the valley. Wine snobs wouldn't be caught dead drinking this wine, but the public loved it whether it was in a gallon jug or in a box.

"I can't imagine LillyHill ever being this big," Selby said. "I'm not sure I'd want it much larger than it is. There seems to be so much to do now. Why are we stopping here?" ·

"I want you to meet someone who works here, if he's in."

Selby thought it strange that Hawk didn't volunteer any more information about who they were to find or why, but she didn't ask as they pulled into the visitor's parking area. While Hawk set out to find the mysterious person he wanted Selby to meet, she wandered through the gift shop, purchasing a sterling silver corkscrew with a deeply etched design of sinuous vines and Bacchus, the God of wine. She also selected a bittersweet chocolate bar as she paid for the corkscrew.

At last Hawk returned and guided her outside, across the broad lawn, away from the public tasting area and touring groups. She couldn't stand it any longer. "Okay, where are we going and who is this mysterious person we are seeing?"

"My father. I haven't seen or talked to him in over two years. He'll meet us in the private tasting room."

Selby waited for more information, but none was forthcoming. It dawned on her that she really didn't know much about this man, her business partner, her lover. What had she gotten herself into?

They entered an unmarked door in one of the huge production buildings and walked down a wide corridor to a large alcove, which had an ornate bar and about a dozen small tables with chairs. A tall, gray-haired man was behind the bar, taking down wine glasses from an overhead rack. Hearing them, he turned and watched them as they came toward him. There was no smile of recognition or move to come from behind the polished bar which seemed to serve as a barrier. At the sight of the man, Selby burst into a wide smile, seeing the resemblance between father and son—the same eyes and nose. However, the older man's hair was short, gray and beginning to recede from his broad forehead. He wore wire-rimed glasses and sported a small goatee.

"Selby, I'd like you to meet my father, Walt Kestrel."

Extending her hand, she said, "How do you do? I'm Selby Browning."

There was an awkward silence as he examined her before acknowledging the introduction and then looked at Hawk. "Would you like to sample some of our premium wines? They won't destroy your delicate palate." There was a hint of a smirk on his face. He poured an inch of red wine into each of three glasses. Turning to Selby, he said, "My son is a wine snob, Ms. Browning. I doubt if jug wine has passed his lips since he left college. However, this is our Reserve Vintage Barbera. You may not be aware that we produce some high-end wines in addition to the jug wines Paul disdains."

Selby sniffed the wine and then raised her glass to examine the color and clarity as the men did, but her eyes were on father and son as they began a strange male dominance ritual, a dance of repartee, sarcasm and one-upmanship.

"Nice color," Hawk said of the black ruby wine. "Complex bouquet of ripe plum and pomegranate."

"Notice the hint of smoke and rose petals?" the elder Kestrel asked.

"Mmm. The undertones of oak add complexity," Hawk said.

To Selby, this was the most bizarre reunion she could imagine. She sipped the wine, trying to taste the plum and pomegranate, the smoke, oak and rose petals. As far as she could tell, it was just... delicious.

"Price?" Hawk said.

"Thirty. That's per bottle, not case," Walt said with a wicked smile that again reminded her of Hawk.

"Touché," Hawk responded.

Walt opened several more bottles of reserve estate wines, pouring a small amount of each into clean glasses. Placing them on a tray, he carried it to a table by a window overlooking the lawns and public building. Selby saw that the father had developed a paunch, probably from too much good food and wine.

They sat, one on either side of Selby. Hawk said, "My father has been cellarmaster here for over 20 years." Selby muttered something vague in acknowledgment, still feeling very uncomfortable by being in the middle of this odd father-son reunion. She felt as if she were here to serve as a deterrent to bloodshed. Hawk continued. "I had the exalted opportunity to be his apprentice until he retired or dropped dead on the job."

The ball being in Walt's court, he said, "That seemed so objectionable to my son that he joined the Navy and learned to cook." He paused as if waiting for a verbal parry from his son. Neither blinked nor looked away. Finally, Walt said, "This is our Petite Sirah. It's for current drinking and will continue to develop over the next three to five years."

Hawk sniffed, swirled, sipped. He turned to Selby and said, "The French Durif grape for Petite Sirahs was introduced in the early 1800s and is used primarily as a blending grape to add tannin and color. It's been the backbone of North Coast jug wines and Burgundies since the 1970s."

Not to be outdone by his son, Walt also addressed Selby. "Even though white wines have taken over much of the market, some of us continue to work with the Petite Sirahs, producing a substantially better product with a more restrained and accessible style that characterizes this particular vintage. Can you notice the aromas of berry and crushed pepper?" Selby sipped and tried very hard to taste something pepperish or berryish.

Finally, trying to get herself off the hook, she asked, "What kind of food do you recommend with this wine?"

Both men chimed in, recommending highly flavored vegetable pastas, cheeses, garlicky dishes and roast pork. Selby stifled a smile and reached for a glass of pale golden wine.

"Ah," Walt exclaimed. "That is our premier Chardonnay. It has an elegance, a complexity you will enjoy." With that the three of them again sniffed, looked, swirled and drank. Selby waited for the men to begin their pretentious pontificating on what she should be experiencing. And it came: the hints of mango, peach, green apple; the wine being round and complex with a lingering finish, a long, creamy finish.

The men looked at her in anticipation. "Well, your knowledge overwhelms me. I can see that you have much to talk about. I think I'll just find a place to powder my nose." With that, she escaped down the corridor, wondering whether they would kill each other or embrace and heal whatever wounds had kept them apart. Her comfort level had dropped at each verbal parry and thrust. Instinctively, she knew the men were headed for an argument. She'd seen it happen too often between Doug and the boys.

CHAPTER FIFTEEN

On her return the conversation became tentatively personal, with Walt saying that he had heard Paul—obviously, Hawk was not a name he used or appreciated—had taken a position in the Willamette Valley.

"So, you are partners in LillyHill Vineyard. The lady has the money and you have the know-how, right?" Turning to Selby, he continued, "Since you are the senior partner, maybe you can get him to get a haircut." Hawk's face clouded over and he pushed himself away from the table.

The blood sang in Selby's ears. She'd been through this scene before when Steve had let his hair go wild. Those were the early punk rock days. Crew-cut fathers couldn't abide the look. Doug blamed her for letting Steve "get out of hand," as he put it.

"Are you ready to go, Selby?"

"Yes," Selby said, eager to escape a scene that was threatening to turn ugly. What is the matter with these two? she wondered. They act like kids. I'd love to send them to their rooms for some time out, she thought in exasperation. This hostility must stop.

Instead of rising, she put on her "mother" face and looked from one to the other, saying, "This has been a very bizarre reunion; since I've been put in the middle of something for some unknown reason, I'm going to give you my two cents worth." She stood, paced a step or two, took a deep breath and shoved her trembling hands into the deep pockets of her shorts.

"I've no idea what your problem is, but life is too short for children and parents to not be open and honest with each other, no matter what age. Seeing you two prance around, trying to wound each other with knowledge, with words, with.....I don't know what. The father of my three sons was killed eighteen months ago. I hope to God that there was no left-over hostility—real or perceived—between them before he was taken from their lives."

Selby felt flushed and her breath came in shallow gulps. "I'm not going to be a buffer between you two. Whatever it is, get it out in the open, say you're sorry, shake hands and get on with life." She quickly left the alcove, almost running down the corridor and out into the sun, her heart pounding from the scene. A low stone wall partially shaded by an oak tree became her refuge. She sat, stretching her pale, bare legs to the sun. Once her heartbeat settled down, she reached for the chocolate bar, took a huge bite and swallowed it with a minimum of chewing. What am I doing? It's their problem, not mine. That damned temper of mine. I'll get myself in deep trouble one day. I didn't used to be so angry. It seems like ever since Doug died, I've gotten mad over simple things.

She settled into a more comfortable position and nibbled at the chocolate, now enjoying the rich, comforting taste. Her thoughts drifted to her own sons. She and Justin were close—always had been. She could never see that they would become estranged. Mike and she were okay, too, as far as she knew. But Steve, well, he was another story. She hated his brashness, his male-chauvinist-pig attitude, his lifestyle. How could she hate the way he acts? He's just doing what Doug did. Did she hate Doug? At times.

But we were good together, too, at first. It was only later—particularly when he cheated on me—that I began to feel differently. A relationship based purely on sex is no relationship—and that's what it was all about. What did we know as high school kids? Selby sighed, not wanting to think of the bad times with Doug. She wanted to keep only the good memories. She needed to do that for the boys. Yet she was her own woman now, not just Doug's widow and the mother of his sons. Marriage and motherhood are so complex. She understood why some women chose to remain alone. Alone could be good, fulfilling, if you had friends and something creative in which to channel your energy. But children were important. She couldn't imagine not having children. If she and Doug had had a more stable marriage and could have afforded it, she might have tried for a girl. She'd often imagined having a daughter to dress up, to take to the ballet, to have fun cooking together. Well, enjoy your three sons. No pretty little girls to raise now. She licked the last of the chocolate off her lips and closed her eyes, soaking up the warmth of the sun and the quiet of the afternoon.

Thirty minutes later the men came to where she was sitting. She watched them as they walked toward her, talking calmly. Well, they hadn't killed each other and they seemed to be having a conversation, not a confrontation, Selby thought as she sat up to meet them, wondering if they thought she was a flake—or worse yet, a meddler. Walt took her hand and said, "You remind me of my wife—all fire and wisdom. You would have liked each other."

With that he kissed her lightly on the cheek and turned to Hawk, offering him his hand, suggesting they call each other soon.

CHAPTER SIXTEEN

Hawk didn't mention the reunion and Selby felt uncomfortable asking. But her curiosity finally got the best of her. "Are you and your father...okay now?"

"Yeah. More or less. It's a beginning." They drove in silence for a few minutes longer, then he said, "Thanks for what you...said...did. I didn't mean to put you in the middle of something, but...I couldn't have gone to see him...alone. He can make me feel...no, I allow him to make me feel... like a dumb little kid at times. I didn't want to play that game today."

"I was afraid that I might have said something wrong."

"You were just fine," Hawk said, placing his hand on her knee and giving it a gentle squeeze.

They tried to recapture their earlier mood of escaping work and responsibility. Hawk had made a reservation at a charming bed and breakfast in the one-stoplight town of Calistoga. The main street was lined with art galleries, boutiques and restaurants, with resorts and spas within walking distance of the commercial area. Hawk and Selby wandered up one side of the street and down the other, reading the menus displayed outside each restaurant. They admired hand-crafted jewelry and laughed at pretentious modern art. They considered going to the one movie theater after dinner, but decided that a shower and early to bed was more to their liking. As the sun set, they chose an Italian restaurant which had sawdust on the floor and a wonderful garlic aroma wafting out the door. They started with deep fried calamari, followed by a Caesar salad made with tiny whole spears of Romaine lettuce, wonderful sourdough bread and chicken ravioli with pesto. Mocha cheesecake and thick black coffee finished their meal. And, of course, wine.

As they strolled hand-in-hand back to their bed and breakfast, Hawk said, "How did your husband die? Would you mind talking about it?"

They walked in silence for a block before Selby spoke. "No, I can talk about it now. There was a time I couldn't...but I've come to terms with it. Let's sit over there."

They crossed the street and settled themselves on a bench in a paved area between two buildings. Hawk stretched his arm across the back of the bench, his hand toying with Selby's shoulder. The light from the street lamp filtered through the leaves of an ancient madronna tree, its reddish smooth bark and shiny leaves enhanced by the soft evening light. Selby took a deep breath and began. "Doug was murdered."

"Oh, God," Hawk said, pulling her closer to him.

"He was hauling a load of micro-processors to Philadelphia. Millions of dollars worth of hi-tech stuff. The perfect score for hijackers. They seem to have ways of knowing who is hauling what and where." She paused, assembling her thoughts, trying to tell a long, terrible story quickly and clearly. "The large cities back East are not fond of truckers. They don't have good truck stops like the West does. They just want them to unload and get out of the city...something about idling diesels adding pollution to their already bad air. So when truckers get tired or have to wait to make a delivery, they just pull over on a side street or sometimes under off-ramps. Even the few truck stops they have are not very safe, Doug used to say." She looked up into the velvet night sky, her mind drifting from the story. "I'll never understand why men—even women—like long-distance driving. Doug says...said...they get addicted to the road and the money. But it's so dangerous—the speed, lack of sleep, poor eating habits, the hookers and homosexuals that are drawn to truck stops."

Selby sighed, pulled her sweater closer around her and brought her thoughts back to the story. "Of course no one really knows what exactly happened, but the police reconstructed the crime as being similar to several other hijacking deaths they had seen before." She paused, and then continued. "Canisters of ether with additional chemicals are sold at truck stops. Drivers inject ether into their diesel engines on cold days to make them start faster. It makes a kind of explosion, I guess. What hijackers do is quietly open the sleeper cab vent windows and fill the cab with ether, knocking out the driver sleeping in the cab. Usually, it just puts the driver into a deeper sleep so that the hijackers can break into the cab, steal the keys to the load and even the driver's personal possessions. Sometimes, they put too much ether in the sleeping area and...and...the driver dies."

Hawk uttered a soft oath and pulled her closer to his side.

"Yes. But there's more to the story. The hijackers brought in another tractor and stole the trailer—cargo and all, according to the police. It was hours later when Doug's tractor was noticed...its doors open. Doug...dead." Again she paused, taking in a deep, ragged breath. "The minute the funeral was over, I was contacted by Micro-Tel—the micro-chip manufacturer—the bank which carried our loan, and the insurance company. Doug kept telling me that once he made this run we'd really make a lot of money and we could pay off the loan sooner. You see, I'd agreed to mortgage our home and borrow on his life insurance so that he could buy the unit. It was a Peterbilt with a refrigerator trailer costing over $200,000, way more than our house. The truck was beautiful, if you like that kind of thing...all shiny with chrome, brilliant green metallic paint, his DB logo on the cab doors..."

She paused again, brushed some imaginary lint off her shorts, smoothing non-existent wrinkles out of the fabric on her lap. Such a silly, charming habit, Hawk thought, watching her struggle to continue.

"Hey...you don't have to talk about it," he offered.

"No. I'm okay." She took a deep breath and continued. "The company and the bank took whatever we had, more or less saying they were sorry I had a bad-luck crook for a husband. Doug...he...forged insurance papers and other documents...anyway, nothing was covered and..." Selby quickly stood up. "Let's go; it's getting cold."

"Okay," Hawk said.

He kept his arm around her shoulders as they walked to their lodging, listening to small town night sounds. He wanted to say something to comfort her, but words wouldn't come. He felt a tenderness for her that he'd never felt for another woman, including his ex-wife. He increased his hold on her. If he could just give her his physical strength, his warmth, perhaps that would help.

They were quiet that night as they lay in each other's arms. The sex was subdued, needy, almost as if they were saying farewell. There was no wildness and giggling, just desperate clinging, a satisfying but strange coupling.

"What happened between you and Walt?" Selby asked as she snuggled close in his arms.

The long pause and deep sigh made her think he would not tell her. He rolled over on his back, his hands behind his head, and stared up at the slowly turning ceiling fan. "I was groomed to follow in his footsteps. I grew up helping him in vineyards, following him around as he worked his way up to become one of the most respected cellarmasters in the Valley. It was a foregone conclusion that I would become a cellarmaster, even though I was more interested in growing grapes than blending wine. We argued a lot over methods of making wine. He always called me a wine snob. Guess I was, still am. And

I didn't want to wait thirty years or more to take his place. I wanted to find my own niche."

They listened to the night sounds: the creak of the old house, an occasional car, far away laughter, the deep warning bark of a dog. Selby waited patiently as he gathered his thoughts. He continued. "He became...harder, more critical after Mom died. She was the one who kept him human, to channel his bitterness over slights or things that he felt went against him. She had a heart problem. We didn't know about it—no one did. She always seemed so full of life. She kept it from of us—Dad, my sister Tracy, me. Mom died about six months after Catherine and I were married. At least she got to enjoy the wedding and miss the messy divorce."

Selby touched him gently, murmuring, "I'm so sorry." He patted her hand as it rested on his bare chest. She asked, "What happened between you and Catherine?"

Hawk gave a low, sharp sound. "We were bad together from the beginning. God, she was a bitch!" He paused again. "I was no prize either. My folks wanted the marriage—particularly Walt. He thought I needed to settle down, and who better than with the daughter of their best friend?" Hawk rolled over on his side to get a closer look at Selby. "Are you sure you want to hear this crap?" She nodded and snuggled closer, inhaling his scent, feeling his skin on her cheek.

"Catherine and I more or less grew up together—neighboring ranches, same grade school, you know the scene. We dated a little in high school, but nothing serious. I went off to college; she went to Europe to finishing school. She wasn't very smart, but she was beautiful, no question about that. She had her heart set on becoming a model." Hawk traced his finger along Selby's nose, chin and down to her breasts, then wrapped her in his arms and continued.

"I was a senior at UC Davis when we met again at a mutual friend's wedding. Catherine was a real knockout—very sophisticated after her European schooling and tour. She was the most beautiful woman at the wedding. Well, anyway, we got caught up in all the wedding stuff—the romance, the champagne, the parties, seeing old friends who were engaged, several others were already married and having babies. We both seemed to feel that we were being left behind. Her modeling career hadn't taken off and her folks were pressuring her to do something—anything. So we began dating heavily, got engaged and were married right after I graduated. Three months from 'Long time no see,' to 'I do.' It lasted just over a year. No kids.

Walt called me a quitter. He was right, but it was the right thing to do. I joined the Navy—which Walt thought was a waste of my time and talents. It wasn't. I needed to grow up. It was the best six years of my life, until now." He kissed Selby's forehead gently.

"Where's Catherine now?"

"Married, lives back East, has two kids. End of story. Now go to sleep. We've got more wineries to see tomorrow." He kissed her on the nose and rolled over.

The next morning, Hawk called Robert to make sure everything was fine at the vineyard and to tell him they would return later in the week. But things were not fine. And it wasn't due to pocket gophers.

They left immediately for San Francisco, throwing their gear in the car and driving as fast as the morning fog and narrow roads would allow. They made a quick stop at the Sheraton Hotel for Hawk to pack and check out, then on to the condo so Selby could pack while Hawk made flight arrangements.

There was no point trying to reach Fiona at LillyHill. She was in the hospital recovering from smoke inhalation.

CHAPTER SEVENTEEN

Liam Walsh rarely took time off from the business. There was always something to do in the greenhouses—checking the thermostats, the sprinkling systems, the presence of insects or disease in the plants. The acres of nursery stock needed tending; bark, gravel and irrigation pipe needed to be ordered for inventory or delivered to customers. Estimates must be made for landscaping projects, workers to hire and train, marketing; managing the employees took all his time and concentration. The business demands also kept him from missing his wife of thirty years, now dead of cancer.

It was nearly a year since she died after the extended illness. He had given her his time and attention freely, lovingly, caring for her until the last. He missed her deeply, but knew he must go on with life for the sake of his four daughters, five grandchildren and the business that he had grown from a roadside flower stand he started at the age of eight, to the multi-million dollar landscaping and nursery operation that was highly respected in the Willamette Valley.

When Justin invited him to LillyHill, he had made a thoughtful decision to attend the brunch. Liam liked Justin. He was a good kid, a hard worker, one of the few young people Liam knew who had sensible plans for the future. He had helped Justin through the death of his father by listening, by understanding that sometimes the young man would not be at his best. Perhaps he could help the mother, too. Losing a spouse could do terrible things to a person. Loneliness could make a person feel worthless, sick. He had enjoyed meeting Selby and the vineyard owners at the brunch. It was an easy social gathering since everyone was interested in growing things. Then he and Justin had worked on the rockery waterfalls that were clogged with winter debris; they had cleaned out the system and started the pump. Selby had been delighted with the results. Yes, it had been a good party. His first social outing since Margie died was successful. He could face life again.

On this late April afternoon, Liam left the nursery early to clean up and take a small gift to Selby. She had mentioned a piece of statuary she had admired on an earlier visit to the nursery. He had found the life-sized stone rabbit crouched among hundreds of birdbaths, jardinieres, deer, ducks, quail, kittens, puppies and assorted replicas of famous religious statuary his business sold to customers for their yards. He hoped this was the one she liked. He would take it to her this afternoon.

This was a big step in his simple life. It took him twice as long to shower, shave and change. "You'd think I was going on a date," he said to himself in the mirror as he patted on aftershave lotion. Was he? he asked himself. No. Just making a friendly call as neighbors might do. The one thing he hadn't been able to do was pick up the phone and call Selby to see if he could drop by for a visit. No, he'd just drive out to the vineyard and take a chance that she'd be home. If she were gone, he'd leave the rabbit with his business card.

As he turned into the vineyard and drove slowly up the hill to the house, he almost hoped that she wouldn't be home. What would he say to her? He could ask how the bonsai was doing. He could ask to see the rockery in bloom. He could ask about Justin. Yes. He'd find something to say.

He parked in front of the paving stone path, which led to the front porch and stepped out of his Chevy Tahoe, admiring how nice his new rig looked. Running it through the car wash on his way here was a good idea, even though he realized it was a delaying tactic. He flicked a speck of dust off the name of his business, which was painted in green on the sides of the white utility vehicle. Can't delay any longer, he told himself.

The gray shingles of the house looked silvery in the warm afternoon sun, yet the windows had a strange, opaque look, not reflecting the oak trees that surrounded the residence as might be expected. Looking up toward the attic with its elaborate gingerbread trim at the peak of the roof, Liam saw a thin stream of smoke. At first, he thought it was coming from the brick chimney, which straddled the high roof beam. No! The smoke was coming from under the eaves—or was it out of the attic window? Fire!

He ran up the verandah steps to the front door, ringing the bell, pounding on the door with his fist, calling, "Selby! Mrs. Browning!" The doorknob resisted his twist. With a last ring and pound, he ran down the steps and around to the sliding glass door at the rear of the house. Locked, too. Trying every door and window on the verandah that wrapped the house, he returned to the front door. Picking up the heavy stone rabbit, he smashed one of the etched glass panes in the front door, reached in and unlocked it. Bursting in, his eyes and throat were immediately assaulted by the smoke. "Mrs. Browning! Selby!" he called. Crouching low, he ran toward the hallway that led to the main staircase and the back of the house.

"Selby! Is anyone home?" he called again, now feeling foolish about breaking into what was probably an empty house. No one here, he thought, turning to find his way back through the smoke. It was then that he the stumbled over a body sprawled at the base of the stairway.

Instinct took over. He slipped his hands under the arms of the woman who lay crumpled on the bottom step. There was no time to wonder if she were injured or if moving her would be dangerous. Get out! Get out of the house was all Liam could think. Stumbling through the gaping front door, he pulled her over to the porch railing and propped her up, her head sagging to one side. "Lady, lady!" he shouted. It wasn't Selby; it was her housekeeper. Her name escaped him. Leaving her propped against the railing, he sprinted to his truck and grabbed the cell phone. After dialing 911, he gave the location of the fire. "We need an ambulance, too!" Liam shouted before hanging up and tossing the instrument onto the front seat of the vehicle. He ran back to the housekeeper—Fiona, that was her name—who was now groaning and coughing, trying to stand, but collapsing when she put weight on her right ankle, which was beginning to swell. "Is there anyone else in the house?" he asked. Fiona shook her head, unable to talk from the coughing.

"Stay here," he said, and dashed down the steps and along the side of the house until he came to a faucet and hose used to water the yard. Unreeling the hose, he began to play the thin stream of water toward the attic window where the smoke now rolled out in greater clouds. It was a useless thing to do, he knew, but he needed to try. After what seemed an eternity, a fire truck and a water tender turned into the vineyard entrance, laboring up the hill to the house, lights flashing, sirens whining their last ear-splitting sound as the units positioned themselves in the driveway. Liam knew that rural fires were compounded by the lack of water pressure and fire hydrants; tanker trucks must haul water to supplement the low-pressure well water that was available in most rural areas.

"Get her away from the house," a fireman shouted to Liam. "Anyone else in there?" Their first priority was safety of inhabitants; next was safety for the fire crew.

"Negative," responded Liam, dropping the garden hose and picking up Fiona's limp body, carrying her to his Tahoe where he sat her on the front seat. She had begun to cry, babbling that she started the fire. The ambulance siren could be heard in the distance as several firemen strapped on their self-contained breathing apparatuses and moved quickly to assigned tasks. The water tender crew set up a portable pool from which water would be pumped. Two firemen unreeled a hose from the fire truck and charged in the front door while another supervised the pumping of water from the temporary reservoir. A sharp sound of breaking glass made Liam look up; smoke poured out of the high dormer window, which had shattered from the heat. Two other firefighters set up ladders and quickly climbed to the roof, axes ready to chop a vent hole in the roof. Another fireman set up a fan-like device inside the door to displace the smoke, making it easier for the firefighters to see.

Amid the organized chaos, the ambulance arrived. Two medical technicians gave Fiona oxygen and prepared her for the trip to the hospital. When she was secure, one asked Liam if there were other injured persons. Liam assured him that the lady was the only one injured, only then noticing his own cut hands when the technician led him to the ambulance for first aid. "You'd better get a couple of stitches in this one," he told Liam. "The rest are superficial."

The whole thing seemed over before it began, as if time collapsed in on itself during the crisis, Liam thought. Now, several neighbors had arrived as well as a county sheriff's officer, who began gathering information. Who discovered the fire? Anyone injured or killed? Where is the owner? Who was taken to the hospital? Liam answered the officer's questions as best he could, staring at the trampled flowerbeds littered with shingles chopped from the roof, water running out the front door. What a terrible homecoming Selby would have, he thought. Would she be coming home any minute or was she out of town? he wondered.

His concerns about Selby were addressed when Robert stopped by the vineyard to see how many gophers had been caught since morning and to reset the traps. He was speechless at the sight of the fire trucks, smoke and commotion. Liam quickly filled him in on the situation and asked how Selby could be reached. Robert stammered that they would have to wait until Hawk called him as he did each morning. All he knew was that they were someplace in the Napa Valley touring wineries.

The firemen made a final room-to-room search, assuring themselves that the fire was out and that there were no additional areas that needed attention. After the sheriff left, Liam helped Robert nail a sheet of plywood over the front door and made plans to cover the hole in the roof the next day. Robert said he'd have his son, Rio, stay at the vineyard until the owners returned, in case the fire flared up again or curiosity seekers took it upon themselves to trespass.

Hawk and Selby talked little on their flight from San Francisco to Portland, each lost in private thoughts. What would they find when they reached LillyHill? Was there anything they could have done to prevent it? How was Fiona? How bad was the damage? Selby castigated herself for indulging in sensual pleasures when she should have been home tending to business. She should have been there, been able to prevent the fire, to keep Fiona safe. Pointless worries and recriminations whirled through her mind.

The uneventful flight from San Francisco to Portland seemed to take forever. After claiming their luggage, they retrieved the Explorer from the long-term parking lot and caught the freeway through Portland to the southwest suburbs where they would swing by the hospital to see Fiona.

"Robert seemed to think she was okay," Hawk said. "Just throat and lung irritation from the smoke."

"Yes, but he said she was hysterical, too."

"Well, that's nothing unusual—or terminal," he chuckled.

"Not funny, Hawk. I know she's not my responsibility, yet she is. Sometimes I think she is more of a problem than managing the whole bequest!"

Fiona seemed to be asleep when they entered her room at the Good Shepherd Hospital, a small healthcare center which served the upper Willamette Valley south of the metropolitan area. She was lying quietly, pale, her head elevated, oxygen tubes in her nose. An intravenous dripped slowly into the vein in her left wrist. Her bandaged right foot and ankle stuck out from the covers, a pillow supporting the injured limb. As Selby took Fiona's thin, wrinkled hand in hers, Fiona opened her eyes, staring blindly for a moment, and then burst into tears at recognition.

"I'm sorry! I didn't mean to burn down LillyHill!" Moaning and struggling, she covered her face with both hands. "My thimbles. I want my thimbles."

"I'll get the nurse," Hawk said, quickly stepping out the door.

"Fiona, hush. It's okay," Selby said. "LillyHill isn't gone. Just smoke damage. Robert told us. It's okay. Don't cry."

"But the fire was my fault! I love that house. Lilly will never forgive me."

"Shhh. Shhh. Fiona, it's okay." Selby put her arms around Fiona, awkwardly trying to reassure her. "Hawk and I are concerned about you, not the house."

Before she could respond, the nurse came in with a mild sedative, which she administered through the IV. The nurse said, "Miss Dermot needs to rest now. Any mention of the fire upsets her."

Stepping into the hall, Selby asked, "Would you have her doctor call me, please. I'd like to know how she is. Is the ankle broken?"

"No. Just a sprain. And her lungs will be fine in a day or so. I'll see if Dr. Stevens is in the hospital; perhaps he could see you now if he is." She returned to the nurse's station to page the doctor. Hawk and Selby wandered down to the waiting alcove, Hawk sitting quietly, Selby pacing. What a strange ending to a lovely, self-indulgent weekend, Selby thought. Guilt slithered in. Screwing instead of tending to business! Could I have prevented the fire? Where do Hawk and I go now in our relationship? Can we go back to being just business partners? There's no future for us. He'll want to remarry, have children. Selby chastised herself, mumbling, "Stupid, stupid!"

"Mrs. Browning? I'm Dr. Stevens. I understand you'd like to know how Miss Dermot is doing."

"Oh, yes, please," Selby said.

"Physically, she's in no danger. Just nose and throat irritation that will heal in a few days. Her lungs look clear, although she'll cough up soot—black gook—for a while. The sprain is fairly serious—mostly painful; with physical therapy, it will be fine. She might feel steadier on her feet with a cane for a few days. However, her emotional state seems...a bit...intense. She blames herself. Whether this is the case or not, she needs reassurance and someone to keep an eye on her until she settles down."

"I'll take care of that, of course," Selby said. "When can she be released?"

"Probably the day after tomorrow. Call me tomorrow morning. I'll know more then."

Thanking the doctor, Selby and Hawk peeked into Fiona's room once more, and, seeing that she was sleeping, returned to the parking lot.

"Hawk, will you drive, please? Suddenly, I'm very tired...and, I suppose, a bit uptight about what we'll find at LillyHill."

"Sure. I doubt if you'll be able to stay there tonight," Hawk said, swinging smoothly into traffic. "You can bunk with me."

"Right!" Selby said sarcastically. "I'll sleep in Justin's room over the garage."

"No, seriously. Even though Robert said only Fiona's suite burned, there's a lot of smoke and water damage. Don't decide until you see the house."

They drove in silence, again lost in private thoughts. Finally, just a few miles from LillyHill, Hawk said, "Would you like to stop for something to eat or take a chance on my cooking?"

"I'm not hungry. Whatever you want." Selby sighed, then continued. "I guess all of Fiona's clothes are ruined. I'll need to buy some things for her and decide where she should stay. Has she ever mentioned friends that live nearby?"

"As far as I know, the Steiners were the only people in her life. Put her up in a hotel for a few days."

She gave a noncommittal sound and leaned forward in her seat as Hawk turned into the winery entrance and drove up the hill. The sunset was turning the house a soft pinkish gray, making the reflection in the windows look as if the fire had returned. Robert's pickup was parked in the driveway. He and Rio were raking up shingles and other debris from the front of the house.

The men shook hands, as Selby stood stunned at the sight. Their deep voices were nothing more than background noise as she surveyed the destruction. Hawk touched her arm and gave her a curious, concerned look. "I'm fine," she said.

At last, Robert led the way into the house, pointing out the worst of the damage with the aid of a flashlight, explaining that the power had been cut. The acrid smell was overpowering, the floors soggy and gritty. Tears welled up in Selby's eyes and a lump in her throat made it hard to speak. She didn't want to become emotional about the house. She had never invested a lot of emotion in material things; they could be lost so quickly. But she felt sorrow for the Steiners. How devastating this would have been to them. She could understand Fiona's guilt even though she had yet to see the mess. I'll need to keep her away until we can get some of this cleaned up, Selby thought.

They climbed to the third floor where the fire had started in Fiona's sitting room. The heat had charred the walls. The hole the firefighters had chopped in the roof was covered with a sheet of thick blue plastic. Robert pointed the flashlight toward the window and said, "This is where the fire started, by the desk under the window. They think it was smoker's carelessness."

"Poor Fiona!" Selby said. "She loved that antique desk. It was one of the things Lilly wanted her to have. I helped her move it up here. It was a beautiful old thing...delicately carved, heavily lacquered. I imagine that it caught quickly...and lace curtains over the window must have helped spread the fire. They were sheer cotton and linen, not nylon that might have melted and not burned, maybe."

Glass crunched underfoot as they carefully made their way out of the room and down stairs. Selby wondered what Fiona had meant about the thimbles. Were they a collection? Had they been consumed in the blaze?

"You can't stay here tonight, Selby. Wait until we get a cleaning crew and a contractor in here. You can consider staying in Justin's room when the power is back on."

"Okay. You're right." Turning to Robert, Selby said, "Thank you for all you and Rio have done. I know you have lots to do with the vineyard and taking time for this was..." She stopped, overcome by emotion she did not want to expose. Selby turned to look at the house again as the darkness softened evidence of damaged. She heard Robert's truck drive down the hill. "Well, I have my hands full now. The only positive thing is that it gives me the opportunity to decorate the house to my taste."

Hawk gently pulled her toward the Explorer. "Come on. Get in. I'll see if I can find something to eat that hasn't turned green and fuzzy in the refrigerator since I've been gone." With that, they drove toward the stables and Hawk's apartment.

CHAPTER EIGHTEEN

"Take a shower while I fix dinner," Hawk said to Selby as she stood in the center of the room looking lost and sad. "You'll feel better."

When she returned wrapped in her robe, Hawk was working a cork out of a bottle of LillyHill Pinot Noir. "Thought we'd try our '96, see how it's holding up. It wasn't the best, but still drinkable." Pouring two glasses, he handed Selby one, saying, "Let it breathe for a few minutes."

Selby sat quietly watching him move efficiently around the tiny kitchen area. A pot of water for pasta was beginning to boil as he sautéed garlic and onion. Then he added a can of diced tomatoes, a dash of balsamic vinegar, a spoonful of tomato paste, a pinch of sugar, some oregano and basil. The aroma changed Selby's mind about not being hungry. She watched him drain a can of tuna and a can of olives, then search the refrigerator for some elusive ingredient. A pleased grunt indicated he had found the tiny bottle of capers that was hidden in a corner. Next he searched a cupboard for pasta, rejecting *spaghetti* and *fettuccine*, settling on *cavatelli*, narrow shells with rippled surfaces. He shook an amount he judged suitable into the pot of boiling water and reached for his wine.

"Is there anything I can do to help?" she asked, not really meaning it.

Hawk shook his head, concentrating on the color and robe of the wine in his glass, sniffing it, finally sucking in a small taste, letting it spray across his tongue. "Is there anything I can do to help you? I know the fire is a shock, but it wasn't your fault. You know that. I'm here; tell me. I don't understand why you're so...upset."

"Forget it. I'm fine" Selby took a sip of the wine, then downed all of it, placing the empty glass on the table in front of her. She shuddered as the wine hit her empty stomach; her temples began to throb. Watching him add the drained tuna and some black olives to the bubbling sauce, she said "You certainly are domestic. Independent as a hog on ice, aren't you?"

"Hog on ice? What kind of folksy colloquialism is that?" he said, trying to turn her caustic remark into a joke.

"I don't know. Seriously, you really don't need anyone, do you?"

"What's your point?" he said, serving her a flat bowl of steaming pasta topped with sauce and Parmesan cheese.

"I don't know. Just ignore it."

"Eat. What do you think of the Pinot?" He poured more wine for her.

She did not respond, so they ate in silence. The past days of laughter, love and learning about each other seemed far away, a fantasy. The fire had cast a pall over their relationship as well as LillyHill. After dinner they sat on opposite ends of the sofa as Hawk surfed through television channels. Nothing caught their interest. Bedtime loomed like a black cloud between them. Finally, Selby said, "If you've got an extra blanket, I'll just curl up here on the sofa."

"No need for that. You can have the bed. You must be tired." He reached toward her. She pulled away.

"No, you take it. It's yours." Selby stood, wrapped her arms across her chest and walked over to the window, staring at the darkness, seeing nothing, not even her reflection.

"Christ! We've been sleeping together for days. What's the big deal now? We don't HAVE to have sex; I'm not some kind of animal." He had raised his voice, exasperated and confused by her attitude, her coldness. "I thought we had something going on between us."

"We did. Lust....and....curiosity."

"So? That's normal. But there was something else...later. Something more. You can't deny it."

"We can't have an intimate relationship. We're business partners. You're too young; I'm too old for you."

The silence in the room seemed to have texture, unpleasantly clotted, dense. With an impatient gesture of his arm, as if to wipe off the surface of the silence, Hawk said in disgust, "What a crock!"

"I just needed to get laid," Selby said softly, almost to herself.

Hawk burst out laughing. "You used me! You took my body. I'm soiled goods now. No one will ever want me again!"

Selby spun around, glaring at him. "That's a stupid thing to say!"

"Not half as stupid as the 'you're too young, I'm too old' crap!" he replied with a sing-song whine. Then he sighed deeply, saying, "Come to bed. Get some sleep," and heading for the bedroom. Then looking back over his shoulder at her, he continued with a wicked smile, "But don't you dare touch me!" His laughter stung.

At that moment, she hated him, his arrogance, his humor, his sexual allure.

She could have kicked herself for mentioning their age difference. How could she have articulated her biggest fear...the fear that one day he would look at her and see 'old woman'? The only relationship possible between them was as business partners.

She could hear him brushing his teeth, going through his nighttime routine that had seemed so normal, so comforting to her the past few days. Still standing by the living room window, she waited until she heard the rustle of the sheets and the ritual pounding of his pillow as he settled into his favorite sleeping position...on his right side, knees bent, the pillow scrunched up between his shoulder and neck. As soon as she was sure he was settled, she quietly took her turn in the bathroom. She felt secretive, not even wanting him to hear her brush her teeth. Intimacy now seemed crude, embarrassing. She slipped quietly into bed, hardly making a sound, clinging to the edge of the mattress and holding her breath. If he reached out for her, would she hit him or melt into his embrace? Please don't make me make that choice, she prayed.

Selby woke to the sound of the coffee grinder, then the shower running. She played possum, eyes closed, not moving, pretending to be asleep. Her ruse was foiled as Hawk held a fresh cup of coffee under her nose. "Wake up, Sleeping Beauty. You've got a messy house to clean. Maybe I should call you Cinderella."

Selby rolled over, scooted herself to a sitting position and took the cup from him, being very careful not to touch his hand. "Thank you." She tried not to look at him, averting her eyes from his face. He hadn't shaved this morning, his jaw dark with a day's growth of beard. It was all she could do not to reach out and stroke his face, place her soft cheek against his prickly one.

He stood quietly, waiting for her to say more, watching her avoid his gaze. "No apology for being a bitch last night?"

"No. Just forget what I said."

"Never! You are the first woman I've heard admit she needed to get laid." His laughter brought a flush to her cheeks as he returned to the kitchen.

The coffee was strong and hot, exactly what Selby needed to face the day, a day of decisions, phone calls, dealing with Fiona. After a few sips, she got out of bed and rummaged through her suitcase, shaking out the wrinkled shorts and blouse she had worn while touring the wineries. Nothing else in her suitcases seemed appropriate for the nasty job she must begin. She slipped on the sweater with the tiger's face to ward off the morning chill, took her empty cup to the kitchen and sat across from Hawk, who was finishing a bowl of cold cereal. "There are bagels in the freezer. I don't recommend having cereal. The milk's turned. Make yourself at home. I've got to catch up on what's happening in the fields...see what damage the gophers have done."

Selby nodded and began making a list of things she had to do: call a contractor for repairs, hire a professional cleaning firm that specialized in smoke and water damage, call the insurance company, buy Fiona some clothes, pick her up at the hospital, put her in a hotel or something, call Liam and thank him...what else? Oh, call Justin and tell him about the fire. It was overwhelming. "Is there a contractor you can recommend?" she asked as Hawk pulled an old sweatshirt over his head.

"Yeah. Frank Cannard of C & M Construction. I think their number is on the pad by the phone. I don't know who the original builders of the house were. Levy might know from handling the Steiners' affairs. Do you remember seeing any blueprints in the stuff the Steiners left you? Gotta go. See ya."

After making the necessary phone calls, Selby walked up the hill to take a look at the house again. The cleaners would be there at ten o'clock. She wouldn't let Fiona see the house until the mess was gone. It would be a shock to her, and hysterics were not on Selby's To Do List. Still mulling over what must be done and what timeframe was feasible, she strolled around the outside, looking at the trampled flowers and shrubs, the bits of shingle and glass Robert and Rio had missed in their effort to rake up debris. Near the front steps, a small, gray stone rabbit lay half buried in the mud. Stooping, she picked it up, its weight requiring both hands. It was scuffed on the nose. Strange. Where had this come from? Placing it on the verandah, she continued her tour, stopping to key in the garage door lock code. The door remained closed; she remembered that the power had been cut. Another thing to do: call the power company and an electrician to check the wiring.

She fumbled in her pocket for the house keys and entered through the back verandah door. She hesitated at going in, yet knew she must. Creepy. That's what Justin would have said. And she agreed.

Thankful for the bright sunlight that streamed in the smoky windows, she made her way carefully up to the third floor, where the fire had done the most damage. Her quest: a clue as to what size shoes and clothes Fiona wore. And a quick look for thimbles. Taking a charred stick that might have been a chair leg, she began raking through some of the debris. A tiny lump of metal caught her attention. Gold? She picked it up and buffed off the soot. Yes, it was gold. Had this lump once been a thimble? She continued her search, looking more closely now. Success! A ceramic thimble, its colors and design altered by the fire, lay cradled in her palm. She'd tell the cleaners to sift through all the debris in this room and look for thimbles.

Next she rummaged near the closet in the bedroom, which was charred less than the sitting room. Still, everything was ruined. However, she had luck in finding one sturdy oxford that looked to be about a size eight. Taking the shoe, the ceramic thimble and the tiny lump of gold, she retreated down the stairs to the master suite. Tears welled in her eyes as she scanned the smoke and water damage. "Well, it could be worse," Selby said aloud, her voice sounding dead in the soggy room. The plaster ceiling sagged dangerously over her bed. There was nothing to do but gather up as many clothes as possible and take them to the dry cleaners; even washing her jeans would probably not remove the smoky smell.

After her third trip between her bedroom and the garage, a white van and a truck with a strange vacuum system bulging from the back turned into the parking area in front of the house. She could see a pickup truck from the power company coming up the lane, too. At least help was on the way. She walked out to meet the crew and tell them about looking for thimbles.

As soon as the power and phone lines were operational, she reserved a two-bedroom unit at the Embassy Suites Hotel. The rest of the day was spent hauling linens and other washable things to the laundry room, which escaped water damage. The smoky smell would be there for weeks, she thought. Being a full-time laundress had never been high on Selby's list of careers, but it kept her constructively busy, her anger at Hawk expunged in physical labor.

That evening, after soaking tired muscles in the whirlpool tub in her Embassy Suites Hotel room, Selby called Elaine. "Come for dinner, a drink, dessert, whatever it takes to get you here. I need to talk to someone sensible. I need my best friend here!"

Within an hour, Elaine was at Selby's door. They settled in the comfortable chairs that faced the now-dark television set, glasses of wine in hand.

"How's the cleanup coming?" Elaine asked.

"Surprisingly well. The professionals really know what they are doing; fire and flood damage is their specialty. Bobbie is working on Justin's room over the garage. It's just smoky. I'll stay there as soon as it's ready. I also need to move the computer up there and see if it still works. Thankfully, I made a backup tape before I left for San Francisco and put it in the vault. I thought it was a bit pretentious to have a home safe; I've never had anything worth the trouble. But, boy, was I glad when I found the tape cool and dry!"

"You'll have fun redecorating the house—in your own style. Will you get some professional help for that, too?"

"Mmm." Selby nodded as she sipped her wine. "Antiques are not my thing, really, so I'm having a restorer come tomorrow and take away anything that can be refinished. I'll let Fiona use those pieces in her room, if she wishes. I can picture the living room very bright and open, with lots of plants. I'd like to bring the outside in. The verandah roof cuts out a lot of light. I'll put warmer colors in the family room. But, yes, I'll need a decorator to give me some ideas."

"You didn't ask me over to talk about redecorating, dear friend. What's really going on? That business partner of yours, is he the problem?"

"You know me pretty well. Yes, he's a problem...or was. I've decided not to have any contact with him unless it is business. I told him we should set up a day and time each week to meet and discuss vineyard and winery issues. No more trips together."

"Uh huh. Who are you kidding? Not me! You slept with him, didn't you?"

"You get right to it, don't you?" Selby looked away, embarrassed, but needing to talk about it. "Well...yes. I just got caught up in the fantasy of being a new person, out of town, really on my own for the first time, in control of the world. Dumb."

"Not dumb...normal, natural. You are a grown woman, a widow, you didn't do anything wrong. Unless, of course, you've fallen in love with him."

"Heavens, no. I hate him!"

"Right."

"No, I really do. He's arrogant. He has a cruel sense of humor. He uses him charm to get whatever he wants...in business, as well as interpersonal relationships. He's a quitter, too, runs away when things get tough. He got divorced after just a year of marriage; he didn't talk to his father for nearly two years when they had a falling out. He...." Selby paused to catch her breath.

"But?"

Selby smiled and shook her head. "I sound like a high school sophomore, don't I?"

Both women laughed, refilling their wine glasses, listening for a moment to the music leaking out of the stereo.

"I'm very drawn to him. He's fun and funny, intelligent, charming, sensual, caring. But there's no point in getting emotionally involved. He's twelve years younger than I am. He'll want to remarry some day, have children. I can't let myself get swept up with a 'boy toy'."

"Why not? Sounds good to me," laughed Elaine.

"Don't give me that. You and Roy are tight. I've never seen a married couple as close and happy as you two."

"Yeah. But even happily married women can fantasize!"

"You want the bottom line? I picked a fight with him last night. I wanted to sever the relationship before he did. I embarrassed myself. I verbalized my deepest fear to him, that our age difference bothered me. I was so...immature, so...bitchy..."

"What's the matter with honesty? It's better to face that fact now than delude yourself, or him, that age isn't an issue."

"I don't think I could handle it if he, one day, looked at me and thought, or said, 'old woman'."

"It could work the other way, too. You could look at him one day and think, 'young punk'."

At that they both shrieked with laughter, the wine having done its relaxing work. Elaine continued, "Is he a good lover?"

"You don't expect me to kiss-and-tell, do you?"

"Of course I do!" laughed Elaine. "Give now. Full details."

Fiona was sitting in a chair by the window when Selby walked into the hospital room the next day, her arms filled with packages. "Ready to get out of here?" Selby asked. "I've brought you some things to wear; can't have you running around in those drafty hospital gowns."

Fiona turned, giving Selby a blank look. "I'll be glad to go home...but there is no home..." Tears filled her eyes and ran down her pale, withered cheeks.

"Pooh! The cleaning crew is there right now. When the contractors do their magic, we'll be back at LillyHill before you know it. It'll be fun to pick out new wallpaper and paint. Here, now. See if any of this fits. Then I'll take you out to lunch. We'll eat something not found on a hospital lunch tray." Selby began to open the packages and sacks. "I don't know what kind of underwear you prefer so I only bought three pair of panties and a camisole rather than a bra. Here are a couple of pairs of socks, a pair of Nikes, a couple of T-shirts and this jogging suit. Hope you like blue."

"I've never worn a jogging suit before," Fiona said, looking helplessly at the array of casual clothing. Polyester pants suits, proper day dresses, pleated wool skirts and Shetland sweaters were Fiona's style. Prim and proper, never overly casual.

"Oh, you'll love it. So comfortable and you can go anywhere in them. I even had to buy myself one. We'll look like twins today," Selby said, holding out her arms to display her new teal outfit, a yellow T-shirt accenting her auburn hair. "You get dressed while I take care of signing you out of the hospital." Selby closed the door softly, rolled her eyes and took a deep breath, thinking, it's like having a child again. Hearing her name called, she turned quickly to see Liam coming down the hall.

"Selby, Mrs. Browning. I'm so glad to see you. I was going to visit Miss Dermot. How is she doing?"

"She's fine. I'm taking her home; well, to a hotel, as soon as she's dressed." Smiling, she took Liam's hand in both of hers and said, "You are quite a hero. We have you to thank for saving Fiona's life and for leaving us a house.

Liam's face flushed as he stammered a "thank-you-it-was-nothing" kind of answer. He kept his eyes on her small hands grasping his. Recovering, he stepped back and gave Selby a shy smile, saying, "I'm glad I was there. Please let me know if there is anything I can do for you. This must be very difficult to face, all the details that need to be handled."

"The cleanup is in motion. The power is back on. It's just going to take time. Say, why don't you have lunch with Fiona and me? I promised her something that couldn't be found on a hospital menu. Please come. I know Fiona would like to thank you, too. No, no. I insist. Stay here while I 'spring' Fiona, then we'll figure out someplace to eat." She hurried to the nurses' station to complete the release forms. A nurse accompanied Selby to Fiona's room with documents requiring the patient's signature.

The sight of Fiona in a bright blue jogging suit and athletic shoes was almost more than Selby could bear. She had to bite her lip and look toward Liam to keep from laughing. It wasn't that Fiona looked foolish; it was the woman's discomfort at not being dressed properly in her own eyes.

"I can't go out in this," Fiona said, turning to look at herself again in the mirror. "You should have brought something from my closet."

"Fiona, the closet is....gone....the fire, you know. Never mind, you look terrific," Selby said.

The nurse said, "Yes, you look great! Everyone wears jogging suits. They're so comfortable that you won't want to wear anything else. Now, please sign here..."

There was no way to convince Fiona that she could enter a restaurant dressed like that. Even Liam had no luck assuring her that she was properly attired for today's world. At last, they drove through a McDonald's take-out window, ordering Big Macs and fries, which they ate in the car. "See, I told you I'd feed you something not on a hospital menu," laughed Selby.

Selby dropped Liam off at the hospital where he'd left his vehicle while they had lunch. "Again, thank you, Liam, for saving us so much heartache. Please keep in touch." It was then that Selby realized the origin of the stone rabbit. "Oh! It was you; you brought the rabbit to the house. Yes. I found it and couldn't figure out where it had come from!"

"Just a small gift for you. Good thing I had it with me; I used it to break the glass in the front door."

"And you cut your hands," Selby said, gently touching the knuckles near the stitches. "Well, Mr. Rabbit will have a place of honor in the rockery."

Liam's cheeks felt warm at her praise. "Thank you for lunch. Perhaps we can have dinner some evening...after you get settled again."

"I'd like that, Liam."

Yes, she'd like anything that would get Hawk out of her system. She hated his arrogance, his pride, his lust. No. She hated her lust for him. It was unbecoming to a woman of her age, a grandmother, for Pete's sake! She didn't need his help putting LillyHill back together either. She didn't need anyone.

Selby climbed into the Explorer, chatting about the weather, asking if Fiona was feeling tired, and telling her that she had made reservations at the Embassy Suites Hotel near the Washington Square shopping center. "You'll be able to walk to the mall when your ankle is well and shop for clothes and other things you need. I'll probably stay at the hotel for a night or two until I can move into Justin's room over the garage. It wasn't damaged...just smells smoky. The cleaners have powerful fans that help with that problem. I'm sure the walls will have to be washed..."

Fiona remained quiet, not responding to Selby's chatter, simply staring out the side window of the vehicle. Selby hardly heard her when she said, "I'll go away. You hate me now."

Selby pulled into the parking lot of the hotel and sat quietly, waiting for Fiona to say more. Fiona had aged ten years, Selby thought. "Fiona, I don't hate you. We'll work through this together. You're not well now. You need to rest, to exercise your ankle. Let's get settled in the hotel. We're going to have to talk to the insurance people this afternoon. They'll be here about four o'clock. Okay?"

Wordlessly, Fiona got out of the Explorer, slowly, carefully, an old woman afraid to move. Selby quickly offered Fiona her arm. She hesitated, then taking Selby's arm, they entered the lobby.

Once Selby had Fiona settled in her room, she returned to her suite and called the insurance company to confirm the meeting. Perhaps now she would find out what really happened on the day of the fire. Up to this time, it had all been secondhand information that came to Selby. The cause of the fire was smoker's carelessness, according to the investigator. How strange, Selby thought at the time. She didn't even know Fiona smoked. Then there was the mystery of why Liam was there. That was cleared up now; he was calling on Selby with a gift. Luck, timing, fate, whatever you called it, was propitious.

CHAPTER NINETEEN

Sidney Washburn was a mousy-looking man—small, with gray-brown thinning hair and a sharp face. At least his eyes weren't black and beady—or worse, pink—thought Selby as she ushered him into their suite. Selby had brewed tea, which Fiona was sipping carefully, tentatively, her posture stiff on the straight-backed chair.

"Would you like tea, Mr. Washburn?" Selby asked, pouring herself a cup.

"No, no. This will only take a minute. Time is money," he said, sitting on the sofa and snapping open his briefcase. "Now. We have statements from the fire department and police officer on the scene that the fire was accidental. We do not see any criminal intent. Smoker's carelessness, probably. So, I just need to take Miss Dermot's statement. I'll record it if you don't mind."

Fiona looked pained, lost. She put her cup on the table, hands shaking, eyes giving Selby a pleading look. Selby flicked imaginary crumbs off her lap, nervous, too, with the agent's brusque behavior. "I'm sure taping the statement is very efficient, Mr. Washburn," Selby said, "Let's keep this as brief as possible. You should be aware that Miss Dermot was just released from the hospital today and is very tired."

"Yes. Yes. Now, if you'll just tell me what happened," he said, placing a small recorder on the table in front of Fiona.

The room was very quiet as Fiona gathered her thoughts. Then, in a thin voice, she began the chronology of events as she remembered them.

"I'd had a late lunch and then went to my room as I usually do. I sat at my desk—in front of the window—to read some travel folders." She paused, lost to the task.

"Yes. Yes?" Washburn urged. "Did you have a cigarette?"

Fiona's gaze wandered about the room, as if looking for a hole to hide in. She swallowed, sighed and finally, just as Washburn was about to repeat the question, said, "Yes. I always have one cigarette after each meal. That's all I smoke. And I open the window so that the room won't smell. I had the window open. It was a lovely day and the air felt good." Her attention drifted away again.

"So. So. You lit a cigarette and were reading travel brochures at your desk."

"I don't know what happened, but one of the brochures must have gotten in the ashtray. I don't know. I just noticed smoke coming from the paper on the desk and I brushed, I tried to stub out my cigarette. Something fell into the wastebasket—"

"What was the wastebasket made of?" interrupted Washburn.

"Ah, er, wicker. I thought the fire was out...but suddenly there was more smoke, flames...I opened the window more...the curtain blew in my face...I..." Fiona put her hands to her face. Painful memories brought silent tears.

Selby quickly knelt beside Fiona touching her, soothing her, encouraging her to go on, to get the terrible story out, be done with it.

"I was so frightened. I picked up the decanter on the table and poured it on the fire...but it flared up..."

"My. My. What was in the decanter?" Bond asked.

"Sherry."

Oh, God, thought Selby. Nothing like pouring alcohol on a fire. Wastebasket flambé. She could picture Fiona's panic, doing everything wrong; but who's to say she wouldn't panic and do the wrong thing in a crisis? She urged Fiona to finish the story.

"The fire flashed up and the curtains caught. The wind was blowing; then the desk just seemed to explode." She paused as a scene from her childhood flashed across her mind. The sound of explosions, sirens, smoke, running to the air raid shelter. "I ran." Again she stopped, her eyes seeing things from the past. "I ran..." She blinked twice, focusing her gaze on Selby. "I tried to use the phone in my bedroom, but the smoke...I think—I thought—I could use the phone downstairs. That's all I remember."

"Ah ha," Washburn said. "This desk, what kind was it?"

Fiona looked at Selby, eyes pleading for her to answer. "It was an antique desk, Oriental, delicate in design, heavily lacquered," Selby said. "I remember it well. It was one of the pieces of furniture that the original owner of the house wanted Fiona to have. I helped carry it up to her sitting room."

"Ah ha," Washburn said again, making notes on a yellow pad. "Is there anything else you can remember?"

Fiona shook her head, eyes downcast, tears running freely down her face.

"Well, Mr. Washburn," Selby said, standing up, "I think that should take care of the rest of the investigation. Please let me know if I can be of further assistance. In the meantime, the cleanup has begun and Miss Dermot and I will stay here until the repairs are completed. Thank you for coming." With that, she walked to the door and opened it, smiling sweetly.

Quickly, Washburn gathered up his recorder, various documents and his briefcase. "Well. Well. I'll complete my investigation and report, and contact you later, Mrs. Browning. Miss Dermot. Thank you."

"Thank you," Selby said, closing the door firmly behind him. "There, that wasn't so bad, was it, Fiona? You did just fine." Now she knew the story, except for the travel brochures. Was Fiona thinking of taking a trip?

"There now, let's have another cup of tea," Selby said, handing Fiona a fresh cup. "Tell me about your travel plans."

While Selby was dealing with the rodent-like insurance agent, Hawk was trying to solve the pocket-gopher problem that was affecting South Slope field. That infestation was compounded by a profusion of voles, often called meadow mice, which had staked out the tender roots of the North Bench field for their dining pleasure. And, as if to add insult to injury, a local deer herd was snacking on new, tender shoots in one field or another each morning. It was going to be one of those years, he decided, as he finished setting out poison for the voles and gophers. It was early in the season for so many varmint problems; Hawk's main concern at the moment was the weather report and the possibility of a late frost that could damage new growth and set back the vines by weeks.

Returning to the office after washing the residue of poison bait off his hands, Hawk accepted a stained cup filled with coffee from Robert's thermos. The two men sat companionably in the winery office, preparing to discuss the work plan for the rest of the summer. The vineyard routine picked up energy as each day passed. There were fertilizers to be applied, special combinations of nitrogen, boron, potassium, phosphate, sulfur, calcium and magnesium. Even zinc, copper, iron and aluminum were important to winegrape growing. Nearly half of LillyHill had the most desirable soils—Bellpine and Bateman. These soils were twenty to forty inches deep with plenty of room for rootstock.

"You know, Robert, grape growing—once you strip away the romance—is mainly just a lot of hard work. I'll admire a large estate, but I'll stick to working a small vineyard," Hawk said.

"Does that mean you aren't going to buy the adjoining acreage?" Robert asked.

"No, I've made an offer. I won't be at LillyHill forever. There are some things I'd like to try on that site. It has good air drainage, elevation and solar radiation. I've had the soil tested; it's Red Nekia and Jory."

"I heard that there was Phylloxera in the one field that's planted," Robert said.

"Yeah. I'll destroy the vines and leave that field unplanted until I'm sure it's clear, then use grafted plants to start. I want to grow Pinot Blanc. I believe there are only about a dozen producers of that variety in Oregon; Pinot Blanc is the coming grape."

"What's it like?

"It's a green-skinned mutation, probably from Pinot Gris, though perhaps directly from the Pinot Noir," Hawk explained, slipping easily into his lecture mode. "When this mutation was first preserved in Burgundy isn't recorded, but by the mid-16th century, Alsation growers had planted 'Clevner.' This 'Clevner' was most likely Pinot Blanc, one of the region's most established varieties, though the word is sometimes used by German, Alsation, and Swiss winegrowers to refer to other members of the Pinot family."

"What's the yield?"

"The average is three tons of to the acre; 200 cases of wine per acre."

"Anyone we know growing it now?"

"I think the first commercial release of Oregon Pinot Blanc goes back to the late '80's," Hawk said. "I understand the 1995 vintage from Amity and Adelsheim vineyards was a breakthrough."

"It's all a gamble, isn't it?" Robert said, putting his mug down and reaching for the clipboard that listed seasonal tasks. "What would you think if I put Rio on varmint duty in the mornings, then he could help me with the trellising in the afternoons. I think he could learn that, but not the pruning yet, if ever."

"Whatever you think best. I'll finish the tipping and heading this week," Hawk said, turning to see a red pickup on high wheels pull into the parking area in front of the office. A powerfully built young man jumped down from the truck and surveyed the vineyard and its buildings with a slow appraisal through mirrored sunglasses. "I'll see who our visitor is," Hawk said, heading out of the office door. His welcoming smile was not returned by the visitor. The truck's passenger, a blonde young man with hi-tech sunglasses, remained in the cab.

"Is this Selby Browning's place?" the driver asked. "Is she around?"

"And you are...?" Hawk said.

"Steve Browning, her son."

"Ah," Hawk said, now understanding why the visitor looked vaguely familiar—the thick auburn hair and freckles. Extending his hand, he said, "Paul Kestrel, vineyard manager. I don't believe she's on the property, but I'll check." He returned to the office and called the house. Bobbie answered, informing him that Selby was at the hotel with Fiona, talking to the insurance agent. Stepping outside again, he said, "Sorry, but she isn't here. We've had a fire at the house and she's staying at the Embassy Suites Hotel on Highway 217."

The young man grunted and swung his arm in an arc at the property, asking, "Is all this hers?" Hawk didn't respond, watching as Steve climbed into his truck. "I'll just look around and see her later." The truck roared up the hill to the house where cleaners and contractors were closing things up for the night. Ten minutes later, the red truck sped out of the vineyard driveway. Hawk dialed the hotel and asked for Mrs. Browning's suite.

"Hi, Selby. How's everything? Fiona?"

Hearing his voice sent adrenaline coursing through her body. Pausing before responding, she took a deep breath and told him how the insurance interview had gone, concluding, "I don't see any problems. I'm just glad I increased the coverage when the property was transferred." Nervously chattering on, Selby asked, "And how is the varmint situation?"

Hawk bit back the response that flashed through his mind: "Speaking of varmints, your son was here," instead saying, "We've put Rio in charge of voles, moles and gophers, much to his delight." Dead air filled the phone line. Then Hawk said, "The reason I called was to tell you that your son, Steve, dropped by. He said he'd see you later."

More silence, then Selby said, "Thank you for telling me. I'll contact him through his employer; I don't know where he's living now. Oh, by the way, I'll probably move into Justin's quarters in a few days. I've bought a new laptop computer and can keep up on the work with that. Let's meet next week and get caught up on winery matters. Thanks again for calling." She hung up and shoved her trembling hands into the pockets of her jogging suit. Then turning with a bright smile to Fiona, who was holding an empty teacup in her lap, Selby said, "Now, what were you saying about visiting your friend in Vancouver?"

"Well, Annie Morcum and I were school chums. When the war came— World War II—we were sent to North America. They called the children, who were sent out of England to safety, Bundles from Britain. I went to a cousin in New York City and Annie went to relatives in Canada. We've written to each other all these years..."

"You've not seen each other since you were girls?" Selby asked with surprise. Fiona sadly shook her head. "Yet, you've kept in touch. How lovely! Well, it's time you two got together."

"Annie has asked me to visit many times, especially since she was widowed. She was a schoolteacher and has two daughters and four or five grandchildren now. So, she really didn't need me..."

"Don't be silly! Need has nothing to do with it. It's time you two got together and this is a perfect time. Wouldn't you rather see her than be cooped up in a hotel room?"

"Well, yes. That would be nice."

"Okay. You call her right now and set up a date to visit in the next week or two. Give yourself a little time to feel stronger. In a couple of days you can walk over to the mall and shop for luggage and clothes. You can easily afford it with the income from your Trust. If you need me to help with airline tickets or anything else, just let me know. Of course I'll drive you to the airport. See, it's really quite simple."

"Nothing is ever simple," Fiona sighed. "But I suppose it couldn't hurt to call her..."

Selby rose briskly from the couch, saying, "After you call her, let's go downstairs for dinner. You might as well give that ankle a little workout."

Later that evening when Fiona had retired, Selby drew a deep bath and soaked her tired body, letting her mind drift to Steve. He had been a difficult child—rowdy, rebellious, idolizing his father, who laughed at his antics. There were times when Selby wondered how she could love him. But love him she did, even if she didn't approve of or appreciate his attitude. He was a male chauvinist who thought of women as handmaidens. Selby blamed herself for spoiling him, always picking up after him, catering to his dietary whims. Yes, she had raised the chauvinist, but Steve's twin, Mike, wasn't like that. Steve liked to refer to himself as "The Evil Twin." Of course that wasn't true. Steve was not evil, just spoiled. No wonder he had yet to find a wife. He always had lots of male friends, but never brought any girls home.

Selby was drying herself when the phone rang. "Selby? Steve."

Hearing her son address her by her name rather than 'Mom' made her pause. "Hello Steve. I was just thinking of you. I heard that you stopped by LillyHill today. Sorry I missed you. Can you come back tomorrow?"

"Maybe. If I don't get a load."

"Do you have a phone...an address...so we can stay in touch?"

He gave her a post office box and phone number, then asked, "Who's the guy with the ponytail? He said something about managing the place."

"That's Hawk...er...Paul Kestrel, my business partner in the vineyard. He knows all about wineries and vineyards."

"Where'd you find him?"

"He came with the estate."

"You mean you inherited him? Weird. Is all that property yours—and the house, too?"

"Yes. And more. Look, Steve, let's get together soon. I'd like to tell you about the bequest and show you LillyHill. Please try to come tomorrow. I'll be working with the clean-up crew and setting up a temporary office over the garage in Justin's room."

"How's 'Joe College' anyway?" said Steve, fondly sarcastic.

"Doing very well. He's particularly happy now that he's at the university."

"Okay. I'll see you tomorrow unless I have a load to haul. Bye."

Her old depression returned, that feeling that Steve was a carbon copy of his father—self-centered, not quite honest. Then there was the sadness of having missed out on a long successful marriage, that feeling always slipped in when she was tired and sad. She missed having an extended family with daughters-in-law and grandchildren nearby for emotional comfort and holiday gatherings, even though the idealized American scene that was more ad agency than reality. Instead, she had experienced the true American life filled with dreams that go wrong, difficult children, philandering husbands, outside forces which alternately deplete and enriched the mix of life.

Loss. What a powerful word. It encompassed so much more than loss by death or theft. Leaving, being left behind, changing, letting go, moving on. That's what it was all about. And impossible expectations, like the perfect marriage.

She recalled the evening she and Doug were sitting on the tiny cement slab they called a patio at the mobile home park. Six-year-old twins Steve and Mike were playing in the neighbor's yard. Selby was eight months pregnant, uncomfortable and sweaty from the August heat. Doug had started his third beer and was complaining about his boss, an old topic that Selby knew by heart. She listened with one ear, shifting her position to relieve the backache, nodding at what she thought appropriate pauses, when she suddenly realized that he had switched topics and had said something about an affair with a waitress.

"What did you say?" Selby asked, turning her full attention to Doug, who was mopping his face with a red bandanna. Trembling, she lowered her glass of ice water to the patio and fixed her eyes upon her high school sweetheart, her husband, the father of their twins.

"I'm sorry about it; it just happened. I met her at the truck stop restaurant in Cody and we got to talking and then we met after she got off work. I only saw her a couple more times whenever my haul took me through Wyoming. It was no big deal."

"No big deal? No big deal! Then why are you telling me...now...tonight...ever?"

"It wasn't my fault. She came on to me. She was young; I was flattered, you know..."

"No, I do not know!" Selby said struggling to rise from the sagging lawn chair. "Of all the..." Selby took a deep breath of the humid air, fighting back tears that fell in spite of rapid attempts to blink them back. "How old was she?"

"Twenty-two."

Responses swirled, collided. She wanted to cut him with words, to strike out in the only way she knew. "Finally found someone with an age to match your IQ," she said.

"That's right, Miss Honor Roll. We can't all be intellectuals like you. We all can't be so smart and know everything about everything. Just because you didn't get to go to college because you got pregnant in high school. Well, it takes two to get pregnant!" Doug raised his eyebrows in triumph at topping her slur on his intellect by reminding her of the college scholarship she gave up to marry him.

"That's right. It takes two to cheat on your wife, too. If you've picked up some disease from that tramp that could damage the baby, I'll kill you!" With that she waddled into the stuffy doublewide to get away from him.

The situation was over, as far as Doug was concerned. He'd cleared his conscience by confessing and apologizing, placing that turd in the other guy's pocket, as he was fond of saying. Of course they eventually moved on past the incident and back to some sense of normality. It took many months, but Selby justified her forgiveness by saying a whole family was better for the children than being raised by a single parent.

Monogamy was a simple concept before the '60s. Since then, her generation would never be absolutely sure that monogamy was the most desirable form of romantic life. If Selby had to choose, she'd choose monogamy, fidelity. Promiscuity had never appealed to her and didn't now, even with her new freedom. But how...when...do you know that one person is right for you? Selby wondered. Spontaneity, freedom from convention, sexual energy had opened the door to a relationship with Hawk. Now she had rejected him before he could reject her. Not a very mature thing to do. Growing up at forty-five is no less confusing than at fifteen, she thought.

Selby rummaged through her suitcase, found the nail file and began to touch up the professional manicure she'd had in San Francisco, thoughts careening from one issue to the next. Losses. Childhood and youth gone. Beauty going. Impossible expectations mellowed, but wealth broadened her options. She knew she must give up something to grow: youth for wisdom, beauty for truth. "I need to separate myself from losses to stand alone, to be distinct," she said to herself "How free and strong do I wish, do I dare, to be? And why do my thoughts always drift back to Hawk instead of solving my relationship with Steve?"

CHAPTER TWENTY

Ten days later, Fiona was ready—suitcase packed, hair done, ticket in her new handbag. Yet, she was still puttering about the hotel room, looking into drawers, checking the bathroom again for forgotten items. "Come on, Fiona. We've got to head out for the airport," Selby said.

"Oh, what if I've forgotten something?"

"Buy it in Canada. You'll only be gone a couple of weeks."

"But Annie said we might fly to England from Vancouver."

"Well, you can't until you have your passport; when it comes in the mail, I'll forward it to you as soon as it arrives. You'll have time to purchase anything else you need. Let's go!"

Selby saw a new side of Fiona as she listened to her chatter happily about seeing Annie, the possibility of going to England. However, Selby had not been able to convince Fiona that she didn't need to see LillyHill before she left. It was as if she needed to punish herself, to inflict pain for causing the fire even though it was an accident. Selby had taken a still-protesting Fiona out to LillyHill earlier in the week. The contractors and cleaners had the worst of the damage cleared up, but the acrid smell, the charred remnants, and the trampled front yard were evidence of the fire. Silent tears streamed down Fiona's face as she hugged herself at the sight. Selby let Fiona feel the needed pain before leading her away, easing into the topic of redecorating her third-floor suite.

By the time they arrived back at the hotel, Fiona had decided upon a sunny yellow wallpaper in a modified Victorian pattern with matching fabric for drapes and quilt from the decorator's samples. White bookcases and a larger casement window would give the room an airy look. Most of the Steiners' antiques, which were being refinished, would furnish the two rooms. Now that Fiona had seen the house and had agreed to the decorating plans, she seemed happily resigned to traveling until she could move back to LillyHill.

After accompanying Fiona to the departure gate, Selby watched as the

747 took off, her spirits rising with it. Progress had been made in her relationship with Fiona. They were learning to communicate, to be less reserved with each other. It was doubtful that they would ever be close, but blatant animosity had been bypassed. Was this a new Fiona, Selby wondered, or was this the real Fiona? Whatever it was, Selby felt good about their current relationship.

Selby's next hurdle was her first meeting with Hawk since the fight she had instigated on their return from California. The ten days of avoiding him did not make the upcoming meeting any easier. However, as long as they kept to business topics, she thought she could present herself well—calmly pleasant, business-like, antagonism gone. She took a deep breath, straightened her shoulders and opened the door to the vineyard office, a cheerful smile on her face. The grand entrance was lost on the empty office.

Damn! Is he going to be one of those always-late people? she wondered.

"Good morning!" Hawk said as he pushed open the door from the tank room. "Did you manage to get Fiona on the plane?"

Selby hesitated before she answered, not knowing if he was commenting on her efficiency or lack thereof, or on Fiona's recalcitrant nature. Deciding to take the high road on their new relationship, she answered in the affirmative and gave him a brief, humorous sketch of the trip to the airport, then continued, "She's applied for a passport. If the documents arrive before she returns, I'll send them to Vancouver so she and Annie can fly to England from there, assuming that the old school chums enjoy each other's company. It would be great to have her gone until the house is ready again. At least there was no problem with the insurance company; supposedly, the check is in the mail." Selby felt breathless from gibbering, from trying to think of Hawk as nothing more that her business partner, not the skilled lover, the charming companion.

Hawk listened to her bright chatter about Fiona's trip as he made a pot of coffee. He hated it when a woman made him unsure of himself. It rarely happened, but Selby had a way of keeping him off balance. His mistake had been to feel tenderness for her at the way she dealt with his father and at her terrible story about the death of her husband. No, he knew better than to take a relationship outside of recreational sex at this stage in his life. If she wanted to ignore the past, fine. He didn't need her in his life, other than as a business partner.

Anyway, he'd had a call from Pam, a flight attendant he used to date. She and a group of other attendants would be in Portland for a two-day layover and planned to celebrate her thirtieth birthday. He'd accepted Pam's invitation for drinks at River Place and dinner someplace in the area. They'd probably end up at Jazz De Opus in Old Town as they used to do. It sounded like a good party. And, Pam was a virtuoso in bed. Yes, it would be a welcome diversion.

Selby placed her new laptop computer on the corner of the desk and booted up the Excel program, its spreadsheet exposing the financial status of Lilly Hill Winery. Hawk set down two mugs of coffee and reached for a clipboard hanging on the wall. It was an awkward moment as they each waited for the other to speak first. They both spoke at once, stopped and looked at each other. Their eyes said it all, the yearning to touch, to erase the past ten days of walking on eggshells, avoiding each other. There was no doubt that a touch, a word—from either of them—would crumble the bitter barrier of pride.

Selby was the first to speak. Dropping her gaze, she softly said, "Now about the last batch of invoices...."

The hour slipped by without mishap. Yes, they could work together. Selby felt herself relax as she filed the spreadsheet and turned off the computer. "Then you think we might make a profit this year?"

"Barring manmade or natural disasters, it looks good. The '97 Pinot is selling well, the '98 will be bottled next week. My main concern is heavy rain during blossoming and its effect on this year's crop."

Rio came crashing in the door, grinning and breathless, asking Hawk for the keys to the car. Struggling to get his hand inside the front pocket of his tight-fitting jeans, Hawk said, "Be careful when you drive out of the garage, okay?" then handed Rio a set of keys.

"Rio drives?" Selby asked.

"On the county roads, but not the freeway. He uses the Jeep for tasks around the property, too."

"That's nice. Well, I suppose I should get back to the house and see how the contractors are doing. It's amazing how far they've come in just ten days. In a week or two, I should be able to bring in the painters; I've already ordered the wallpaper and fabric for Fiona's room. The new appliances are in crates in the garage."

The sound of a deep-throated muffler purring outside the office made Selby look out the window. A black Trans Am stopped in the driveway and Rio stepped out, shoulders back, head up, a young man with a hot car.

"What's with the Batmobile?" Selby laughed.

"Hey. I don't make fun of your car, Miss Stuffy Mercedes."

"But I didn't have a choice," she said, giving a friendly smile. Mistake, Selby. Don't look at him, don't play games. Walk out of here. But her feet would not move. Touch me. Hold me.

"Rio's going to wash it for me. I've got a date tonight." Damn. Why did I say that? Cheap shot, Hawk.

"Well, then, I won't keep you. In fact, I've a date with Liam. See you later." You liar. It's not a date. Liam just said he'd take me out for pizza tonight. She stumbled out the door, gave a friendly wave to Rio and walked briskly up the hill to the house. All the way back to the house she muttered to herself: "Hawk's nothing but a self-styled stud. Not your type at all, Selby. You've got assets to manage, a house to redecorate, and three sons, a daughter-in-law and a granddaughter to love. You don't need a man in your life. Particularly him."

At the house, Selby opened the wall safe and placed the back-up disk inside. The safe had protected her business data from the fire and now she was a believer in copying everything and locking it away. Just as she was closing the door, she noticed a small box tucked back in the corner. That's funny. I don't remember seeing that before. Guess I didn't think there would be anything in the safe when I first used it.

The box was old, a nutmeg brown, its thick paper edges scuffed, the corners rounded from repeated handling. Gently lifting off the lid, she saw a small dark blue velvet jewelry box. Tipping it out into her hand she opened it carefully, exposing an ornately engraved locket on a heavy gold chain. With her thumbnail, she pushed the locket open, revealing two sepia-toned photographs—one a mustachioed young man in a stiff collar, the other a plump-faced young woman with wild hair piled high on her head. She was wearing a dress or shirtwaist with leg-o-mutton sleeves and a white high-necked inset. A locket lay on her breast. Was it the same as the locket Selby now held in her hand?

Selby walked over to the window to get a better look at the piece. The chain was particularly lovely with short straight pieces of yellow gold attached with tiny double rings of pink gold. The locket itself was heavy, deeply engraved with flowers and birds. It would take a magnifying glass to see if the locket in the photograph was the same as this, but she felt it was. This must be a family heirloom from either Frank's or Lilly's side of the family. Fiona might know. She wondered if Lilly forgot about this piece of jewelry or if she didn't want Estelle to have it. It should certainly stay in the family. She carefully placed it back in the velvet box, then the paper box, which she locked in the safe. I'll have to talk to Levy about this, she thought as she wandered upstairs to see the progress that had been made on the refurbishing.

The workmen returned her smiles and made passing comments. "Won't be long now." "Everything look okay?" She nodded and made mental notes to herself: she needed to decide on paint and fabric for the master suite and the other bedroom, to confirm her choice of hardwood for the floors since she didn't want wall-to-wall carpeting throughout the house and to select area rugs for each room. So much to do!

She'd stay at the hotel tonight and then move into Justin's rooms over the garage tomorrow. It would be much more convenient and, with the kitchen appliances installed in the next day or so, she could cook again. Besides, she had a freezer full of meals Adelina had prepared last month. Bobbie had done an excellent job of cleaning Justin's rooms, she thought. The smoky smell was gone now that the walls were washed and painted. Yes. Things were coming together now. Just forget Hawk. Let him till the soil, prune the vines, blend the wine. Tomcat around. Stay out of her way.

Maybe she should drive the Mercedes back to the hotel tonight. She had avoided it, preferring the Explorer for some unknown reason. Once the decision was made, she transferred a few personal things into the sedan, adjusted the seat and mirrors, and backed out of the garage. It felt like she was wearing someone else's coat, which was two sizes too large. But it handled well and in five minutes she felt as though she had been driving a luxury car all her life. Well, this isn't so bad, she said, tuning the radio to a station that played '60's hit songs. Pure luxury!

Selby met Liam in the lobby of the Executive Suite Hotel at seven o'clock. Dressed in a denim skirt, a soft T-shirt and sandals, she felt relaxed and comfortable, looking forward to having a dinner companion, even though they were just going for pizza. She watched him as he came in the hotel entrance, looking serious, perhaps a bit nervous. He's really quite sweet, she thought.

He broke into a broad smile seeing her walking toward him. "Hi. Hope I'm not late."

"No, no. I was just telling the desk clerk that I'd be checking out tomorrow. I can move back to LillyHill now. It'll be like camping out for awhile, but I need to be there for the decorators and sub-contractors."

Taking her arm, he guided her to where he'd parked his Tahoe. He had washed it, vacuumed the inside, and made sure that business papers were stowed away. He'd taken much more time getting ready for seeing her than was necessary. After this first date he wouldn't feel so nervous, at least that's what he kept telling himself.

Izzy's Pizza Parlor was crowded, as usual. Families were lined up at the all-you-can eat buffet. Liam and Selby found a corner booth and sipped beer while their medium everything-but-anchovy pizza baked. Conversation came easily. They talked of Justin, progress on the house, the weather and when to plant roses. She told him how the rockery looked and asked whether the bonsai needed pruning. Selby felt pleasantly relaxed, unchallenged; Liam seemed shy and tense. It surprised her when he suggested a weekend at the beach.

"I thought we could drive down on a Friday night and come back on Sunday. We could stay at Schooner Landing; it's right on the beach." He almost sounded a bit breathless, she thought.

Selby's mind raced to come up with a noncommittal answer. Did she really have the time to be away from the house? Did she want to commit a weekend to Liam? What kind of sleeping arrangements did he have in mind? "Well, that sounds like fun, but I need to check my calendar, to see what construction...decorating...things are scheduled. And I think Justin is coming home either this weekend or next. Umm...can I get back to you?"

"Oh, sure, sure. I just thought it would be a good way to get better acquainted."

So, he wants to get better acquainted. Do I? Draining the last of her beer from the thick mug and placing it on the table, she said, "Well. I really must get back to the hotel and pack so that I can check out tomorrow. This has been such a nice break for me. I'm glad we could get together."

As they walked back to his vehicle he said, looking hopefully at her, "I thought we might drive around a bit, maybe stop for ice cream."

"Sounds like fun, but give me a raincheck, okay?"

The conversation during the drive back to the hotel concentrated on crazy drivers, a safe topic as they both agreed that most people should never get behind the wheel of a car. When he found a parking space in the hotel lot, he turned to her and reached for her hand. "I really enjoyed seeing you tonight. Even if you can't get away for a weekend, I'd like to take you out for a nice dinner, or a movie or anything you'd like to do. And if you have any gardening questions, I'd be glad to drive out to LillyHill."

Selby thought he looked like a worried puppy. He was sweet and she did enjoy his company, but.... "That would be lovely. Let's do stay in touch. Perhaps when Justin comes home you can come out to the house and see how things are coming. I know he would enjoy seeing you—telling you about his classes."

His face radiated pleasure at the invitation. "I'll walk you to the hotel. No matter how nice a place is, it can still be dangerous for a single woman."

While Selby and Liam were enjoying their pizza, Hawk was on his third scotch. The laughter and conversation were loud; the crowd of flight attendants, pilots and other guests seemed to increase exponentially. Pam was clamped to his arm, her lush breasts pushing into him as she introduced him to the others, as they kissed her and offered birthday wishes. There was much discussion about where to eat, half the group opting for seafood at Captain Andy's, the other half choosing Chinese. Since it was Pam's birthday, Hawk let her choose; their small group walked six blocks to the Oriental Palace restaurant. Upon arrival, they all ordered Tsing Tao beer while waiting for a table. Hawk had only a moment's concern about adding beer to the scotch-on-the-rocks he had consumed. This was way out of character for a man who saved his palate for fine wines.

Finally, a waiter led them to a large round table in a corner on the upper tier of the restaurant. Someone decided that they would all have the Emperor's Banquet, rather than order individually. The food began to arrive on great platters, in steaming bowls, course after course. Pam insisted that everyone eat with chopsticks, which she handled with expertise. Hawk had trouble getting the food into his mouth, finding it easier to drink his dinner. The dim light obscured what they were eating, which was probably just as well, Hawk thought, until he bit into a particularly hot pepper. His misery amused everyone. Pam offered to kiss away his tears. Sated, they complained that they had eaten too much. A walk to the jazz club ten blocks away was just what they needed.

However, once out on the street, the ten blocks seemed too far to walk and they settled for a once-popular club called East of The Sun. The clientele had changed since they had frequented it years ago. The interior was smoky, noisy and crowded, the customers young and rowdy with outrageous outfits of black leather, clear plastic and Lycra. Jewelry featured chains and leather thongs; body piercing and odd-colored hair set them apart from the sophisticated thirty-something group that wandered in off the street.

"I love slumming!" cried Pam as she led the way to the remaining empty table.

Hawk had given up "slumming" years ago and was beginning to wish he and Pam could have just gone to her hotel room. He didn't find the punk rock music and the weird young people amusing at all. He was squashed between two male flight attendants, Lawrence and Martin, who made no secret they were a couple. However, Hawk found them interesting and very knowledgeable about fine wines. They were just about to tell him the best way to cook sweetbreads when a disturbance across the table drew their attention. Pam was pulling her arm away from a young drunk who wanted her to dance. "No, I don't want to dance! Beat it, kid."

His reply was lost as Hawk vaulted across the table, whirled the would-be dancer around and hit him square on the nose, splattering blood, broken glass and drinks over nearby customers. The bouncer, a huge black man, separated Hawk and his opponent, telling them to take their problem outside. The crowd inside picked up on the fracas like sharks at the scent of blood, hoping to get a piece of the action. Several pushed their way outside to join in.

Lawrence and Martin escorted Pam out of the club with the rest of their party just as the bouncer tossed Hawk and his opponent onto the sidewalk. Picking themselves up, Hawk started to leave when the man grabbed him by the sleeve, saying, "You fuckin' queer! We'll see how gay you'll feel when I get through with you!"

Hawk attempted to walk away from his assailant, ducking wild punches, when one caught him along the side of the head. The blow enraged and stunned Hawk. He turned and brought his knee up sharply, catching the man in the crotch. The assailant dropped to the sidewalk, clutching his genitals, as Hawk staggered into the arms of two policemen who had arrived on the scene. In the next ten minutes, the crowd was dispersed, Lawrence, Martin, Pam and others caught a cab back to their hotel and Hawk was escorted to the police station. Booked for being drunk and disorderly, he slept off his hangover in a cell with six other social outcasts.

The next day, while Hawk was paying his fine, retrieving his car and taking his bruised body and a black eye back to LillyHill, Selby was unpacking her things in Justin's quarters over the garage. It was a beautiful spring day with puffy white clouds forming and reforming into fanciful beasts and castles. She raised the casement window, took a deep breath of the soft air and scanned the vineyard, each field different from the other. Newly planted stock—short brown sticks inserted into long strips of black plastic—would one day become mature vines to march sedately between wires trellising that denoted older plantings. The fields seemed to tip toward the sun. Pale green foliage alternated with emerald ground-cover; red soil drifted over the edges of the black plastic strips. Selby squinted her eyes and imagined the fields criss-crossing, forming an agricultural plaid. Could she find a similar scheme for the family room area rug or upholstery?

Justin had called, saying he'd drive up from the university on the weekend to see how the house was coming along. He also had a proposition for Selby. He sounded so excited that she could hardly wait to hear what he had in mind. On a day like this, she'd promise him anything.

Another reason she felt so good was that she had a phone call from her daughter-in-law Rhonda in Germany. "Amanda plays with her toy telephone all the time," Rhonda had said. "It was a wonderful gift." After the two women had shared their news, Selby and Amanda had a long talk on the real telephone. Rhonda had urged Selby to fly to Frankfurt for a visit. She could do that, would do that. Before the inheritance, money and time away from work had kept her from even considering a trip to Germany, but now, things were different. It was hard to believe that she had only seen her daughter-in-law and her grandchild once and under sad circumstances.

When Doug had been killed, the Army allowed Mike and his family to fly from Germany to the funeral. Amanda had been just six months old, a beautiful baby with silky black curls like her mother's. This was the first time Rhonda and Selby had met. Mike and Rhonda had eloped, so the usual wedding events where fiancée and parents get acquainted had been circumvented. And, considering the circumstances, any kind of meeting would have been uncomfortable at best.

Mike and Rhonda's quick marriage had been in response to her parents' vehement disapproval of the young people's relationship. Rhonda's father, Brigadier General Richard Elliot, and her mother, Gloria, were appalled that their daughter would fall in love with a corporal from the motor pool, an enlisted man, a nobody from Oregon. The young people had met when Mike was assigned to drive the Brigadier's wife. Gloria had a drinking problem; Brigadier General Elliot did not want an "incident," as he so carefully put it. Mike hated the duty; there was something unpatriotic about driving an alcoholic wife to play golf and tennis. The tennis games ended on the clubhouse verandah with gin and tonics. Then there were the bridge games that went late into the afternoons, followed by cocktails.

To keep Mike busy, Gloria often sent him to pick up Rhonda from the private high school when she stayed late for track or for play practice. To break up the romance, Elliot had simply arranged to send Mike to Germany. The young lovers sealed their fate at a local justice of the peace and embarked on a concerted effort to get Rhonda pregnant.

Selby worried about them. They had made the same mistake that she and Doug had made, letting their sexuality overrule any long-term planning. At least Mike and Rhonda had gotten married before she got pregnant. That was more than she and Doug had done. Well, things work out for the best if everyone keeps the lines of communication open, she thought. She had lost Doug, but had gained a sweet daughter-in-law and a beautiful grandchild. So, with the time and the money she now had, she'd go to Frankfurt as soon as the house was finished. Life was wonderful! She even thought Liam was a good friend to have. Yes. She was blessed.

The decorator had left dozens of wallpaper books, fabric samples, paint chips, tile samples and room sketches for Selby's consideration. These were spread over Justin's bed, desk and table where Selby studied each item, making notes and placing each sample in either the "No" pile or the "Maybe" pile. Just as she started downstairs to find something for lunch, a red, high-wheel pick-up truck roared up the drive. It must be Steve. It has been more than a week since he said he'd come to see her. At last they would have time to talk. This really made her happy day special.

CHAPTER TWENTY-ONE

Two men climbed out of the gleaming red Dodge Ram loaded with chrome, extra halogen headlights, a roll bar, and over-sized wheels and tires. It was the kind of truck that elicited one of two responses: macho or stupid. Selby's was the latter, but she kept that opinion to herself.

She ran down the front steps and threw her arms around her son. "Oh, I'm so glad you could come!"

Steve gave her a quick hug and then turned to his companion. "Selby, this is Chris."

Selby extended her hand, saying, "Welcome to LillyHill, Chris." The tall, thin young man was beautifully handsome, deeply tanned with short blonde hair. His eyes were hidden behind mirrored sunglasses, as were Steve's. He was wearing bright blue running shorts, a sleeveless T-shirt and expensive athletic shoes. By the looks of his thighs and his lean build, Selby guessed that he was a runner. Selby shifted her gaze from Chris to Steve. "It's chaos inside but come in and I'll find you a beer while I fix lunch. There's so much to tell you I hardly know where to start!" She led them through the front hall and past the living room where workmen on stilts were plastering the ceiling. "Come into the kitchen; it's almost finished. At least the refrigerator is installed and the microwave works. Turkey and ham sandwiches okay?"

They nodded as they twisted off the beer bottle caps and looked around the family room. "You said you had a fire? What happened?" Steve asked.

Selby gave them a quick overview of the fire as she made sandwiches. Placing the impromptu lunch on a tray with paper plates, she said, "Let's go sit on the front steps. That seems to be the best place to eat on days like this."

Steve asked many questions. Selby responded as openly as she could. The queries seemed to dwell more on the money she had inherited and less on how the bequest affected her life. And as the questions became more pointed, Selby found herself being evasive. "It's hard to put a dollar amount on the bequest. Most of the trust is tied up in California real estate investments. I simply serve on the Board of Directors for that part of the estate. Dividends are distributed quarterly. I'm still learning, so don't expect me to be able to answer all your questions when it comes to such complicated financial matters."

"Well, in round figures, just how much are you worth?'

Steve's blunt question hit her hard. He didn't want to hear about her or Justin or Mike and his family. He didn't want to tour the winery or hear about the complexity of running a vineyard. He wanted something.

"I don't honestly know and it really doesn't matter, does it?" She smiled sweetly, uncomfortable with the conversation in front of a stranger. Chris sat to one side, never saying a word, simply sipping his beer and eating his sandwich, listening intently. It was disconcerting not to see his eyes. Who was he, really?

"You do stuff for Justin, don't you? Like tuition for college."

"Of course. He's doing so well in school. It's a good investment."

"Yeah. I saw him a couple of week ago. You going to give him the Explorer? Old Blue is a junk heap."

Selby laughed. "So, he's sent you to soften me up about the Explorer!" This was more like it—big brother helping out little brother. "I'll think about it. He said he was coming up this weekend and had a proposition for me. I guess I know the bottom line now. Depending upon his presentation, I just might let him have it." She relaxed now that she knew what was going on.

Steve gestured toward the car in the driveway. "You like the Mercedes?"

"It's okay. I think I'd prefer something else. When I have time, I'll trade it in."

Steve put down his empty beer bottle and stood up, stretching. He took a pack of cigarettes out of his T-shirt pocket, lit one, slipped the book of matches back under the cellophane wrapping and tossed the pack to Chris. "I have a proposition for you."

Selby felt a chill. Was it because he was standing in front of her, blocking the sun, or his tone of voice?

"I want my own tractor-trailer, like Dad had. I don't need a college education or a car. How about you investing in me?"

The way he intoned "investing" made Selby feel ill. So. He wanted his share of the inheritance. He had ignored her for years and now he saw her only as a money pot. She was no longer "Mom"; in his eyes, she was "Selby," his personal bank. Anger and guilt choked her response. Think Selby; don't get emotional.

"Why would you want to face the same dangers Dad did? I still have nightmares about the way he died."

"Hey. Life's a gamble. Anyway, that was a real freaky thing with Dad. I'm driving cross-country now, so what's the difference if I own my own tractor-trailer or not?" Selby shook her head and stood, moving away from Steve's shadow. The sun's warmth helped her think. She looked toward the winery buildings. Hawk's Trans Am was parked in front. She wished he were here to defuse the situation, to give her some thinking space. If he were here, she wouldn't feel threatened.

"Have you developed a business plan? If this is to be an investment, I'll need to have something in writing—cost, what you're bringing to the table, projected return on investment. "

"Shit." He turned away and ground out the cigarette butt on one of the paving stones that led to the porch. "You're worth millions and you won't give me...say, $150,000 for a unit?"

"I don't have $150,000 in cash to give you," Selby said, her jaw tightening. "And even if I did, I wouldn't. If you want an 'investment,' then go about it in an adult, business-like way." Her temper was up, and she could see Steve's was too.

"Everything's for Justin. And what have you given Mike? I know you've given him something."

"You know nothing of the kind. You want the same amount as Justin? Fine." Selby turned on her heel and entered the cool, dark house, hearing the soft slapping sound of plaster being trowelled on the ceiling and the distant whine of a Skilsaw cutting molding upstairs. She trotted up the garage stairway to Justin's room, took her checkbook from a cardboard box that served as her temporary office and wrote a check to Steve for $5,000, approximately what she had spent on spring term tuition and books for Justin.

When she emerged from the house, Chris and Steve were leaning against the truck, smoking and talking softly. The way they were standing close together made Selby uncomfortable. What was it about the silent, beautiful young man that made her wary? Was he the one behind the request for money?

They looked up and came toward her as she walked down the steps, the small, blue check in her hand. Was she afraid of her own son? Perhaps a little. This is not the way things are supposed to be. Damn money! Not enough—or too much—and it screws up relationships. Pulling herself to her full five feet five inches, she said, "If you're truly interested in a business arrangement to secure funding for an eighteen-wheeler, then get a proposal on paper and we'll see my attorney. I'll listen to any reasonable request, but get this through your head: I am not mother moneybags." She extended the check to Steve. He took it without looking at the amount, turned and walked back to the truck.

She watch them until the truck left her property, then sat down on the porch, her arms across her knees, head down, crying softy in the warm May sunshine. Had she handled it all wrong? Maybe she was overly concerned with Steve's safety. If only she knew what really happened to Doug. The police reconstructed the hijacking and murder as best they could, but they didn't know all of it. The truth of the matter is that Selby would not have felt better about knowing the details of Doug's last hours on earth. Hearing a vehicle coming up the hill, Selby shook her head and mopped at her tears, thinking to herself, sometimes a person isn't meant to know everything. Perhaps this is one of those times. She was relieved to see the truck was the tile contractor and not a visitor.

CHAPTER TWENTY-TWO

Hawk had a beautiful black eye and the mother of all headaches. He'd endured Robert's teasing, and, after a hot shower, was back to work. Stupid, damn fool! You're way past acting like that, he told himself. No more flight attendant action. All he needed now was to have Selby drop into the winery office and see his misery. Wouldn't she just have a laugh! Well, what did he care what she thought? She had Liam by the nose. Nice, safe widower. Well, the two of them were welcome to each other.

Hawk was attending to the pile of mail on his desk when the phone rang. It was his Realtor. "Hawk? Dick. The owners of the property took your offer."

"Great! How soon can we sign?"

The details were discussed, and as Hawk hung up the phone, he smiled, pleased at his acquisition, yet dreading telling Selby. How would she take it when he told her he'd be leaving? She should understand that he wouldn't be at LillyHill forever. She'd just have to take over and hire what physical labor she needed to replace him. He'd not leave Selby—LillyHill—until after harvest and crushing this fall. That's the least he could do. After all, he had a financial interest in LillyHill, too. She could buy him out if she wished. Then they'd really be done with each other.

Hawk rose from the battered swivel chair and stretched, feeling the stiff muscles and bruises from his brawl. He was getting too old for that kind of stuff. He hadn't felt this bad since he fell off Tucker last year. Tucker. He'd forgotten the horses since the trip to California and the fire. Better go see the old fellow. "Rio," he bellowed.

The young man burst in from the aging room, wiping his hands on a paper towel, a big smile on his face.

"Ya want me to wash the Trans Am?"

"No, just put in it the garage. Be careful now, okay?" Hawk chuckled at the small things that gave Rio such pleasure. He wondered if Robert and Adelina ever got over seeing their eldest child in this condition. Well, it could have been worse and they did have three other kids. Nice family. Would he ever have a family of his own? Right now it didn't seem likely. He just didn't have the time or the inclination to find the right woman. Just getting his own vineyard and making it the best was what he wanted now. That's where he'd put his energy, he told himself.

As he walked down to the barn and around to the back corral to find Tucker, the perfect May afternoon improved his spirits. In a couple of weeks, he'd own seventy acres of prime land with Neika soils. He could fix up the old house, build a small barn for Tucker and Zephyr, maybe get a dog. Perhaps the brawl knocked some sense into him, he thought. Rounding the corner, he stopped. Selby was sitting on the top rail, crooning to Zephyr and feeding the mare carrots. Damn! What's she doing here?

Hearing footsteps, she turned, her smile fading at the sight him. "Oh, hi, Hawk. I was just...my God, what happened to you?"

"Nothing. I'm fine. What're you doing here?"

"You told me to spend time with Zephyr so I wouldn't be so afraid to ride her. We're getting along fine. I've brushed her and I would have ridden, but I don't know how to saddle her."

Glad for a neutral topic, Hawk said, "You want to ride now? I was going to take Tucker out." This will give me a chance to tell her about buying the adjacent property, he thought.

"Sure." She slid off the rail into the corral and took hold of the mare's halter. Hawk whistled for Tucker; the gelding trotted toward them, head up, ears forward.

"Yeah, old man. You think I've got something for you but I don't."

"Here, give him one of these carrots." Taking a second look at his black eye, she said, "How did you... Are you sure you're okay? Have you had a doctor look at your eye?"

"It's nothing. Don't ask. I'm fine."

He helped her get the bridle on Zephyr and gave her verbal instructions about saddling the mare while he brushed Tucker, who had been rolling in the corral. Twenty minutes later they were riding up the hill toward the house and over to Bench 7. The horses were eager to run. Once the riders reached the old lane between LillyHill and the adjoining property, Hawk told Selby to hold Zephyr back as he was going to run Tucker down the road. "The mare will want to follow, so keep a tight rein on her. Come when we're around the corner—out of sight, only trot or canter at a speed that's comfortable for you. I'll see you around the bend." He dug his heels into the gelding and galloped down the old road.

Zephyr started to follow, but Selby held her back, walking the mare in a small circle until Hawk and Tucker disappeared from view, then she clicked softly and let the horse trot down the road. Zephyr seemed to know when her rider relaxed, changing her gait to a smooth canter and then a full gallop. An adrenaline rush hit Selby as the horse thudded down the soft dirt road. It was exhilarating, yet frightening to have the horse in control. As she rounded the bend at full gallop, a piece of opaque plastic sheeting snapped in the breeze from a pile of trash. Zephyr shied to the left; Selby's momentum took her straight ahead.

She felt suspended in air, watching the ground come toward her. It was patterned with rich brown earth, tufts of emerald grass, twigs and gray stones. Instead of hitting the ground, she descended into a sea of black champagne, its bubbles winking like tiny vigil lights. Her breath was gone; she struggled to swim to the surface, gasping for air.

Hawk was off Tucker and over to Selby almost before she hit the ground. Both horses snorted and trotted away, eyes rolling, ears laid back at the commotion. Selby hit face-down in the road, knocking the wind out of her. Tiny points of light danced in her head. Hawk carefully rolled her onto her back. A gash over her eye began to bleed, running into the soft earth that was ground into the side of her face.

Calling her name, Hawk carefully ran his hands over her body, seeking broken bones or odd angles to her limbs. Finding nothing obvious, he cradled her shoulders and lifted her slightly to ease her gasps while supporting her head.

Selby finally surfaced from the dark, effervescent sea, struggling to take a full breath. Blinking, she saw Hawk's face close to hers. He was calling to her. I'm here, I'm fine, she tried to say, but her words didn't make sense. She reached up to clear her eyes, finding her face warm and sticky. "What? I'm fine. I'm fine," she mumbled.

Still holding her, Hawk removed her neckerchief, folded it into a small square and told her to press it over her eye. "Looks like you have a cut, so hold this on it. Got your breath yet? Feels terrible to have the wind knocked out of you, doesn't it?"

Selby, struggling to sit up, said, "I'm fine. Aren't I? Let me up."

"Easy. Put you weight on me. Hurt anywhere?"

"Zephyr just went the other way...."

"The trash in the road spooked her and she shied. You just kept going. Tucker did the same thing."

"But you stayed on."

"We've got to get you back. I'll get the horses. You want to ride double with me or on Zephyr?"

"I'll ride Zephyr, but would you take the reins?"

They returned to the winery, walking the horses, which seemed to know that something had gone wrong with the ride. Rio greeted them, saucer-eyed and slack-jawed.

"Take care of the horses, Rio; I'm going to take Mrs. Browning to the hospital. Tell your dad we think she's okay."

The Emergency Room staff was having an unusual lull in their daily parade of broken bones, cuts and burns, real and imagined heart attacks. Selby was whisked to an examining room while Hawk took care of the requisite admitting paperwork. The physician was thorough in his examination and probing in his questions, asking again and again how the accident happened.

As he cleaned the cut over her eye and applied a butterfly bandage, he said, "Are you sure it was a fall from a horse? I noticed that your husband has a black eye."

"Oh, we're not married."

"Domestic violence isn't something to hide. You mustn't let yourself be a victim, married or not."

"But you don't understand...."

Adjusting a large foam rubber neck brace, the doctor said, "I'll write you a prescription for something stronger if aspirin doesn't take care of the pain."

Hawk peeked into the examining cubicle. "Okay if I come in?"

"Oh, Hawk, he thinks I'm a victim of domestic violence! Guess he thinks I gave you your black eye."

This struck both of them as particularly funny, their laughter easing the tense situation.

"Well, we can't ignore suspicious injuries," the young physician said with a sheepish smile. "You wouldn't believe what comes in here, especially on Saturday nights. Now I want to you take it easy and if you have any dizziness, blackouts or severe headaches, come back or contact your family physician immediately. You shouldn't be alone tonight. You need someone to check your pupils periodically because of the concussion."

"No problem. I'll stay with Elaine tonight," Selby said to Hawk. "Will you take me there?"

"Sure. You want to go home first and get cleaned up and pack some things?"

"I'll call from here first to make sure it's okay."

Elaine was away from home for three days attending a Human Resources Conference in Seattle. Selby sat quietly, trying to think of who else she could ask to be her night nurse, but her brain seemed to be in neutral.

"I'll take care of her," Hawk said to the physician. "And I promise not to blacken her other eye, if she won't blacken mine."

Driving back to LillyHill, Selby kept up a feeble protest that she didn't need a nurse for the next 24 hours. In the end, she agreed to let Hawk watch her. "Okay. You win. Take me home so I can get cleaned up."

"You were lucky that the ground was soft from yesterday's rain. For once, moles are a blessing. Doing a face-plant in the fresh mole hill probably saved you a fractured skull."

"Does this mean you're going to quit killing them?"

"Absolutely not!"

Hawk looked in the freezer for one of Adelina's enchilada casseroles to bake for supper while Selby showered. She put on a gray sweatsuit and tossed a sleep shirt, toothbrush and comb into a small tote bag. Her head and neck were beginning to ache. She longed to sit quietly in a far away corner and wait for the aspirin to do its work. With the adrenaline rush gone, the let-down miseries settled upon her.

They returned to Hawk's apartment and settled in for a quiet evening. Dinner was tense, both remembering the last meal they'd had in Hawk's apartment and determined not to quarrel tonight. At 8:30, Selby said, "I'm really tired. If you don't mind, I'll go to bed. Thanks for everything today."

"Let me check your pupils before you go," Hawk said, looking intently at her eyes. She was going to have one beaut of a black eye, he thought. "They look fine. I doubt if you'll have a scar from the cut. It's in your eyebrow so it probably won't even show."

"That's good," she said sleepily as she wandered into the bedroom and closed the door.

She awoke with a start, disoriented and uncomfortable. Rolling over carefully, she saw Hawk sitting up in bed reading, the high-intensity lamp casting its light on his book, his bare torso veiled in shadows.

"What time is it?"

"Ten-thirty. Sorry if I woke you."

"No, you didn't. This foam collar is so hot. Suppose it would be okay to take it off?"

"I don't know. You could see how it feels without it. Here, let me help."

Selby sat quietly, her back to him, while he disengaged the Velcro fasteners on the foam collar. "Let me see your eyes."

She turned, kneeling on the bed, her face lifted to him. Gently taking her face in his hands, he said, "I think they're okay; the pupils contracted when the reading light hit them." He continued gazing at her. She slowly closed her eyes. Bending his head, he kissed her slowly, tenderly, unsure of her response. There had been so much anger between them.

Selby responded by sliding her arms around him, pressing her palms on his smooth back, feeling the movement of his muscle as he broke the contact and looked at her questioningly. She recognized the look—his eyebrows arched, eyes wide. The look asked, "Do you want to make love?"

Her response was to take off her sleep shirt. Hawk lowered her gently into the bed, supporting her head and neck, stretching out beside her. This may not have been what the doctor ordered, but it was what both of them wanted.

The next morning at the breakfast table, Hawk said, "About last night...."

"Oh, it was my fault...."

"I know I stepped outside our business arrangement...."

"We were both under a lot of tension yesterday...."

"I don't want us to be distant...."

"No, no. I understand. We can get back to business...."

They paused in their mutual apologies, smiled and finished their bowls of cold cereal. Neither was upset by the night of love; both understood the need to get their relationship back on a solid footing.

"I feel like I've been hit by a truck this morning!" Selby said, moving her shoulders carefully, trying to stretch out the stiffness.

"I've never had that kind of complaint before."

"There's a first time for everything." They smiled companionably at each other. "I suppose I'll be stiff and sore for several days. Maybe I'll get that prescription filled so I can function a little bit better." She paused, sighed and looked up shyly at Hawk. "Are you going to tell me how you got your 'mouse'?"

"No."

"I'll bet you ran into a door. Men would rather say they got a black eye in a street brawl than to admit they were clumsy."

"That's right."

"Hah! I knew it!"

Both of them smiled, pleased with the relaxed morning-after breakfast, yet cautious with their conversation. As Hawk helped Selby put on the neck brace, he said, "Feel up to a walk in the vineyard? I'd like to discuss the frost protection options I mentioned last week."

"Isn't it too late for a frost now?"

"No. We can have them into early June."

"What would happen?"

"Primary shoot damage. However, I'm more concerned about an early fall frost that can damage leaves and delay cane hardening,"

"And....?"

"It would make the vines susceptible to winter damage.

"That would affect the following year's crop?"

"Yup." He smiled at her, pleased that she was beginning to grasp the intricacies of growing wine grapes. There was so much for her to learn, but she was a good student.

They put their breakfast dishes in the sink. Selby moved slowly and painfully down the flight of steps from Hawk's quarters. Rio was coming out of the barn where he had been tending to the horses. He waved and shouted hello. They waved back and walked slowly across the winery yard to the nearest field. The morning fog seemed to evaporate before their eyes, the sun warming their shoulders. Every muscle in Selby's body protested as she walked; the aspirin did little to dull the pain.

By the time they reached the field across the road, Hawk had slipped into his lecture mode about viticulture, leaving Selby to mentally catch up with the technical terms and the "big picture" as he often said. "We can use heaters, but I prefer overhead sprinklers; however, we'll need sufficient pond capacity to operate them. What would you think of enlarging the irrigation pond to the west?"

"I have no problem with that. Just give me the cost estimate as soon as you can." Examining the delicate new growth on the mature vines at hand, she noticed some strange markings and ridging on one of the vines. "This looks weird. What is it?"

"Borers. We found some branch and twig borers last week and have given the fields a shot of pesticides. The borers are a late spring problem, but I think we have them under control. In June and July we have to watch for black vine weevils."

Before he could launch into another technical lecture on insects, an old blue Honda turned into the driveway. They waved at Justin as he turned into the winery parking area.

"Wow! What happened to you two?" Justin exclaimed as he unfolded his lank frame from the small car. "Did you win or lose?"

He embraced his mother carefully, planting a kiss on the unbruised cheek. Then he reached out a hand to Hawk. Shaking the young man's hand, Hawk said, "Zephyr zigged and your mother zagged. I got mine in a street brawl."

Selby beamed at the two men and their ease with each other. "Hawk was just giving me a lecture on pesticides. Don't get him started or you'll learn more than you want to know about root rot, thrips and weevils."

"I think that class comes next term," Justin laughed. "At least I'll know who to ask if I get stuck." He looked back at his mother's swollen and bruised face, her eye beginning to take on a sinister hue. "Hey. Did you really fall off Zephyr? Are you sure you're okay?"

"I'm fine. Hawk took me to the hospital and they patched me up. Give me a ride home so Hawk can get back to work. I'm completely useless today." Justin held Old Blue's door open while his mother seated herself carefully on the passenger side, her movements painful and slow. They both waved to Hawk as they drove to the house. It was good to have Justin home for the weekend. She loved to hear his enthusiastic chatter about school, his plans for the future. And she needed to talk to him about Steve.

"You must have left the dorm early. Have you had breakfast?"

"Yeah. I stopped in Salem. But I could use some juice. Do you have any cookies around?"

"I think Adelina put some in the freezer. Have your snack and then I'll give you a tour of the house. You'll have to sleep on the family room couch since I'm still in your quarters. The new furniture won't be here until the painters are finished."

It was relaxing and pleasant to have Justin home, interested in what she had been doing and sharing his college life with her. He'd be home mid-June after final exams. He'd talked to Liam about a summer job, but hoped to help Hawk, too. He wanted to learn as much as he could about the vineyard. "And I have a special favor to ask."

Here it comes, Selby mused, the request for the Explorer.

"Well, you see, we need to have a junior project and I thought I'd get started on mine even though I am still a sophomore. We have to have complete architectural drawings and specifications for a major landscaping project, like a corporate headquarters or city park, but we can do a residential project if it's more than a regular lot." He stopped, took a deep breath before continuing. "I'd like to landscape LillyHill—really expand what's here already. Make lots of changes: fence both sides of the driveway down to the winery, put in a lily pond over there with koi—you know, Japanese fish—a gazebo out back, and...what'd you think? I know it'll cost a lot of money, but I'd give you an estimate and I'd stay within budget?" He looked at her as if he'd asked for the moon.

"What a wonderful idea! Do it! The timing is perfect since much of the front area was damaged by the fire," she said. "I ask only that you treat me like a client and not your mother."

"Oh, yeah, sure. That's part of the deal. It will cost thousands of dollars and take two years, so...."

"I understand. A business deal. I like it." They shook hands to seal the deal and then hugged and laughed at the pleasure they both felt. "Now, I need you to do something for me. I have a prescription to be filled and we need some groceries. I don't want to go out in public looking like this."

"Really! You look like you've been in a fist fight. Sure, I'll shop for you after I see Liam about a summer job."

Handing him some cash and the keys to the Explorer, she said, "You need to try out the Explorer if you're going to take it back to school."

"Huh? You mean it? Wow!"

"Old Blue doesn't look safe to me. Let's junk the thing."

Two hours later Justin was back with the groceries, the prescription and a large jardiniere planted with brightly-color flowers—petunias, sweet alyssum, pansies.

"Look what Liam sent you. I told him you were hurt and he wanted to send you flowers. He wanted you to have the biggest bouquet he could find. Where shall I put it?"

"Hey. You're the landscape architect; you decide." Selby couldn't help but laugh at Justin struggling to get the planter out of the Explorer. "Come in when you're finished with the monster bouquet. I've got to take a pain pill. Lunch'll be ready when you're done."

Just as she finished loading a tray with sandwiches, chips, pickles, cookies and milk, the phone rang. It was Fiona.

"Thank you for sending me my passport. It got here just in time. We leave for England Tuesday."

"I'm very happy for you, Fiona," Selby said. And for me, she thought to herself. She told Fiona of the progress on the house and Fiona chattered on about the ferry trip from Vancouver to Victoria and having tea at the Empress

Hotel. Then she began a recitation of all the things they planned to see in England.

"We're going to spend two weeks in London. My ankle is strong enough now so that we will take walking tours around the city. We'll see St. Paul's, Trafalgar Square, Buckingham Palace and, of course, we'll take in the theatre, too. Then we'll take the train to the Cotswolds for a week...."

Selby listened more to Fiona's enthusiasm than her actual itinerary, which included Scotland and Paris after England. Fiona was a new person. Perhaps she just needed to find a life of her own, a life that was more than serving others. She sounds young again, if she had ever been young, Selby thought.

"Oh, I almost forgot, Fiona. I found an old locket in the wall safe. Can you tell me about it?"

"Oh, that must be Lilly's mother's locket. It was one of just a few pieces of jewelry Lilly wore in later years. She kept it in the safe when she wasn't wearing it. It was very special to her, even though it didn't have the dollar value that some of the other pieces had."

"I think it should go to Estelle with the other jewelry, don't you?"

"Well, I suppose so," Fiona said with hesitation. "I hope she will appreciate it. Maybe she could save it for little Lilly when she grows up."

"Okay. I'll call Mr. Levy and see that he gives it to Estelle. Have a wonderful time, Fiona. We'll see you in September. Just let me know when you'll arrive and I'll meet you at the airport. Have a wonderful time! Good-bye."

Selby and Justin sat on the porch steps in the sunshine and ate. This lunch was so different from the lunch she had shared with Steve. She hugged herself with happiness. But thinking about the other lunch saddened her. Like it or not, she was going to have to mention Steve. "Have you talked to Steve lately?"

"Yeah. He and Chris stopped by the dorm one night and took me out for a beer."

"You're not old enough for a beer!"

"I know, but I didn't get carded. We went to a place they know, not one where students go. Those places check everyone!"

"Who is this Chris?"

Justin shifted uncomfortably on the steps where he was sitting. "Er. You don't know?" Selby shook her head and waited. "Well, Steve and Chris are friends. Good friends. Close friends." Selby frowned and waited for more, an uneasy prickle running up her spine. "You've met him, I guess. He's a nice guy." Justin looked closely at his mother. "You really don't know?"

"If I did, I wouldn't be asking. Is there a problem?"

"Oh, Mom. You really don't know? Ah. Steve's gay and Chris is his...."

"Oh my God. Are you sure?"

Suddenly her headache returned with a vengeance. How could she not have known? As she thought back...years back, it did make sense. Had she knowingly disregarded indications? Girlfriends were few and never serious in high school. Steve always liked the company of men, but that seemed perfectly normal to her with his interest in athletics and trucks. What had Doug told her one time? The trucking business was filled with homosexuals and some of the drivers were quite overt in prowling the truck stop showers. Yes. But that seemed so strange. Her stereotyped view of gay men was one of swishy waiters and ballet dancers, not truck drivers. But then she compared all truck drivers to Doug. Perhaps it did make sense; long-distant driving, like the military and prisons, was a man's world.

"Do you have a problem with that, Mom?"

Selby took a deep breath, trying to gather her true feelings about gays. It had never been an issue with her. She accepted them as long as they weren't publicly blatant in their affection toward each other or militant in the streets. She really hated the overly strange ones who went out of their way to shock people. "I can accept it, but I don't understand it. If Chris is truly a good person, then I'm happy for Steve. Why didn't he tell me? Does Mike know? Did Dad know?"

Justin shrugged his shoulders. "I doubt if Dad did. He'd of had Steve's head on a plate. I would guess Mike does. How could twins not know everything about each other?"

How could I have been so...out of touch? She was at a loss for words at the moment; her train of thought had been knocked off the track. There were so many questions she wanted to ask Justin. How long have you known? Did Steve just come out and tell you? How do you feel about it? Instead, she tucked the new information away for further, private consideration. Closing her eyes against the bright June sun, she said, "Well. There's an issue between Steve and me that is more of a concern than his sexual orientation. He seems to have no respect or love for me, yet looks to me as his personal bank now that we have this bequest. He's very upset because I wouldn't give him the money to buy a tractor-trailer. How could I put him in harm's way, like Dad? I just couldn't bear it if I made it possible and something happened to Steve on the road."

"He's driving now. It won't...wouldn't...be your fault if he had an accident. Odds are that he'll be fine, safe. What happened to Dad was so freaky!"

They sat quietly, side-by-side, arms on knees, staring down the slope to the vineyard. There was no easy answer. Finally, Selby said, "I really didn't say absolutely 'no'—just that he had to bring me a business proposition. Perhaps that was a delaying tactic on my part. I wonder if he thinks I said no because he's gay? Does he know I didn't know?"

Justin shrugged his shoulders. "Look. I'll do what I can, when I see him again...to explain."

"No. This is my problem, not yours, not Steve's. I'll talk to him—clear up whatever misunderstanding there is between us."

CHAPTER TWENTY-THREE

The weekend with Justin went by quickly. Selby spent most of her time on the family room couch nursing her bruised body and stiff neck, while Justin visited friends, took photographs of the house and surrounding area for his school project, and told glowing anecdotes about Liam's qualities. "Promise me you'll call him when he can come see you? He's really worried about you."

"Yes, yes. But stop trying to play Cupid! My life is much too busy right now for any outside interests." You're a liar, Selby said to herself. You already have an outside interest even though it's going nowhere. Maybe Justin's right. I should give Liam a chance. It might be fun to be courted again. At least it would take my mind off Hawk. But would it be fair to Liam to use him that way?

By Monday, with Justin back at the university and the soreness from the fall all but gone, Selby was ready to get back to the tasks at hand. First, she confirmed dates and tasks for each sub-contractor, then confirmed shipping dates for furniture and area rugs. She'd found the perfect area rug for the family room—a geometric pattern in colors that echoed the vineyard. The new black leather sofa would look great on it in front of the fireplace, she thought. The next item on her list was to call Levy and tell him about the locket, to see that he gave it to Estelle. However, that was not to be.

"I'm sorry, Mrs. Browning, but Mr. Levy is on an extended vacation," his secretary said. "He won't be back for six weeks. Is there something I can do for you?"

Without thinking it through, Selby said, "Oh, no I can handle it. I'll talk to him when he gets back. But could you give me the telephone number of Estelle Jacobs?"

The call to Estelle had gotten away from Selby; the next things she knew, Estelle was coming to LillyHill to pick up the locket the next day. What have I done? It would be risky to see Estelle. Stupid, stupid! Oh well. Maybe it will be fine. She must be over her upset to want to drive out here. However, no matter how much Selby told herself that it was acceptable for Estelle to visit LillyHill, instinct told her it was a mistake to have made contact with the volatile woman.

The muggy June day was oppressive. Selby discarded the foam neck brace and told herself she was well. The butterfly bandage on the cut over her eye fell off, revealing an angry scar that would need time to fade. The yellow and green bruises on her cheek accentuated her naturally pale skin. She looked vulnerable. Bulldog Estelle could devour me in one bite, Selby thought with a wry smile at the pathetic creature in her mirror.

At two o'clock on the dot, a white Lincoln Towncar eased up the dusty driveway and stopped in front of the house. Selby watched from inside the shadows of the living room. Estelle seemed to be giving little Lilly a piece of her mind, the child responding with flailing fists and unheard wailing. At last, the two guests were out of the car and coming up the walk. Selby flung open the door and walked to the edge of the verandah. "Welcome to LillyHill. Come in." Her smile felt tight, painted on.

Estelle was taking in every detail of the yard, the house and Selby. Her eyes could have been cameras with automatic shutters. Snap, snap, snap, recording everything in sight. "It looks like you are doing a lot of remodeling. I'm surprised. Aunt Lily had impeccable taste...."

"Oh, she did, indeed, but we had a fire several weeks ago. Fiona's rooms were destroyed and almost everything else was damaged by water and smoke," Selby said, and then went on to give a brief overview of the incident.

"Were you injured in the fire?"

At first Selby had no idea what brought on that question, then she remembered her bruised and cut face. "Oh, no. We...I was out of town when the fire happened. These bruises are from a fall from one of the horses," she said indicating her face. "Would you care for some iced tea? I'm sure little Lilly would like a cookie. While I get them, here is the locket. It's really very beautiful—a nice heirloom to hand down to little Lilly."

Conversation was strained and interrupted by Estelle correcting everything the child did. Little Lilly was restless and curious, but not destructive. Selby's heart went out to her. Estelle didn't seem to realize how special it was to have a daughter. She imagined how explosive the relationship would be when the child became a teenager. Yet who was she to criticize? She didn't even know until yesterday that one of her adult sons was gay!

Finally, Estelle stood and looked around the room for little Lilly. The child had wandered outside where the plumber and his assistant were installing a hot tub off the rear verandah. The two men were red-faced and disconnecting some of their final work.

"I helped the men, Mommy," little Lilly said proudly. It was obvious that her "help" had caused a problem.

Estelle yanked her away, shouting, "What have you done?" The child began to cry. Estelle smiled, picking her up, saying she was a naughty girl, but crooned to her and patted her gently on the back. Selby couldn't interpret the mixed message. She wondered if little Lilly could.

While Selby escorted Estelle and little Lilly to the car, Hawk was on the telephone with Adrianna, his former fiancée, who was calling from the University at Davis, California. "Hey, baby, great to hear from you! What's up?"

"Miss me?"

"You bet. Things got even duller around here after you left."

"I didn't think the place could!"

Hawk liked her laugh, a boisterous, unfettered burst of sound. She was a large-boned woman, tall and well-shaped. Lush. That was the word that came to mind when he thought of her. Intelligent, too. She began telling him about her doctoral dissertation.

"I'm researching climates in wine-growing areas in Texas, Idaho, Washington, and Oregon, then comparing them to wine grape-growing regions in England, Chile and Australia. There's already a lot of research on France, Spain and California, so I'm trying to find a new angle. I'll be in Oregon early next month. How would you like LillyHill to be in the data?"

"Sounds great. Some people will do anything to travel and write it off as an expense!" They both laughed. "I'd love to see you and do whatever I can to help your research. I'm part owner of LillyHill now and I've bought adjoining acreage. I'd be very interested in your research methods and the results on both properties. Count on my help."

They chatted about mutual friends and inquired about each other's love life. What had been between them at one time was gone, except for a deep friendship based on intellectual respect and a common interest in viticulture. They agreed on the first week of July for her visit.

The white Towncar lumbered down the driveway and off the property as Hawk hung up the phone. His curiosity had gotten the best of him, so he saddled up Tucker and rode up to the house. His excuse was that he needed to tell Selby about acquiring the adjoining land before she found out from someone else.

As he rode up the hill, Selby was in the driveway talking to the plumber. She was animated, smiling and gesturing. Hawk wondered what could be so amusing. It seemed to him that she could always find something positive about any given situation. She might be depressed, but always rallied to meet the situation head-on and deal with it.

Selby and the plumber turned at the sound of Tucker's hoof beats. "Howdy, cowboy; the rustlers went that-a-way," she drawled.

"You want to saddle up, ma'am, and join the posse?"

"No thank you! I want this batch of bruises gone before I risk another tumble. Come in and see my new hot tub." Turning to the plumber, she said, "Thanks for being so patient with my mischievous little visitor."

"What was that all about?" Hawk asked as he looped Tucker's reins loosely on a shrub by the driveway.

"You didn't see my visitor? Estelle Jacobs came by to pick up an heirloom locket that I found in the wall safe. Anyway, little Lilly wandered out where the men were working and managed to drop sticks and dirt in one of the fittings that the plumber hadn't secured. It was a small mess, but nothing serious. What was funny was Estelle's reaction. She'd been giving the child all kinds of grief about touching things in the house, but when that happened, she almost seemed pleased, as if she was glad that something could have been damaged, yet she laid into little Lilly like she committed a terrible crime. Weird lady."

"Why did you ask her out here? Was that wise?"

"Didn't mean to. Levy is on a vacation and I thought I'd just tell her she could pick the locket up at his office, but before I knew it, she had invited herself to come to the vineyard and I didn't know how to get out of it graciously. I'm sure there was no harm. Maybe she's accepted the idea that LillyHill isn't hers."

"If you believe that, then I have a bridge in New York to sell you."

They walked to the back of the house where a hot tub was positioned next to the rear verandah. Nestled in the sheltered slope of the hillside, it would give users a view of the west slope of the vineyard.

"That's a beauty! How many gallons does it hold?"

They examined it in great detail and flipped through the owner's manual to see how it worked. "How about some iced tea before your ride?"

"Sounds good. Anyway, I wanted to talk to you about the property next to Bench 7; you know... where we were riding last week? Well, I bought it."

Selby's heart gave an odd thump. "How nice...ah, what are your plans?"

"I'm going to work with varieties that aren't popular or are just coming on like Pinot Blanc. I may even try a Spanish variety called Tempranillo from the Duero region in Spain. It's a red table wine that takes cool nights and hot days to grow. Might not have any luck with it here, but it would be fun to try." He looked at her sad face, which brightened up when she saw that he was watching her. "Hey. It'll be okay. When my contract is up, you might decide that you don't need me any longer. You're a quick study; you'll know more than I do pretty soon."

"Don't be silly...I mean...you have half interest in LillyHill, so you'll always...." Selby's mind careened from one possibility to another. Hawk not at the winery? How would she manage?

"Look. I've always wanted my own place. This way, as LillyHill matures, I'll have time to work my own vineyard. The transition will be smooth. And someday you might not want me around...to buy me out."

There was no response she could make to this suggestion. Yes, it did make sense for him to invest in his own future, but to leave LillyHill? Of course. Nothing is forever. She knew that. She just didn't want changes so soon, particularly any thought of his leaving.

He continued. "You'll be able to run everything in another season. Justin seems interested, too."

"I guess it does make sense. I just wasn't thinking very far ahead. I'm afraid my mind has been on Steve and then this visit from Estelle...."

"What about Steve?"

Turning, she walked back into the house to get the iced tea. He followed.

Did she want to tell him? She really wanted to talk with Elaine about it first. But maybe he would understand...could give her some insight.

They leaned companionably against the counter, sipping their tea while she decided. "Okay. I'll tell you. I guess I need to hear myself say it out loud, to see how it sounds." She brushed off the front of her denim skirt, smoothing it in preparation to voice what she had learned about Steve.

"Justin told me that Steve is gay and that Chris, the young man who came here with him, is his lover."

"Jeez."

"Yeah. I feel so stupid for not knowing. Where have I been all these years for him?"

"How do you feel about it?"

"Funny, I'm more shocked at my not knowing than I am about his being gay. That's a strange mindset, isn't it? What really bothers me is that he asked me for money...a lot of money...to buy a tractor-trailer and I turned him down. I'm worried that he thinks I said no because he is gay, but I didn't know then. I didn't give him the money because I don't want him to die on the road like his father did."

"And you're not sure he understands that's the real reason?"

"Mmmm." Selby nodded and sipped her tea.

"You'll have to talk to him—and soon—to get it straightened out."

"I know. Well, I've got to get back to work getting the house ready for the final touches and you need to exercise Tucker."

"And you need to get back on Zephyr soon. The longer you wait, the harder it'll be to ride again."

"You're right, of course. Okay. Next week?"

By the end of the week, the subcontractors had finished their work and Bobbie and Selby began to replace all the items that had been stored in the garage during the renovation. The area rugs and new furniture would arrive over the next few days. Except for the bedrooms, everything was complete. Her final chore was to select linens for the bedrooms. She looked at dozens of colors and patterns. The small bedroom had a white daybed with the trundle; it begged for pink candy stripes and eyelet ruffles. Selby kept telling herself that it was too feminine, too...fluffy. At last, she succumbed to the whim and purchased the linen and accessories. She justified the color scheme as it being a guest room for Amanda when Mike and Rhonda came to visit.

The other bedroom featured a queen-sized brass bedstead, which gleamed against the hyacinth blue walls. She selected a design-quilted comforter and full-platform petticoat with an all-over rose motif in soft shades of blue, ivory and white on a buttercup and cream background. The tailored shams and comforter were edged in twisted ivory cording. The window coverings were the same print in a tucked valance and lined tie-back curtains.

While she was pleased with her final choices for the guest rooms, she was less sure of the master suite. It was as if she had lost interest in decorating, of marking her private territory with special touches. A quilted headboard and matching bedspread in off-white nubby cotton fabric was as far as she had gone. I'll do something special later, she told herself. The king-sized bed she'd always wanted seemed too big now, empty and lonely.

The sitting room had become her office. Sleek, modern modules held her PC, printer and files. Nearly every day there was an email from Liam; simple things like, "Isn't this a lovely day?" to "When can we get together?" The email she most enjoyed was from Rhonda. In addition to the messages she sent Rhonda, once a week she sent a message specifically to Amanda even though it would have to be read to her.

The sitting room-office also had a comfortable chair, reading lamp and side table placed by the windows which overlooked the fields to the northeast. Stacks of books on growing grapes and making wine were within easy reach, as were materials from the Reed-Steiner & Company. Another board meeting was scheduled for August in San Francisco. Perhaps she'd ask Elaine to go with her for a wild weekend of shopping, dining and the theater.

Selby left a message on Steve's telephone recorder asking him to stop by the vineyard as soon as he had an opportunity. Her message was not returned and she continued to fret about it.

"He's probably on an east coast trip, Selby. He'll get back to you. Here, let me see if you have the cinch tight enough," Hawk said.

After their weekly business meeting, Selby agreed to ride Zephyr over to Hawk's property. "Is it true horses can sense fear? If so, Zephyr is probably picking up all kinds of bad vibes from me," Selby laughed.

They rode slowly, companionably together up the hill past the house and over to Bench 7 field, then walked the horses along the lane where the accident had occurred.

"I had Rio pick up the trash that frightened the horses. I'll post the property and do what I can to secure it from dumpers and hunters."

"Do you have a name for your vineyard and the wines you'll make? I noticed some wine label sketches in an album on your coffee table the first time we met."

"I've lots of ideas, but haven't settled on one. One of the names I really liked was recently taken by another winery: *Abadela*. It's Castillian and means 'planting sticks in the ground'."

She laughed. "That's what they look like. When I first saw what you were planting in the new field I thought you were out of your mind. I didn't think those tiny sticks could never become anything, but look at them now!"

They urged the horses up a steep draw to a grove of old oak trees at the top of a hill, which overlooked Hawk's property. A weathered old house and several rickety outbuildings were situated about halfway down the hill.

"Looks like I have my work cut out for me. I may have to drill a new well. That'll be one of the first things I do, and see what can be saved in the house. The sheds can come down, except for the pumphouse for the water system."

"I can see why you like the property. The view from here is magnificent." She turned to him and touched his arm. "Glad to have you as a neighbor."

The ride went smoothly and Selby again began to feel comfortable on Zephyr. "Can we go back a different way? Maybe make a loop back to LillyHill...."

"Sure. We'll have to cross the creek and open some gates, but that's no problem. We'll end up on the south side of the barn."

By riding cross-country, they approached LillyHill from the south, avoiding the roads and the driveway. They were unaware of a visitor parked in the shade of the winery.

Hawk and Selby led the horses into the cool, dark barn and began the post-ride ritual of wiping down the horses' sweaty backs and rationing the animals' first drinks of water. The brushing finished at last, they hung up the tack and embraced casually, pleased with themselves and their comfortable relationship, unaware of the observer in the shadows.

Bending his head to hers, Hawk whispered, "Ever do it in the hay?"

Giggling, she whispered, "No. That's Hollywood stuff. It sounds scratchy and dusty! I like my creature comforts. Anyway, business partners don't do it at all, even if they want to." They both laughed and walked out into the bright sunshine, their arms around each other. The sight of a red pickup truck and Steve leaning casually against the fender brought them to a halt.

"Steve! What a surprise! I didn't expect you...." She and Hawk released each other, feeling like guilty teenagers.

He had a smug, knowing look on his face. "You said to come. I just got in from Houston last night."

"You've met Hawk Kestrel...." The men shook hands, acknowledging their previous meeting. "Give me a ride up the hill in your macho truck." Turning to Hawk, she said, "Thanks for showing me your property. I'll see you tomorrow."

Back at the house, Selby told Steve to help himself to something cold to drink while she washed the dust off her hands and face. When she returned, Steve was sitting on the new black leather sofa in the family room, running his hand over the soft texture, and sipping a beer. "Pretty nice."

"Thank you," Selby said, placing two coasters on the square coffee table as she sat next to him. "Basically, all the repairs are completed. It's just a matter of adding personal touches...getting some of our family treasures out of storage...that kind of thing."

"What happened to your eye?"

"I fell off a horse. Today was the first time I've been riding since the accident. The horses belong to Hawk." Now that Steve was here unannounced, she'd had no time to think through again what she wanted to say to him and how. She felt lost and clumsy. "Justin was here a week or so back and we talked about you and Chris. He thinks Chris is a nice guy." Steve sat quietly, watching her, waiting. Selby put her iced tea carefully on the coaster. "He said...I wasn't aware...you and I haven't been close for the last eight or ten years...." A deep sigh escaped as she looked at her handsome son, so like Doug in his younger days, before he lost his hair and developed a pot belly.

Finally, she put her hand on his arm. "I want you to know that the only reason I turned down your request to finance the tractor-trailer was my concern about your safety. Nothing else figured into my rejection. Do you understand what I'm saying?"

"Yeah. Chris said you didn't know. I thought you did. You always seemed to know everything when we were kids. I couldn't believe you didn't see the obvious. Guess you were too busy working and raising Justin."

"Nothing is ever obvious to me, never has been," she smiled. "It's an act all mothers put on."

"So? Now what?"

"So, nothing, I guess. I just wanted to clear the air, to let you know that I love you, always have and always will."

"No rig?"

"Only if it's a solid business deal. I'd be willing to loan you the money, but you need to handle the transaction like you were borrowing the money from a bank. Consider it part of your education." She gathered her thoughts in preparation to tell him what she'd really like. "And speaking of education, would you ever consider a different career from truck driving? It's dangerous work. It's hard on the body...too much sitting, greasy food, no exercise. I'd give you college tuition without a moment's thought, if you wanted to prepare for another field of work."

"You remember what Dad used to say, that driving is addictive; guess I'm addicted."

"The offer still stands, whenever you're ready."

They sat quietly, listening to the old family clock tick away the silence.

"Haven't seen that piece of junk for a long time," he said, nodding at the

Seth Thomas sitting on the fireplace mantel.

"That clock's been in your dad's family for years. I had it cleaned. Sometimes I forget to wind it." They continued to listen to the clock as if it would alleviate the tension between them.

"Well, I have to get back. I leave for Seattle tomorrow." He stood, placing his beer bottle on the table, ignoring the coaster.

"Yes. Thanks for coming. Please feel free to come anytime...and bring Chris."

"Yeah." They walked out of the cool house and into the late afternoon sun. The gleaming red truck seemed to be absorbing the heat, pulsating, eager to go. Steve lit a cigarette, flipping the match into the gravel driveway. "Justin going to live here this summer?"

"Yes. He has a job at the nursery again and plans to help here in the vineyard. I understand harvesting grapes can be a lot of fun as well as a lot of work. Perhaps you and Chris would like to join in this fall...if you aren't on the road."

"Maybe." With that, he climbed into the high-wheeled pickup, started the engine and revved up the motor, his chrome tailpipes and muffler breaking the summer silence with a snapping growl. "See ya."

Selby nodded and lifted a hand in farewell. Well. Now what? Nothing, I guess. The tears came. She'd failed, but she didn't know how or when or where.

The ringing of the telephone jarred her out self-condemnation. A familiar voice asked how she was feeling.

"Oh, hi, Liam. How are you?"

"I'm fine. It's you I'm concerned about. Justin said you'd call me when you were feeling better."

"I'm fine now, really. Just been busy and vanity's kept me from calling you. Come for supper tonight, if you're free. You'll have to take pot luck."

"Sounds great to me. About seven o'clock?"

This impromptu invitation spurred Selby into action. First into the shower, then to find something to eat. Yes. It was a good decision to invite him—a distraction. She needed something to get her mind off Steve—and Hawk, too. Liam was a good antidote.

CHAPTER TWENTY-FOUR

The vineyard settled into its summer routine. Robert, Rio and Hawk were busy cultivating, irrigating, fertilizing, and controlling pests. Final exams over, Justin moved home and began his job at Liam's nursery and helping at LillyHill when he had time. Selby happily immersed herself in the role of mother, business owner, housekeeper, cook and gardener. Her energy seemed boundless. It was as if her whole life had finally come together. To top it off, she was being courted by an attractive contemporary who thought she was the most beautiful and charming lady he'd ever met. Their dates had been simple affairs—a movie, a mid-week picnic at a nearby scenic place, a day trip to the coast. They held hands, laughed at each other's jokes, shared family reminiscences and parted with chaste kisses. However, Selby could tell Liam was becoming more serious, and she didn't know what to do about it.

Liam suggested a night on the town in Portland. The evening of dinner and dancing at a posh establishment followed by a romantic walk along the river made it obvious that Liam had something in mind. Selby was amused, curious to see what he had planned. Fingers entwined, shoulders touching as they strolled the Riverplace Promenade, he paid her numerous compliments— what a good mother she was, what excellent taste she had in decorating, how quick she was in learning the winery business. As they were driving back to LillyHill, he said, "You know, I've never shown you my home. Would you like to see it?"

"I'd love to." He'd been so circumspect in their relationship up to this point that she was beginning to think she had lost her sex appeal. The invitation to see his house came as a surprise.

His home was a quaint farmhouse, which had been remodeled and expanded. The board-and-batten siding and cedar shingles gave it a cozy, traditional look. A separate building served as garage and workshop. Parking at the front walk, he hurried to the passenger side and opened the door for her.

"I should have brought you out sooner—in the daytime—so you could see the yard. And the vegetable garden. But my housekeeping isn't always the best now...."

"I'll bet you cleaned house all morning so you could lure me here in the middle of the night."

"Well, you can't blame a guy for trying!" This amused both of them and they were laughing as he unlocked the front door and entered first, switching on the lights. "There are two bedrooms and a bath upstairs that I don't use anymore, unless the girls come with their families," he said as he took on the role of nervous tour guide. "I use the dining room as an extra office now, so it's a mess. This is the kitchen and there's a screened porch off the master bedroom over there."

"Very cozy. I like the corner fireplace in the living room."

"Its not as elegant as your home, but...."

"It's lovely! I'm sure you have good family memories as well as sad ones."

"Yes. We were very happy here. It seems so quiet now with Margie and the girls gone." He cleared his throat, smiled and reached for her hand. "Would you like a glass of champagne?"

Oh, dear. He's trying too hard. Shall I just put him out of his misery? Be a brazen hussy and throw him to the floor? Or kill the seduction by asking to go home? "I'd really prefer a cup of coffee."

This seemed to stop him for a moment, but he recovered quickly and led her into the kitchen. "Instant is all I have. I hope that's okay." She gave him a smile of approval. She was being mean, throwing his plans out of whack. Why didn't he just grab her and kiss her? But she knew why: he wasn't the grabbing kind. He was a romantic—flowers, champagne, little gifts.

"I have something for you," he said as they carried their mugs of coffee into the living room. Seated side-by-side on the sofa, he opened a drawer in the lamp table and pulled out a small package, beautifully wrapped in gold paper. "Open it."

A gold charm bracelet on black velvet gleamed in the lamplight.

"Oh how lovely! But I don't understand...."

"I like to give presents. I just thought you might be tired of flowers and garden statuary."

"Thank you. But this is so nice; I really can't accept it."

"Put it on; let me help you."

She held out her wrist, his trembling fingers fumbling with the tiny clasp. Three charms hung from the chain: a tiny Victorian house, a bunch of grapes and a rabbit.

"It's wonderful! I remember my mother having a silver charm bracelet. They were popular when she was in high school."

"My mother had one, too. Lindy, my youngest daughter, told me charm bracelets were back in style now."

So, he checked with his daughter about selecting a gift. She must have approved, Selby surmised.

After he fastened the chain, he brought the sensitive inside of Selby's wrist to his lips. His mouth lingered over her pulse; his tongue sensing her heartbeat, which had increased. She felt a rush of desire. No longer an observer, she was a participant in the seduction. It seemed that only moments had passed between chaste kissing, upright on the couch, to full body contact. Stretched out full length on the couch, she could tell that he would go as far and as fast as she wanted. But what did she want? Heavy necking on the couch was fun, but rather pointless at their age. Either fuck him or go home. Suddenly, her self-centered musings were interrupted.

"I love you, Selby. Marry me."

A bucket of cold water couldn't have been more effective in breaking the mood. Her body stiffened. Sensing this, he pulled away. Disentangling herself and sitting up, she gasped, "What?"

"Marry me. I've been in love with you ever since we met. I feel as if I've known you for years. Justin's told me so much about you. I'd take good care of you—not that you can't take care of yourself...." He sat back, flustered, sensing he had said the wrong thing. This woman did not need anyone to take care of her. "What I mean is...I love you. I want to spend the rest of our lives together. I'm going to retire early. My son-in-law, Bryan, and Justin, when he finishes college, can take over the business. We'll travel anywhere you want." He paused, heart pounding and breathless. "I've been looking at motor homes. If you'd rather go to Hawaii or Europe, that'd be fine, too. We're meant for each other, I just know it." He stopped, looking at her intently and waiting for her answer.

Every response that came to Selby's mind sounded trite. She certainly wasn't going to say, "This is so unexpected," even if it were. "You've got to be kidding," wasn't appropriate; "Let me think about it," was lame.

"Wow!" That sounded so silly that they both laughed.

Pulling her into his arms again, he said, "I really mean it. It's more than being caught up in the moment—and it was such a nice moment. I'd planned a proper proposal with a ring and everything later this summer, but we—I—

just got carried away. Think about it; meet my daughters. Talk to Justin. You can even pick out your own ring."

One afternoon several days later, Selby and Elaine sprawled on thickly tufted patio furniture, nibbling cookies and sipping iced tea. "This is the life!" Elaine said, savoring the view from the shaded verandah. "One of these days I'm going to quit my job and become a lady of leisure."

"So you think I'm a lady of leisure, do you?" Selby laughed. "Let me tell you, refurbishing a house gets old very quickly."

"I can imagine! I really like the way you've lightened up the rooms—personalized them. Your office is really great, too. Makes more sense to use that space for something you need every day."

"Um hum. I just couldn't see having a sitting room. I've never been the type to just sit, unless it's with you!" They smiled at each other, secure in their friendship. Their gaze shifted to a red-tailed hawk circling the vineyard.

"What do you think she'll find for lunch—a mouse or a rabbit?" Elaine asked.

"Hard telling. Rio is in charge of predator control. I doubt if he's as tough on rabbits as he is on gophers. Rabbits don't seem to be as much of a problem to the vines as rodents."

They watched the hawk's ever-widening circles until it was out of sight behind a hill. "How's the love life? You still using Liam to keep Hawk at bay?"

"That's an interesting way to put it!" Considering a response, she passed the cookies to Elaine and poured more tea for them. "Hawk and I've been so busy that there hasn't been time for unbusiness-like encounters. And having Justin around certainly eliminates opportunities for me to get into trouble, even though it's pretty nice trouble!" They laughed. "I see Liam at least once a week for dinner or a movie. Sometimes Justin comes with us. That keeps Liam where I prefer him, at arm's length. But he's a darling. Really. I do like him."

"He hasn't made a move on you yet?"

"Well—yes."

Elaine waited for Selby to expand her brief response. "'Well yes' what? Don't keep me in suspense!"

"He proposed to me."

"And you said....?"

"Wow."

"You said 'Wow' to his proposal?" Elaine laughed. "That was very mature."

"I know. I felt so...stupid. I didn't have a clue he had anything serious in mind. I was in my own little world. A proposal wasn't in the mix. It wasn't what he had in mind that night either. He just got carried away."

"So?"

"I've been thinking about it, about him. He's certainly pleasant, thoughtful, caring. I probably know more about him and his background than I do about Hawk."

"How'd Hawk get in this conversation?"

"Well...you know what I mean."

"Yeah, I do. Hawk really turns you on, and Liam is a safe choice. The question is: Do you even want a choice?"

"Exactly! Why does there have to be an either-or? Right now I'm perfectly happy to have two interesting but very different friends. I like the sexual tension between Hawk and me, the flirting, the challenge to keep things on a business-only level. But I like being courted by Liam, too. You know what I mean?"

"Not really, since I don't have a lover and no one is courting me except Roy!"

"He's still courting you after all these years of marriage?"

"In his own way. He lets me know that I'm still the love of his life." Elaine reached over and squeezed Selby's hand. "I'm so glad everything has come together after all you've been through. Just don't feel pushed into a decision. Have it all, if you can!"

"Wouldn't that be great?" They gazed across the vineyard, watching a flock of Starlings swoop to the ground, then explode into the sky at some mysterious signal. Selby thought about Elaine's friendship, how easy it was to talk with her. "Come to San Francisco with me next month. I have a board meeting to attend. We'll stay at the condo, shop, go to the theater. Can you get away?"

"I'm going to have to think that offer over for about two seconds. Of course I'll go!"

"By the way, I'm having a small dinner party to christen the new dining room table. Liam's coming and I'd like you and Roy to come too. I may even invite Hawk...."

"You've got to be kidding! Are we playing sophomoric jealousy games?"

"I guess it would look weird. Okay. Just the four of us. Then you can tell me what you think of Liam."

Their afternoon of girl talk came to an abrupt end when a registered letter arrived. It was a notice saying she was not in compliance with the Oregon State Liquor Control Commission and questioned the current status of county commercial and agricultural permits.

"What in the world? I don't have anything to do with the OLCC, do I?" She looked up at Elaine. "There must be a mistake."

"You make wine."

"I just assumed...I've got to talk to Hawk. He should know if we are in compliance."

"It's no big deal, Selby—just standard over-reaction in a government office," Hawk explained.

A county agriculture permit had expired, but other state and county regulations had been met. However, the process of hopping through bureaucratic hoops took several days and a good amount of emotional energy.

"But I felt like a criminal! Now that I know about the permits, I'll make sure that they don't lapse again."

The business partners were settled in for their weekly meeting. Hawk brought Selby up to speed on the status of the vineyard from the newest plantings to the flowering of the mature vines. They talked about the fall wine festival and when to finish bottling wine that was aging in the French oak casks. Then Selby booted up her laptop and went over the latest profit-and-loss statement. As the session came to a close, a car pulled into the parking area in front of the winery office.

Emerging from the car, two serious-looking men in suits and dark glasses took a long look around before coming to the office door. Selby opened the door with a smile. It faded when one of the men took out his wallet and flipped it open to an identification badge.

"Mrs. Browning? Federal Bureau of Alcohol, Tobacco and Firearms to inspect the premises."

The sound that came from her mouth could have been a call for her partner or an exclamation of surprise. "Awk!"

They stepped into the office and introduced themselves. Selby shook hands numbly, her mind stuck in neutral. Hawk shook hands with the visitors and suggested that they step into the aging room where there was more space to discuss whatever was on their mind.

"We had a call about improprieties at the LillyHill vineyard. If you would just show us around and answer a few questions, I'm sure we can get this cleared up."

"Improprieties? Impossible. All the permits are current and the liquor commission inspector was on the property a year ago. I'm sure we have a letter of compliance on file," Selby heard herself saying.

"Your background looks fine, assuming the IRS audit is clean. Since we had a team in the area, we thought we'd respond to the tip."

"Who...?"

Hawk gave Selby a swift look, winked and turned his attention to the visitors. "It's quite a coincidence that you're here; we've just finished updating our county and state permits. Is there something of particular interest?"

"Do you have a greenhouse or other areas under cultivation other than this acreage?"

"No. We grow and produce three types of wine under the LillyHill label."

The men wandered around the steel fermenting tanks and oak casks. They looked at the current permits. Declining an invitation to sample the wines, they left without further explanation or apologies.

"What....?"

"Dear, dear Selby," Hawk said, shaking his head. "Doesn't this whole thing smell of Estelle?"

"Oh, surely not. No one in her right mind would joke with the ATF!"

"You got that right. But who said Estelle was in her right mind?" Laughing, he hugged Selby and told her to go home so he could finish up. "I'd put money on it. Estelle just wanted to annoy you. Didn't one of the agents say you were being audited?"

"I am; but other than the hassle, there's no problem according to my accountant. I have an appointment next month with the IRS auditor."

"And you see no coincidence in these hassles? For being a tough, independent woman, you are also naïve and trusting, Selby. Guess that's what I like about you."

Although the visit simply had been two ordinary-looking men in one nondescript Ford sedan, to Selby it had the feeling of a SWAT team raid complete with Kevlar vests and Kalashnikov automatic rifles. She called Elaine to tell her about the raid. Hearing Elaine's laughter and agreement that Estelle must have had something to do with it and the audit brought the situation into perspective for Selby. Hanging up, she logged on to the Internet and sent e-mail to Mike and Rhonda, telling them of her latest adventure. Just another little bump in her road, a road that was widening, straightening out and taking her higher than she had even been before. She had financial security, a lovely home, an interesting business to run, a marriage proposal and/or a lover.

However, that night, sleep would not come. Her bedroom seemed hot and stuffy. Perhaps her office would be cooler. She'd review plans for participating in the Labor Day Wine Festival held by area growers. This would be the first year that LillyHill would hold a large-scale wine-tasting event. So many considerations had to be addressed: parking, staffing, supplies, seating, food, selection of wines to offer to the public.

After an hour of work, Selby wandered downstairs for a dish of ice cream and a prowl through the house, flipping lights on and off, critiquing room decor, jotting down an item or two on the grocery list. Then went back up stairs for another try at sleeping.

After another hour of tossing and turning, she got up, stripped off her shorty pajamas, grabbed a towel and padded barefoot out to the hot tub. The tepid water felt cool and relaxing to her warm, restless body. She let her mind drift with her body. If her life was so perfect, why was she crying?

Tears ran down her cheeks and dropped into the water. She rested her head back on the edge of the tub, her arms stretched out along the rim. Now that her face was turned to the star-studded sky, the tears ran into her ears. A silly, old country-western song came to mind: "I've got tears in my ears from lyin' on my back in my bed while I cry over you." Who is 'you'? she wondered. She didn't need people around her all the time, but now that the house was completed, it seemed so empty. She almost missed Fiona's daily puttering—dusting, watering the plants, sweeping the verandah.

Even though Justin was home from college this summer, he was up and gone by six a.m. After a twelve-hour day, he still had the energy to clean up and go out with friends, especially one friend—pretty brown-eyed Sara, who lived in Eugene where her father was an English professor at the university. Whenever Justin had a day off, he drove 140 miles round-trip to be with her. He was there now and would get up early to be back to work tomorrow. Ah, young love!

She turned off the noisy bubbler so that she could enjoy the night sounds—crickets, a distant dog barking, mysterious rustling in the grasses. Gazing at the night sky, she watched a man-made object move from northwest to southeast. Was it a satellite or the space station? Did the astronauts have tough personal issues waiting for them when they returned? Probably. But for months they could concentrate only on the tasks at hand. No. She wouldn't trade places with them. She liked the land, the earth with its ability to regenerate, to grow things that pleased the eye and the tongue. Earthbound was fine, so don't complain about having to deal with life's unexpected complications, she admonished herself.

But why was Liam's proposal more of a complication than an opportunity? She'd enjoyed being married, even though things weren't always the best with Doug. She liked having someone there to share life's daily pleasures and problems. When Doug was on the road for days, weeks at a time, she'd learned to be self-reliant. Problem-solving skills improved; decisions came easily to her. And now, it was nice not to have to get another opinion, unless she really wanted one. No more games: "What do you think of this, dear?" "Do you think we could afford that, dear?"

She submerged herself in the tub, then stretched out and floated to the surface. Night noises were muted in her watery cocoon. Her buoyant body released mental and physical tensions. A feeling of well-being returned. A breeze sprung up, sending a slight chill over her wet, exposed body. She stood and reached for her towel.

"Like Venus rising from the sea," a male voice said.

She clutched the towel to her mouth, smothering the scream that filled her chest. Before she could move, a figure stepped out of the shadow.

"Hey, it's okay; it's me."

"Hawk! How could you do that to me! You son-of-a-bitch!" She tossed the towel on the deck and slid back down into the water. Her knees would no longer hold her.

"I'm sorry. I didn't mean to frighten you. I thought you'd recognize me, but I guess it's too dark out here."

"What are you doing prowling around my house at this hour?" The mixture of anger and relief gave her voice a metallic sound. Her heartbeat was still at a gallop.

"I couldn't sleep. I saw your lights going on and off, so I thought I'd—I don't know. I walked up the hill and by the time I got here the lights were out, but I heard the bubbler on the hot tub."

"Damn! You scared the wits out of me. I guess I've learned my lesson not to be out here when I'm home alone. It could have been anyone." They were both silent. Hawk was embarrassed; Selby was angry, but relieved. "Well, the least I can do is to invite you in."

"The house or the hot tub?"

"Whatever."

He chuckled, quickly stripping off his shorts and briefs, and joined her in the cool water. "Ahhhh. That's wonderful."

"I was just getting out. But the adrenaline rush you gave me took off the chill," she laughed. "Damn. I don't think I'll ever forgive you. I think I'll get a big, vicious dog and train him to attack you on sight."

They soaked companionably, commenting on the sky and the night sounds. The quiet conversation lagged. Their toes touched at the bottom of the tub. Selby's mind and emotions kicked into gear. *Here we are again, alone and naked. I swear I look for opportunities to be with him. That's no way to keep our relationship businesslike, especially if I do stupid things like invite him into the hot tub. Get real, woman. Either put a stop to the relationship by buying him out or accept recreational sex for what it is.*

They ran their feet up and down each other ankles. The next step was inevitable.

CHAPTER TWENTY-FIVE

The day of Selby's dinner party dawned cool and cloudy. Out in her garden at first light, she picked strawberries for pie, snipped tender spinach leaves for salad, and cut flowers for the centerpiece. The tiny cherry tomatoes and snow peas she harvested would be served with seasoned cream cheese as one of the appetizers. A grilled salmon fillet, walnut wild rice, and Adelina's whole-wheat dill bread would complete the meal. She'd marinate the salmon in oil, lemon juice, garlic, soy and thyme, and then cook it on the outdoor grill. LillyHill's '95 reserve Chardonnay and a competitor's '95 Pinot Blanc for comparison were chilling. She felt at ease with the menu.

However, she was uneasy with the guest list. What was to be a companionable foursome had become six. How compatible they'd be, she couldn't guess. First, Elaine would look askance at Hawk being there; second, Selby knew nothing about his friend, Adrianna. He said she was doing research, that they had known each other for many years and would be visiting the winery. There was nothing to do but extend an invitation to dinner. At least that was Selby's justification.

A few minutes before seven that evening, Liam arrived with an indoor fountain. "What in the world?" Selby said, opening the front door to welcome her first guest.

"I saw you looking at this at the nursery the other day when you were there. Where would you like it?"

"My goodness! Just because I look at something doesn't mean you have to give it to me," she laughed. "I was thinking that something like that would be nice in the corner of the dining room. The sound of running water is so soothing."

"It'll only take a few minutes to set it up. It needs to be near an electrical outlet. The motor is very quiet." He carried the box into the dining area and Selby showed him where she thought it would look nice. "If you'll bring me four quarts of water, I'll get it started." He quickly assembled the unit, arranged stones on the ledges and in the pool and poured water into the base. A few adjustments, a flip of the switch and a trickle of water spilled over the ledges and rocks of the waterfall into the basin at the bottom where it would be recycled, providing peaceful sight and sound.

"It's lovely. Thank you. You are too good to me."

Liam encircled her with his arms and kissed her gently. "You can have anything you want, as long as I can have you forever."

Pulling way, she smiled and said, "If my dinner burns because you are distracting me, it'll be all over before it begins." She was glad that he took the remark as she had intended—a nice way of saying "this isn't the time for serious considerations." They heard a car in the driveway and went to the front door to welcome Elaine and Roy, then escorted them to the back verandah for wine and hors d'oeuvres.

After serving the wine, Selby said, "Hawk and a friend will also be joining us." She felt, rather than saw, Elaine's look. "Adrianna Dyhr is an old friend of his. She's doing research on vineyard climates for her doctoral dissertation and asked to include LillyHill in the data. Hawk felt that it could be of value, as well as an opportunity to reconnect with a former colleague." The little speech left her breathless. Had she handled the explanation well? Did it seem offhanded enough? She smiled at her guests, who seemed unconcerned, except for Elaine's one raised eyebrow. At the sound of a vehicle coming up the hill, Selby said, "Excuse me while I greet the others."

Before stepping out onto the front verandah, she watched as a blonde woman parked a white van next to the other cars. Emerging from the vehicle, Hawk and the women paused at the end of the path to the house. He was talking animatedly, pointing out something with his right hand, his left resting on the small of the woman's back. Selby knew the feel of that hand and had thought it was his special touch for her. Obviously, it wasn't.

This moment of show-and-tell gave Selby an opportunity to have her first look at the mysterious Adrianna: tall, very tall, silvery blonde hair pulled back into a high ponytail that hung half-way down her back. Built like a "brick chicken house" as Doug used to say of women with fully-developed bodies. She wore tan safari shorts and a matching sleeveless blouse; leather woven sandals and a gold ankle chain drew attention to her long tanned legs. Selby felt small and pale in her yellow silk jumpsuit. She had felt very beautiful this evening until she saw this goddess. That was the only word to describe her guest.

Meeting them at the edge of the porch, she said, "Welcome to LillyHill, Adrianna. I'm so glad you could join us."

"Thank you for including me. It's been so good to see Hawk again." She flashed perfect teeth at him and placed her hand possessively on his arm.

"Come in and meet the others," Selby said, leading the way into the house. Her face left like a plastic mask; she hoped it was a pleasant one.

Once all her guests were settled, Selby excused herself to tend to last-minute dinner details, not that there was really anything to do. She was so organized that she could have stayed with her guests until it was time to put the salmon on the grill. She just needed a few minutes alone. However, that was not to be. Elaine and Adrianna joined her in the kitchen.

"Your home is lovely, Selby. Hawk told me about the fire; that must have been terrible."

"It was, but it gave me the opportunity to put my own touches to the house. Would you like to see the rest of it?" Showing this woman her house was the last thing she wanted to do, but it seemed like one of those things women do for each other, an obligatory ritual.

"I'd love to! It might encourage me to settle down one day," Adrianna laughed. "I'll be doing field work for at least a year in the Pacific Northwest, Australia, and Chile."

Elaine sighed and said, "Suddenly my office job sounds really dull!"

"Don't forget," Selby said, "We're going to run away to San Francisco next month. We'll go so crazy that you'll be happy to get home and back to work!" Selby led them into the living room, then upstairs to the bedrooms and Fiona's suite. She pointed out major changes, which had been made and mentioned where the fire had started in Fiona's room. Selby listen carefully to Adrianna's comments, pleased to see her home through a stranger's eyes. While Selby respected Elaine's opinions, they were through the eyes of a close friend.

As they returned to the kitchen, Adrianna said, "The house seems so much lighter than it did before. And by the way, what happened to the Dragon Lady?"

"You've been here before?"

"Oh, yes. When Hawk first came to LillyHill, I came too. I did some field study for my master's program. The housekeeper took a dislike to me. I don't know why, other than she was very protective of Hawk. I pity any woman who tries to get between Hawk and her."

Seeing Selby's stunned look, Elaine distracted Adrianna by saying, "The Dragon Lady is traveling with a childhood friend. When did you say Fiona will be back, Selby?"

"September, I think."

"She's coming back? Well, enjoy it while she's gone," laughed Adrianna. "But watch for fire and brimstone if Hawk brings a fiancée to LillyHill. No wonder he bought his own vineyard. He's not the type to live the life of a monk!"

Selby felt as if her jaw had dropped to her chest. She quickly turned to the refrigerator and took out a plate of sausages. Handing it to Elaine, she said, "Will you please see if one of the men will grill these and cut them in bite-sized pieces? We can nibble on them until dinner is ready."

"Sure." Elaine and Adrianna left Selby tending imaginary last minute details.

Selby went into the powder room to see if her face looked like it felt: permanently frozen into surprise. She stretched her jaw, practiced smiling and joined her guests, telling herself that 'Life is imperfect, and things just happen. Deal with it!'

"Let me refill your wine glasses," she said. "Those sausages are chicken with basil and pine nuts."

Murmurs of "These are wonderful" and "Really good," came from her guests. Adrianna was stretched out on the chaise, her long tan legs crossed at the ankles. Selby sat in a chair across from her, noting that the gold ankle bracelet was deeply etched with a hawk in flight.

Looking at Hawk, Selby said, "Adrianna tells me that she's met Fiona."

"Ah...yes." Everyone looked at Hawk, expecting some elaboration; none came. He searched his mind for an appropriate comment, but all he found was self-condemnation for not being candid with Selby about Adrianna. Why hadn't he told her that he and Adrianna had lived together at LillyHill? Too late now; he'd explain later. His thoughts were interrupted when Adrianna spoke.

"I always called Fiona 'Mrs. Danvers'—you know, the housekeeper at Manderley in *Rebecca*?" She paused to see if the others got the literary connection.

Hawk laughed and said, "I'd forgotten about that...."

Adrianna beamed and continued. "She seemed to think Hawk was her responsibility, as well as the house. Fiona was probably one of the most difficult people I've ever met. A dried-up old prune! Always meddling, criticizing. Ugh! And a firebug at that...just like Mrs. Danvers! I can't believe that you'd let her live here after that."

Selby rose to Fiona's defense. "Fiona had a very difficult life—being taken from her parents when she was young, sent to America. She never saw her parents again. They were killed in the London blitz. I'd say that would impact anyone's personality."

Sipping and nibbling, the other guests nodded in agreement. Selby's anger rose—but anger at whom? Adrianna or Hawk? Right now she didn't care. Face flushed, the pupils of her eyes dilated, she was as angry as she had ever been. How dare this woman—a guest—say such cruel things about someone who couldn't defend herself? Selby leaned forward in her chair and continued.

"Fiona spent her entire life serving others. She never had the chance to have a life of her own until now. I've seen changes in her." She searched her mind for a change, latching on to the smallest thing. "She's smiling more. She sounded happy when she phoned last month." Selby's voice had risen; her back had straightened. "Perhaps now she can find some joy for herself instead of always making sure others are well cared for."

The guests shifted uncomfortably in their chairs. Selby's indignation notched up; she was on a roll. To emphasize her point, she slammed her wine glass down on the ceramic tile tabletop, sending stemware shards and wine flying. Nearly shouting, she said, "Fiona's welcome to live at LillyHill for as long as she likes! Even if the bequest didn't have that stipulation, I'd insist that she stay! She needs love...and care as she gets older. And I'll happily do that!" Selby stood and pointed a finger at Adrianna. "I doubt if you would understand that!"

The guests sat stunned. This wasn't their Selby. She was always pleasant, always in control of her emotions. What had set her off on this tangent? The sound of chirping crickets and the sight of blood dripping from Selby's outstretched hand lent a surreal aspect to the gathering. Elaine was the first to move, reaching for Selby, quickly pressing a napkin to the bleeding palm. The men stood, but before they could do anything, Elaine gestured with her hand, saying sharply, "Sit!" In unison, they sat. "Stay!" And they did, as the two women entered the house.

Roy was the first to move, stooping to pick up the broken glass and mop up the wine with paper napkins. Ignoring Elaine's command to stay, Liam followed the two women into the house.

Adrianna sat up, swinging her long legs to the patio floor. "Hawk, I'm sorry. I didn't realize... Perhaps I should leave." Now she was standing, looking confused and unsure, not a common situation in her life. Hawk stood, too.

"Wait a minute while I see how badly she's cut," Hawk said, as he stepped over the stooping Roy and entered the house. He found Liam standing at the bottom of the stairs. "She okay?"

Liam glanced at Hawk and said, "I don't know; I should go up...or...."

"Come on. Elaine can't do more than kill us." The two men walked up the stairs; Hawk led the way to Selby's bedroom. It was empty, but they could hear the women's soft voices in the bathroom. Liam looked around the room, his love's inner sanctum. He liked its simplicity. He noticed her scent. Then a disturbing thought came to him. How did Hawk know which room was hers? He seemed to know exactly where he was going.

Elaine had cleaned and bandaged the cut in Selby's palm, wrapping it tightly to stem the flow of blood. The blood-spattered silk jumpsuit lay in a on heap in the floor. "I'd better soak that in cold water before it dries," she said to Selby, who was looking in her closet for something else to put on.

"That'd be great. Thanks for the first aid. I feel so stupid, losing it like I did. My reaction was way over the top. I don't know why."

"She was thoughtless, so don't beat yourself about the head and shoulders." Hawk called out. "Everything okay?"

Elaine poked her head around the door jam, saying, "You guys don't follow orders very well, do you?" She was smiling. "We'll be down in a minute. Go away, make yourself useful."

Selby slipped into a batik tunic and pants in cream and sienna. With difficulty she ran a comb through her hair with her left hand. "Do I apologize to her or act as if nothing happened?"

"Never apologize, never explain. It drives people crazy!" laughed Elaine. Then she looked sober and gently hugged Selby. "We'll talk later. You just need to figure out who you're really mad at."

Selby nodded and swallowed hard. "I already know. And I'm not pleased with myself."

Elaine smiled, saying, "I'll help you get dinner on the table."

The two women found Liam standing in the kitchen looking as if he'd be glad to do something, if he only knew what. Hawk was out on the verandah, telling Roy and Adrianna that Selby was okay.

Liam rushed up to Selby and embraced her. "Are you sure you're all right, darling?"

It was the first time Selby had heard him express an endearment in front of others, even if it were just Elaine. It seemed as if her shy suitor was not as shy as she had thought. "I'm fine, really. Just very, very embarrassed. I shouldn't have lost my temper." It was then she noticed Hawk standing in the doorway with a bemused look on his face. She pulled away from Liam, giving Hawk a look that could remove paint from a battleship.

Hawk said, "Selby, I'm sorry. Adrianna was way out of line, but she meant no harm. That's just her way." Selby looked at him with such hate that he couldn't believe she was the same woman who had invited him into her hot tub and then into her bed a week ago. "Adrianna would like to leave."

"That's not necessary. Assure her that I will not attack her verbally or physically for the rest of the evening." She paused, then added, "However, I won't promise the same about you." She turned away, opening the refrigerator with her left hand. "Your first penance is to grill the salmon."

Liam was completely confused now. Were Hawk and Selby just friends and business partners, or was there more to their relationship? Why did she seem angry at Hawk? Because his friend was rude or because....? Love and hate are two closely related emotions, he thought. It didn't make a lot of sense to be upset with Hawk, yet ask him to grill the salmon as if he were the host. His musing was interrupted when Elaine spoke.

"I'll toss the salad. Liam, would you please slice the bread? The salmon won't take long. Woe unto Hawk if he overcooks the fish!" Both women laughed. Liam didn't have a clue as to what was going on.

The rest of the evening went off without a hitch, although there was tension in the air. The guests rose to the occasion, complimenting the food, the table setting and the new waterfall. They discussed the weather in great detail and avoided anything that had political or religious overtones. Even the house and the vineyard seemed taboo subjects. They bid their farewells earlier than usual, leaving Liam with Selby.

"I'll help you clean up," he said.

"There isn't much to do. Stop worrying about me. I'm fine. Just embarrassed."

He embraced her, kissing her tenderly, sliding his hands down her back and pressing her hips to his. He could administer the world's best relaxation, if she'd allow it.

The warmth of his embrace and his concern stirred something in Selby. Desire? A flutter, perhaps. More likely the need to be cuddled after losing her cool. She stayed in his arms, swaying slightly with him as he murmured in her ear, suggesting what he could do to make things okay. Her mind was a ping-pong ball. It would serve Hawk right if she jumped into bed with Liam. Hawk was probably bedding the bitch goddess right now. But did she want to bed Liam? He would take it as a sign that she'd marry him, a decision she had yet to make. Besides, her hand hurt. She was tired and just wanted to be left alone, to nurse her pride and her cut.

"You are verrry persuasive," she purred in his ear, "but I'd rather not have an injured hand to distract me. Give me a rain check?"

He groaned in frustration and disappointment. "A rain check. Sure. I'll go home and do a rain dance. But first, I promised I'd help you clean up."

"There's nothing more to do, really. A few napkins to pick up. Elaine did it all." She walked him to the door, thanking him again for the waterfall, promising that she would call him the next day.

He kissed her deeply, passionately, telling her how much he loved her, temper and all, saying, "I'm going to Boston in two weeks. Come with me! My granddaughter, Christine, turns sixteen and I promised I'd be there for the party, and take her to New York for lunch and a matinee. Come with us. I want you to meet everyone! We'll drive up the coast, see the sights...."

"That sounds wonderful, but I have a Board meeting in San Francisco."

"Can't you miss it?"

"No. Anyway, Elaine's going with me; we've planned it for a long time."

"Okay, busy lady. You'll miss me."

"I'm sure I will." Then she kissed him gently, saying, "Go home now. I'm exhausted."

She watched his vehicle go down the hill and out through the vineyard gate. But she was really trying to see whether Adrianna's white van was parked at Hawk's quarters. She couldn't tell; perhaps it was behind the winery building. Well, it wasn't any of her business. "You're jealous," she said aloud to her reflection in the hall mirror. "Not a pretty sight at your age."

Just as she was turning out the kitchen light and heading upstairs, she heard a car stop in front of the house. Liam must have forgotten something, she thought. Flipping on the front porch light, she saw Hawk coming up the front walk. She opened the door but left the screen door closed and locked.

"You're the last person I expected to see. Thought you'd be in bed with...." Selby said, stopping in mid-sentence.

"I owe you an explanation."

"You don't owe me a thing. Anyway, how'd you know all my guests had gone?"

"I saw Liam's car leave."

"Where's Adrianna?"

He gave his slow, knowing smile. "It's not what you think, Selby. You going to let me in?"

"No. The screen door stays locked. And if I had a Doberman or a pit bull,

I'd sic him on you." She couldn't help it; a smile broke her scowling face at the thought.

"Come on, open up. Let's talk. You're scarier than I am. Such a temper! I never would have thought it of you." Now he was chuckling, his hand pulling gently on the screen handle, rattling the door. "Come on. You know you're dying to hear what I have to say."

"Damn! You're an arrogant piece of work. All right. Come on, but just five minutes." Selby flipped the screen door catch and walked into the kitchen, cradling her right hand in her left. The cut was throbbing, fresh blood soaking through the bandage.

Hawk pulled a chair away from the kitchen table and slumped in it. "How's the hand?"

"It hurts. I made the mistake of loosening the bandage, but my hand was getting numb. Elaine did a great job stopping the bleeding, but the bandage was really too tight."

"Let me see it."

"No. You don't need to. I'm fine. "

"You aren't either. Let me see it." Selby sat across from him and placed her hand on the table. He carefully unwrapped the cumbersome bandage exposing the jagged cut, which was oozing a stream of bright blood. "Jeez. You need stitches."

"Oh, no! Really?"

"Every time you move it's going to break open. I'll take you to the emergency room." He stood, reached for a kitchen towel, which he quickly folded into a sling. "Here. Put this on. Keep your hand up and it won't throb so much."

"I'm fine. I'll go tomorrow."

"Don't be such a stubborn...." He looked at her, his jaw tight. She was the most exasperating woman he had ever known. She ran hot and cold, sweetly efficient and solemnly hostile. He didn't need this. Then, in a gentle voice, he said, "You really need it looked at by a doctor. You could have seriously damaged something in your palm."

"Oh, all right! But take my car. The keys are on the hook by the door to the garage. I don't like riding in the open Jeep on the freeway."

Hawk adjusted the Mercedes seat to fit his tall frame, then the rear view mirror.

She was turned away from him, but watched his reflection in the window, her mind careening from anger at letting him in the house, to gratefulness that someone was there to help her with her hand. The cut was much worse then she had originally thought. In fact, she nearly fainted at the sight of it when Hawk unwrapped it. She still felt a bit queasy.

Once they were out the property gate and on the road to the local emergency room, he asked how she felt.

"A bit...pale. You always seem to be rescuing me. I'm really very self-sufficient, you know."

"I know."

"Well, explain. You said you wanted to explain something...about Adrianna?"

He gave her a quick look, then returned his attention to the dark, narrow county road. "Adrianna and I were together about six months, the last three at LillyHill. She left last fall. We had similar career interests, but she found Oregon boring. She missed San Francisco, LA, the Napa Valley, and her friends. Besides that, she and Fiona didn't get along at all. It was mutual hate at first sight." He chuckled and paused in his explanation, merging onto the freeway. Traffic was heavier at midnight than he had expected. Probably half of the other drivers were drunk or stoned, he thought. "We enjoyed each other, but there was nothing...solid...nothing spiritual between us."

Selby nodded, waiting for him to go on. So far it wasn't much of an explanation. She could have guessed that much. He seemed to have finished. "Well, you certainly are a handsome couple." He gave her a questioning glance, frowning.

"We haven't been a *couple*, as you put it, for a long time."

With a giggle she added, "A beautiful couple with his and hers ponytails...."

Her sarcasm surprised him, but two could play that game. "I thought you liked my ponytail." He grinned at her, knowing that the remark would remind her of their first night together.

"Go to hell."

"You *are* feisty tonight! Maybe we ought to put a stitch or two in your mouth while we're here." He pulled into the parking lot of the emergency entrance and escorted her to the admitting desk.

As luck would have it, the emergency room doctor on duty was the same one who had treated Selby after her fall from Zephyr. The look on his face as Hawk and Selby walked into the examining room caused them to burst out in laughter.

CHAPTER TWENTY-SIX

The next two weeks rushed by as Selby prepared for the August board meeting in San Francisco. She studied for it as she would for a mid-term exam, reading every document and letter sent to her. She scrutinized the materials—financial statements, graphs and proposals—making a list of questions to submit to the office. The responses came by FAX, phone and e-mail. The San Francisco office was very cooperative; if they thought she was slow at catching on to the nuances of real estate investments and management, they didn't let on. Chairman Reed was always gracious when responding to her questions, perhaps pleased that she was at least making an effort to understand the business and her role on the board.

While preparations for the business trip went well, the easy, loving relationship between mother and youngest son had cooled. Something was bothering Justin. At first, Selby put it down as too much work and too many trips to see Sara in Eugene. When he wouldn't tell her what was bothering him, she guessed that young love was not running smoothly. Finally, one evening when they were alone, he seemed willing to have a conversation over dinner, instead of giving monosyllabic answers to her questions. This was more like it. Yet, he seemed to be giving her the third degree about something.

"You don't seem to be going out with Liam very much lately. How come?"

"No reason other than being very busy preparing for the board meeting in San Francisco on the eighteenth. And he's getting ready to fly east to see his daughter and family. One of his granddaughters is turning sixteen. We talk on the phone almost every night."

"Hawk going to San Francisco, too?"

"Of course not. He has nothing to do with the board. Anyway, he has too much to do here to leave the vineyard. But Elaine's going with me. We're really looking forward to getting away."

"Why'd you let Hawk take you to the doctor for your hand? Liam would have taken you."

Selby felt a chill at his accusing tone of voice, his implication—at what, she didn't know. She stumbled over her explanation. Guilty of nothing, yet feeling like she had done something terrible, she said, "Hawk just came back after everyone else had left to, ah, to apologize for his guest's behavior. He wanted to look at my hand. It was throbbing and bleeding again. I said I'd go to the doctor the next day, but he insisted on taking me then. They put in six stitches...see?" She held out her palm to him.

He gave it a cursory glance and then pushed away from the table. Picking up his dishes and taking them to the dishwasher, he said, "I don't think you're being fair to Liam. If you're going to marry him, you need to pay more attention to him."

"What in the world are you talking about?"

He kicked the back of his left shoe with the toe of his right, a gesture from childhood when he couldn't put his thoughts into words. "Nothing. Never mind. I gotta go."

Selby's mind flashed back to the last time she and Hawk had seen each other. Nothing had happened! He brought her home from the emergency room, put the Mercedes in the garage and left. He hadn't touched her. Justin had never been at LillyHill when she and Hawk had.... She was completely stumped. It was as if he knew, or guessed. But that was impossible. Wasn't it?

"Wait. Something's really bothering you. Tell me."

He sighed, averting his eyes. "Liam's my friend. He loves you. I think you should marry him. And soon. That's all." Turning, he went out to the garage and upstairs to his quarters. Flopping down on his bed, he stared at the ceiling, going over in his mind what Steve had told him. The brothers and Chris had met for pizza and beer a few weeks ago. Their conversation bounced all over the map—cars, television, rock vs. rap, jobs, future plans and finally family. Steve had said something like, "Mom seems to be enjoying her widowhood. I think she's sleeping with that vineyard manager of hers."

The remark had almost gone over Justin's head. His mental leap was that Mom was enjoying dating Liam. When he realized what Steve had said, he denied it, rising to her defense. "Don't be stupid. They're just friends. Anyway, he's too young—not much older than you are." Steve just laughed and shrugged his shoulders.

Leaving the pizza parlor, Steve draped a brotherly arm across Justin's shoulders. "Don't be naïve about Mom. Or Hawk. There's something between them. Trust me."

Jerking away from his brother, Justin shouted, "You're a goddamn liar! Mom wouldn't do that. He's nothing to her—her business partner, that's all. She loves Liam."

Steve laughed and punched him gently in the shoulder. Justin returned the shoulder punch, a little harder than was necessary. "Hey, lil' bro, let's not get heavy with the fists."

"I'll get as heavy as I want to," Justin said, kicking gravel at Steve.

"Jeez, man, lighten up. I don't want to get in a fight about this. I don't care who she sleeps with."

Justin swung his fist at Steve's face, catching him in the nose. Responding by instinct, Steve grabbed Justin's arms. Before Chris could separate the brothers, they were wrestling on the ground like a couple of ten-year-olds. "You goddamn liar! Take it back! You hate Mom because she won't give you money!" Justin yelled.

"Okay, okay," Steve said, breaking loose, getting up and brushing himself off. He gently touched his nose to see if it were bleeding. "Take it easy. Forget it. Come on, Chris."

Dusty and disheveled, Justin stood and watch them get into their pick-up. He spat a mouthful of dirt and blood from biting his own tongue in the scuffle. Swallowing the anger that had nearly brought him to tears, he returned to his car and muttered to himself as he squirreled out of the parking lot, spraying gravel on the parked cars. His mind was full of things he should have said to Steve. Mom was special. She wasn't some tramp who'd sleep around. Where'd you get such a crappy idea? Where's the proof? She was Mom! But after that night, he was uncomfortable around Selby. He was torn between avoiding her and following her, watching, trying to figure out if there was any truth to what Steve had said.

How many times had the scene gone through his mind? Too many, Justin thought. Sitting up, he grabbed the TV remote control and began to surf the channels, looking for something to take his mind off the real or imagined problem. There was nothing he could do, except to get her married to Liam as soon as possible. Then no one could even think anything bad about her.

CHAPTER TWENTY-SEVEN

Elaine and Selby's flight to San Francisco was uneventful: no luggage was lost, the cab driver spoke English, and the condo was clean and stocked with delicacies to please a couple of women on the loose. Settled in after an afternoon of shopping and haircuts, the women kicked off their shoes and sipped wine while making dinner plans.

"Here's a list of restaurants that Mr. Reed had his secretary FAX me when I asked for suggestions. What do you feel like? French? Chinese? Greek?"

Elaine perused the list. "Why don't we just start at the top and work our way down?" she laughed. "It shouldn't take more than a couple of weeks! I'm open to eating anything that I can't get at home."

"We'd better decide and make a reservation. If they're booked, I'll have Mr. Reed's secretary try. It's who you know at some of these fancy places." They scanned the list again and agreed upon French cuisine.

It took a call from Reed-Steiner & Company to get a reservation for that evening at *Vaucluse*, but it was worth it. The women were chasing the last crumb and bit of sauce on their dessert plates. "Absolutely marvelous! I may give up eating anything unless it's as good as this meal. If fact, you can't really call what we just ate a 'meal.' That sounds so—ordinary," Elaine said.

"That would be a unique diet: never eat anything that wasn't prepared by a famous chef—or at least a very good cook. That means I could eat your cooking."

"And I could eat yours." They both laughed at their silliness, sitting back as the waiter refilled their coffee cups.

"All right, dear friend," Elaine said. "I've avoided the topic of the men in your life long enough. What's going on with the three of you?"

"You make it sound like a *menage a trois*! Well, to be quite honest, neither Hawk nor Liam has been on my mind for the last two weeks. I've seen Hawk at a distance in the fields and Liam calls or comes over almost every night. He's pushing for an answer to his proposal, but I just haven't wanted to think about it. I realize that I'm probably being unfair to Liam—taking so much time to think about...us together. And Justin's been pushing me to marry Liam, and soon. Why, I have no idea. My son's been very weird lately—like he's mad at me or something. That's about it."

"No, that's not about it. Are you in love with Hawk?"

"Wow." Selby took a deep breath, gazed around the elegant dining room and their fellow diners. A flaming dish of some sort arrived at the table next to theirs. They watched the serving ceremony, fascinated by the flair of the waiter and the flames from the chafing dish. With no other excuse to avoid an answer, Selby repeated Elaine's question. "Am I in love with Hawk? I don't know. At first it was just curiosity. Then...I guess you could call it common old lust. There is something more, though, but I'm not sure what. I like him; he's fun, funny, considerate, intelligent. He's also aloof, selfish and pre-occupied with his own agenda, as I am with mine." Again she stopped, studying her coffee before raising the cup to her lips. After replacing her cup, she looked at Elaine and said, "I have more feelings for him than I want to have. He always seems to be there when I need him, but I suppose that's just because we live on the same property. I like him very much, but love? I'm not sure what love is anymore."

"How does he feel about you?"

"You know, we've never exchanged endearments. Neither of us has ever said, 'I love you.' We tell each other...things...when we make love; in fact, we talk up a storm! But as for his feelings about me, your guess is as good as mine."

"And Liam?"

"I have good feelings about Liam, too. They're different from those I have for Hawk, although I consider both of them good friends. Liam and I certainly have more in common than Hawk and I do. First, there's our ages— or perhaps I should say our generation; then there's our children and grandchildren and the fact that we've each lost a spouse. He's generous, sensitive, steady." Once again she paused to gather her thoughts. "The other night he suggested that we get married this fall as soon as the grapes are harvested. He's buying a huge motor home and wants us to spend the winter traveling to meet his relatives and friends. We'd head down to Arizona and New Mexico, seeing the sights. Then on to Texas, especially San Antonio, then along the gulf to Florida. I may be odd, but that doesn't appeal to me at all!"

"Why?"

169

"I finally have a home and business, something I've always dreamed about. True, the business is a lot more than the secretarial-bookkeeping service I'd envisioned in my younger days. But I find the challenge of learning—of stretching my mind—very exciting, empowering. And, I love LillyHill. It is so beautiful. I just want to stay there and enjoy it.

"Have you told Liam this?"

"Not in so many words. As usual, he said for me to think about it, as if it would take me a long time to know what I want. I just hate to shoot him down. That's not being fair to him to make him wait, is it? I just wanted these days with you without other distractions. Fortunately, he flew to Boston to help celebrate his granddaughter's sixteenth birthday. He was telling me that he prefers the older grandchildren to the babies. Guess the little ones are just too noisy and busy for him." Selby smiled at the waiter when he placed the leather folder with the check and her charge card on the table. She perused the bill and said, "I'd really like to be away from both of them for awhile to see how I feel completely on my own. As you know, marriage isn't high on my agenda. Friendship and physical comfort are. I don't need a full-time man in my life, yet I don't want to become a frantic old woman who's always looking for approval in the eyes of every man she meets. You know the type I mean?"

"You mean like Sue Perahta?" Again they laughed, recalling a former co-worker who was obsessed with collecting men any way she could. Elaine leaned forward and lowered her voice. "Did I tell you she's a redhead now? And she's had breast enlargement! She's referred to as Sue Perstructure now."

Smiling, Selby signed the check, retrieved her Visa card, and looked at Elaine. "What would you like to do now?"

"To be honest, I'd like to go back to the condo and get into my nightie. Suddenly, I'm exhausted. Anyway, we need to try out the facial stuff I bought today. You said you'd try it, too! And I've got all day tomorrow to sightsee and prowl around on my own while you're dazzling the corporate world."

An hour later, the two women were wrapped in towel sarongs, their hair in plastic shower caps, and blue-green goo spread over their faces. "I hope this stuff washes off," Selby said as she finished massaging the concoction under her jaw.

"You'll definitely make an impression on the board tomorrow if it doesn't!"

"What are your plans tomorrow?"

"I've always wanted to stand on the Golden Gate Bridge. I assume that people are allowed on it—to walk across it. I just want to go part way and look over."

"Sounds like fun. Just don't fall off! We've got a date for Irish Coffee at the Buena Vista. I'll meet you here about four o'clock. I also want to order the watercolor we saw of the mother and child for my bedroom. It's time I finished decorating my room.

"I think you should get those hanging glass frames with the pressed flowers and leaves, too. They'd look great in your bedroom window."

The friends relived the day's events and the shopping. They talked of plans for the rest of their time together in the city and fell into bed, with glowing skin, free of the blue goo. This was the perfect get-a-way, as far as they were concerned. It couldn't be better.

The board meeting had gone well the next day. Selby understood more about the business interests and activities of Reed-Steiner & Co. She could see the importance of taking an active role running the business, not just letting the other partners handle it. And she saw how the partners never made a decision without a reliable calculation which showed that it had a fair chance to yield a reasonable profit. As old Mr. Reed often said, "Keep away from ventures in which you have little to gain and much to lose." Selby wondered if he were referring to life, too. If she made a thoughtless decision to marry, she could lose her newfound independence.

Following the meeting, board members gathered around the table in the corporate dining room. Crisp dry wine was poured to accompany the *Salad Francillon a la Tapenade*. As far as Selby could tell, the dish was a cold potato salad with mussels in vinaigrette. She had a difficult time swallowing the mussels, but the Tapenade—a mixture of Greek olives, capers, anchovies, olive oil and garlic—spread on crisp rounds of toasted French bread made up for the strong seafood that was not to her liking. She would have been happy to just have the Tapenade, bread and wine. Following the salad, an artichoke stuffed with prosciutto ham, breadcrumbs and parmesan cheese was served in a broth of chopped fresh tomatoes, herbs and white wine. Wonderful whole grain bread accompanied the dish. Just as the *Tarte Aux Abricots* was being served with the coffee, an emergency phone call came for Selby.

Excusing herself, she follow Reed's administrative assistant, Joseph; he guided her to an empty office. Sitting at the desk, she paused for a moment before reaching for the telephone. What could possible be so important that Joseph would use the term "an emergency"? Lifting the receiver, she cleared her throat and said, "This is Selby Browning."

"Selby? Hawk. I'm sorry to be the bearer of bad news, but...."

"Not another fire?"

"No. Much worse. Are you sitting down...is someone there?"

"Oh, God. It's Justin."

"No." He paused again, hating to tell her. "It's Mike."

At first she didn't comprehend exactly what he had said. "What? Tell me again. I'm okay." But she wasn't. Her heart rate accelerated and a fine perspiration broke out on her forehead. She looked up to see Joseph hovering just outside the door. He must know, but what?

"Mike and Rhonda were killed in a car wreck on the Autobahn." Hawk stopped, alert to any response she might make. Hearing nothing but a sharp intake of breath, he continued. "The military sent two officers to the winery. I told them you were out of town and that I'd contact you."

Selby's mouth wouldn't work. Her tongue felt thick and dry. Finally, she asked, "The baby?"

"She's okay. She was staying with neighbors."

"Thank God!"

Hawk listened intently, giving her the opportunity to speak, to ask questions. He could hear nothing, but could picture her trying to compose herself, to hold in her emotions, to take control of herself. "Are you there?"

"Yes. Yes. Give it to me, everything you know."

"The accident happened in the early evening on a rain-slicked stretch of the Autobahn south of Frankfurt. They say death was instantaneous. Rhonda's father, Brigadier General Richard Elliot, will meet you at the Frankfurt airport. We're to let his staff know your flight number and arrival time. The General is handling all the details in Germany. As soon as he was notified, he got a military 'hop' from Dover, Delaware.

"I just talked to Rhonda two days ago! She sounded so happy. Mike was safely out of Kosovo. They were going to have some time together. Going to a spa for a long weekend."

The silence between them hung heavy. Finally, Hawk said, "What can I do for you?"

"I don't know; let me think." Joseph was placing a tray on the desk. It held a carafe of water, a glass and a bottle of Cognac. Selby began thinking out loud. "I'll fly from here. Will I need a passport? I don't have one. Elaine has to fly home tomorrow. She can close the condo and take my car home from the Portland airport. Oh! I must call Justin! And Steve. I don't know where he is...Oh, God, Hawk...."

"Look, I've already told Reed's assistant the situation. He said he'd tell the board while you were on the phone. The office can help with reservations. Do you need a visa for Germany?

"I don't know...."

"Can Elaine go with you?"

"No, she has to go back to work. Look, I need to call Justin. And would you check with Steve's company to see where he is? You could call Chris, his—friend. The number is—someplace. Either that or...."

"If Elaine can't go with you, will you have Justin go?"

"No. I don't know. Maybe." Tears came. A glass with a splash of cognac was placed in her hand. She gripped it, feeling the scar tissue from her cut pull painfully across her palm. It's not possible for Mike—and Rhonda!—to be gone. They—we—never had a chance to really become family. She stopped talking. Tears slid silently down her cheeks.

"Selby? You still there? I'll have Justin call you there—at the office. That would be easier than you trying to catch him. Steve, too. I'll see if I can prepare them for you, if you wish. Okay?"

"Yes. Thank you. Oh, Hawk. What have I done to deserve this? Have I been too happy?" Before Hawk could respond, she hung up the phone and looked into Joseph's eyes. He handed her a box of tissues.

"Mrs. Browning, Mr. Reed has put the staff at your disposal. Just tell me what you would like done. We can make airline reservations and take care of the travel documents you'll need." He touched her hand gently, reminding her of the cognac. She took a sip and put the glass back on the tray. A drink wasn't what she needed. Then the most bizarre thought popped into her mind: She didn't get to eat the apricot tart that was served for lunch! She felt as if she had lost her mind. How could she even think of dessert at a time like this? It was the money. She'd give it all back to have Mike and Rhonda alive. Was this some kind of punishment?

She shook her head, blinked and said, "I'd like the first flight out of San Francisco to Frankfurt. Thank you for handling the documents. I wouldn't know where to begin. And I'm expecting a call from my son, Justin... and maybe one from Steve—another son." She looked toward the door as the elderly Reed wheeled himself into the office.

"My dear Selby," he said, reaching out to her with his mottled hand. "I'm so sorry. My staff will handle everything. Just let Joseph know...."

"Yes. Thank you." She felt quite numb. She had been through the death of family members before, first her mother, then Doug. She had been too young to remember much about her father's death. Stay calm, she told herself. Think of the living. Oh, poor little Amanda. What will happen to her now?

After Selby hung up, Hawk held the receiver, staring at it, listening to the dial tone. At last, he replaced it and began the tasks he'd volunteered to do. He wanted to be with her, to hold her and tell her he'd always be there for her. More than anything, he wanted to be part of her life, a more important part than just business and occasional sex partner. Are you in love with her? If this isn't love, it is damn close, he told himself.

As the Lufthansa airliner lifted off through the San Francisco morning fog, Selby was gently pressed into the soft leather seat. The past fifteen hours blurred. Special travel documents were arranged, phone calls from Justin and Steve completed. Hawk had done a good job finding and preparing them. Steve was on the East Coast and would see her when she returned from Germany. She'd asked Justin to handle all matters at home, to work with Hawk on whatever needed to be done. Perhaps if they worked together on something this serious, he'd see that Hawk wasn't a threat to the family. Justin was also to tell Liam when he called.

Elaine's flight left an hour after Selby's. The two women had clung to each other and cried, as they had the night before. Selby felt drained, puffy-eyed. At least for the next thirteen hours, she could crawl into her shell and prepare for meeting General Elliot, the man she now blamed for Mike's death. Elliot was the one who sent Mike to The Balkans. If Mike and Rhonda had been...if, if, if. Think about something else, she told herself. The baby. Yes. It was bittersweet that she'd finally see Amanda, hold her, tell her she loved her. At last, Amanda would have something more of her grandmother than just a voice on the telephone.

Selby let her gaze drift over fellow travelers. There were the obvious businessmen—in fact, one sat next to her now, his laptop computer displaying colorful graphs. There were the vacationers—older couples, two academic-looking women, and a family of four that looked...Swiss, she decided. Several younger-looking passengers defied categorizing; they looked too scruffy to be flying first-class. Rich and spoiled? Successful and not interested in appearance? Computer designers? Rock stars? Drug dealers? She felt the eyes of fellow travelers on her, too. What category had they placed her?

Could they read her grief? Tears seeped quietly down her cheeks. Would she ever feel joy again?

CHAPTER TWENTY-EIGHT

On arrival in Frankfurt, Selby was whisked through customs and escorted to a private room where Brigadier General Richard Elliot was waiting. Stiffly she held out her hand to him. "General. Thank you for everything you've done to expedite this situation. As soon as possible, I'd like to see my—our—granddaughter." It was all Selby could do to be civil to this man, the one she felt was responsible for Mike's death. On the flight, she thought of all the damning things she would say to Elliot when she saw him. She wanted to strike out, to blame someone, something; Elliot seemed the most logical choice at the moment. But seeing him in person for the first time, she remembered that he, too, had lost a child, that Mike might have been assigned to The Balkans even if he and Rhonda hadn't fallen in love.

Elliot took her hand, briefly, acknowledging her greeting. "I have a car waiting. If you'll come with me." How he hated this woman and her no-class son for killing his daughter. Rhonda would be in college now, the darling of her sorority, if it hadn't been for.... But it was really Gloria's fault. If his wife weren't an alcoholic and could have driven herself places, then Rhonda and Mike would never have met. Gloria had blamed him for sending Mike away, saying that the army should have kept the young soldier close by so that Rhonda wouldn't have married and run away. The marriage could have been annulled, or divorces were.... What's the point of thinking about it anymore? When he did, he always came back to his daughter's brutal injuries. She had been thrown through the windshield on impact, cutting her beautiful face to ribbons, while that husband of hers simply broke his neck.

Escorting Selby to the car, he sneaked quick glances at her. His son-in-law's mother wasn't anything like he expected. Instead of the frumpy truck driver's wife he'd pictured, here was a petite woman, elegantly dressed in a black pantsuit. Her emotions under control, ready to get on with the difficult task of viewing the bodies and making arrangements. He had expected an hysterical woman making an embarrassing scene at the airport.

"Is your wife in Frankfurt?" Selby asked as they settled themselves in the rear seat of the limousine.

Elliot gave instructions to the driver, who pulled away smartly from the curb into the thick airport traffic. "No, Gloria is not well. I'll be taking Rhonda back to Virginia. What are your plans for...Mike?"

Selby gave him a searching look, trying to read this military "stone." "Did the kids indicate what they wanted? Was there a will? Did they make arrangements for Amanda in case....?" She had to stop; tears were beginning to form. She would not cry in front of this man.

"As far as I know, nothing like that was decided beyond the military's required documents. Rhonda never told me...we were not close...since...." Elliot looked away, his sense of command and power fading under the gaze of this questioning woman.

Selby said, "I got the impression from Rhonda that she and Mike were very happy. Perhaps they should be together...now; they didn't have much time together before...."

Elliot did not reply. He understood her inference: he'd tried to keep the young lovers apart and had failed. Then it dawned on him that she hated him as much as he hated her.

Selby continued. "I'll have Mike cremated and take him back to LillyHill, if that is what you'd prefer."

"It doesn't matter what I prefer. If you want them buried together in Virginia, that's fine with me. I'm sure Gloria will agree."

What a weird conversation, Selby thought. She'd like to see his eyes, to see if she could read his grief. He was wearing dark glasses, as was she. Selby removed hers, hoping he would do the same.

Elliot said, "Would you prefer to go to your hotel before seeing your son?"

"I didn't make reservations. After seeing Mike, I thought I'd go to Amanda, perhaps stay in their quarters, care for her. I assume that Carla and John are as stunned by this as...we...are. They might appreciate some help."

"Carla and John?"

"The Gardners, who are caring for Amanda." Amanda had been left in the care of Mike and Rhonda's next-door neighbors in the housing complex reserved for military families. With two children of their own, Carla and John Gardner had become close friends with Mike and Rhonda, exchanging baby-sitting, playing cards and going on picnics.

"Oh, yes, I remember."

"Does Amanda have any idea of what has....?"

"Ah... I don't know. I've not yet seen her nor talked with the Gardners. In a day or so, perhaps."

Selby couldn't believe what she had just heard. Were the Elliots so unfeeling, so estranged from their daughter that they could ignore their first and only grandchild?

"If Rhonda and Mike have made no...arrangements for...Amanda, then I shall take her home to Oregon with me."

"Our attorneys should probably meet to...."

Selby exploded. "What do you mean 'our attorneys'? We are talking about a two-year-old who has just been orphaned. Are you out of you mind? You cold-hearted son-of-a-bitch!" Tears gushed from her eyes; she quickly mopped them away with her handkerchief and replaced her sunglasses. As she slipped them on, she noticed the driver watching the back-seat drama in the rear view mirror.

"Really, Mrs. Browning! You're upset; I understand that. But there is no call for a scene. Perhaps you'd like to go to your hotel now." He had been right: she had no class. She obviously was a person who did not believe in going through channels. Impulsive. Volatile.

"A scene? I'll give you a scene if you so much as try to stop me from taking Amanda with me. The dead may be precious to us, but the living are what count now, particularly a child. Have you no feeling for your granddaughter? Some curiosity? My God!" Selby was as surprised at her outburst as was Elliot. She took a deep breath and with what dignity she could muster, said, "As I told you, I'm not going to a hotel, I'm going to Amanda as soon as I see...Mike."

The rest of the day had gone off without a problem. There was an unspoken truce between the grandparents. Late that afternoon, Elliot's driver dropped Selby off at the Gardner's quarters. Carla Gardner welcomed Selby with hugs and tears, delighted that she had come to care for Amanda. Amanda was less than enthused about the visitor. The child sucked her thumb and clung to Carla, asking for her mama. Selby choked back tears, wondering what, if anything, to tell the two-year-old. With Carla's help, Amanda finally made the connection between the telephone voice and her visitor. At last, the child lost her shyness and brought toys, depositing them one by one in Selby's lap. The first toy she brought was the telephone with the recorded messages from Selby. Amanda began calling her "Gamma."

Two days later, Elliot visited Amanda and Selby, finding them at the Garland's quarters. The meeting was awkward. Once again, Amanda clung to Carla, rejecting the toy the stranger—her grandfather—offered her. Elliot seemed uncomfortable with the whole situation—the tiny room, the two women and most of all the children. Carla's two rambunctious boys were fascinated by his uniform; they insisted on touching the gaily-colored ribbons and brass. Selby was alternately amused and appalled at the General's discomfort around youngsters.

"Come on, boys. Let's get a snack," Carla said to her children, taking them into the kitchen, leaving the two grandparents alone with Amanda.

"Well, what do you think of your granddaughter?" Selby asked, touching the dark silky hair of the toddler, who now sat on the floor between them, stacking wooden blocks.

"She's...beautiful, just like...Rhonda...when she was a baby." He swallowed hard and looked away, struggling to say something appropriate. Their conversation jerked along with mundane comments about Amanda and her future.

"Carla says she's very bright, although she seems to have reverted to some of her babyish habits this week," Selby said. "Children are adept at picking up on adult stress."

"I imagine so. Rhonda said Amanda was learning to speak German as well as...."

"Yes. Now is the time for children to learn foreign languages."

"Rhonda took French in school; I think she was quite good at it."

"We'll have to make sure that Amanda receives the best education...."

"Oh, yes. Private schooling, college, of course."

"But that's not for a few years. I hope you will agree that I should do what I can for her now."

Finally, after a long silence, Elliot covered his face with his hands, his elbows on his knees, crushing the knife-edged creases in his uniform.

He *is* human, thought Selby. She could see him struggling with his emotions, leaving her at a loss for words. Kneeling on the floor in front of him, she clumsily put her arms around his shoulders. She could feel him shake. Her touch seemed to release the tears he had been fighting. The tears that she had vowed not to shed in front of him joined his. They stayed that way until Amanda's curiosity and offer of a toy broke the grief-stricken tableau.

Over coffee that Carla had left discreetly on the table, Selby said, "I'll take Amanda back to the states as soon as I finish here. LillyHill is a wonderful place for a child—room to run, a lovely old oak tree that's just right for a swing. She'd have her own room, of course, and I'd get her a puppy or a kitten...." Selby's mind raced for more details to put into the sales pitch. She didn't want Elliot to have any objections to taking Amanda to LillyHill. "I believe you said Gloria was not well, so it seems that I should...."

"Yes, yes. That's fine. I know Gloria will want to see her soon, though, when things settle down. She's very...upset...right now, as you can imagine." Elliot studied Selby. An intelligent woman, strong. She wouldn't lose herself in the country club scene or drink herself into a stupor during times of crisis. What had she said about running a winery and serving on a board of directors?

"Rhonda was our only child, as you probably know. This has been devastating...to all of us. I know the baby needs a home, at least until we can...."

"I'll stay in touch with you, of course. And please feel free to come to Oregon as soon as Gloria is feeling better. Perhaps next spring I could fly to Virginia with Amanda. It's very important that she know all of her grandparents."

"Yes. That would be fine. Fine." Elliot seemed distracted now. The issue of where Amanda would stay, at least for the time being, was settled. He was anxious to leave, to get back to making simpler decisions, decisions without messy emotions. Overseeing thousands of soldiers and multi-millions of dollars in equipment was easy compared to this. "I have some documents for you," he said, handing her a folder from his briefcase. "That should finish up all the paperwork. My Virginia office address and phone number are there," he said pointing to one page, "and our home address and telephone number are on the last page."

Selby reached for one of her business cards and gave one to him. He studied the small white card with the LillyHill winery logo, address, phone and e-mail address. "Rhonda told me that you bought them a computer for e-mail. That was very generous of you. It helped...bring us closer."

"I'm glad. Sometimes a long letter seems so formal, hard to write, but an e-mail message can say, 'I love you' without saying it." The grandparents looked into each other's eyes. At last, a connection had been made, an understanding relayed. Selby gave him a bright smile, saying, "I'm sure Amanda will soon be keyboarding her own e-mail to you. Kids catch on to this computer stuff so quickly."

Elliot smiled, stood and extended his hand to Selby. "Thank you. I've made arrangements for a car and driver. Use it for as long as you wish."

The following days were filled with decisions, sorting out Mike and

Rhonda's personal things and turning the quarters back to the military. Selby offered the computer to Carla, a small token for taking care of Amanda and showing such kindness during the grandparents' difficult visit. Amanda helped Selby pack a suitcase for the trip to LillyHill, putting in a favorite stuffed animal, her "blankie" and her footie PJs. It was all a game to the toddler, but it got a difficult trip off to a pleasant beginning.

CHAPTER TWENTY-NINE

One week later, Selby and Amanda were on their way home to LillyHill. The flight from Frankfurt to London was uneventful, but then the delays began. No sooner were all passengers loaded and prepared for their over-the-pole flight from London to Seattle than a mechanical problem was discovered. This necessitated that everyone deplane and board another aircraft at a different gate. Head winds, customs, and delays in Seattle stretched out the trip to eighteen hours of travel. Even though Selby and the baby flew first class, they were exhausted by the time they arrived in Portland, Oregon, that evening.

Selby had purchased a seat for Amanda so she wouldn't have to hold the baby all the way home. With a seat of her own, Amanda had room to wiggle and to sleep. The flight attendants did all they could to make Selby's flight easier—from taking the dark-haired toddler for walks around the first-class cabin, to warming her bottle and the jars of junior food. Once Amanda had finally settled in for a nap after they left Frankfurt, Selby allowed herself a glass of champagne. Sipping the effervescent wine, she wondered what the flight attendants would think if she asked them to just leave the whole bottle. Of course she didn't ask; even one glass would probably give her a headache, but she hoped the wine would help her relax after a week of making decisions, of going through the apartment and sorting the young couple's possessions. She had packed Mike's personal things in a footlocker and had it shipped home via the military. Carla had packed Rhonda's things for shipment to Virginia. Mike's belongings would take several weeks to reach LillyHill. By then, Selby thought, she could face looking at the bits and pieces of his short life, things that were special to Mike—books, photographs, souvenirs and clothing. Justin and Steve would need go through the trunk, too, making a last connection with their brother.

Their plane landed at Portland late in the evening. Selby had phoned Justin from the aircraft to let him know they'd be about forty-five minutes late. He said that Hawk was coming with him; Liam wouldn't be back from

Boston until the next day. He sounded disappointed that Liam wouldn't accompany him to meet them, but Selby was relieved, and happy at the thought of seeing Hawk.

The first-class passengers disembarked ahead of the other travelers. Selby staggered along the ramp, a diaper bag and her carry-on case slung on one shoulder, with Amanda draped sleepily over the other, her blanket clutched tightly in a dimpled fist.

"Mom!" Justin called out and rushed to her.

"Easy. She's tired and a bit skittish with strangers. God, it's good to be home," she said, accepting his kiss on her cheek.

"You're not there yet," Hawk said, taking the bags from her shoulder, "but it won't be long."

They were swept along the concourse, which was filled with passengers on their way to the luggage carousel. Conversation was difficult, but they managed to exchange bits of information about the trip and home. Awake now, Amanda studied the two men who smiled at her. She began a game of peek-a-boo, flirting first with Justin, then with Hawk.

As they entered the luggage pick-up area, Justin said, "I'm going to get the car and pull it around to the loading area right out front...there," he said gesturing toward the exit. "Hawk, you stay here with Mom and get the luggage, okay?" It was obvious that he had taken on the man-of-the-house role.

"Good idea," Hawk said to Justin, before turning to Selby. "You look like you've been pulled through a knothole backwards."

"Thank you. I really needed to hear that." Selby smiled back at him. "I'd like to see how you'd look after eighteen hours on a plane with a two-year-old."

"Let me hold her; she must be getting heavy." Selby gave him a tentative look, reluctant to hand over the child. "Hey. I know all about kids. I babysat my nieces and nephews when I lived near my sister, Tracy." He held out his hands to Amanda, fluttering his fingers, enticing her. She hid her face in Selby's neck, peeking at Hawk. Finally, she reached out to him. He held her confidently, allowing her to touch his eyes and nose.

"You've cut your hair!" Selby said. "Why?"

"You seemed to have taken a dislike to ponytails," he said. They continued to stand there, grinning at each other, neither wanting to say anything that might spoil their mutual joy at being together again.

One of Selby's fellow passengers stopped beside them, saying, "So there's Daddy! She was such a good baby on the plane; no crying at all. She looks just like you!" Patting Amanda's hand and addressing the child, she asked, "Are you glad to see your daddy? That's right, give Daddy a hug," she continued, as the shy child tried to hide from the aggressive stranger. "Oh, the luggage is coming. Good-bye."

"Have you noticed how people are always jumping to conclusions about us?" Hawk said. "First the emergency room doctor, now a stranger. Here come the bags. Which are yours?" he said, handing the child back to Selby.

Justin was waiting outside the exit with the car, its trunk and doors open. "I got the car seat just like you asked. See? It's top-of-the line and it's installed correctly. Here, let me put Amanda in it."

"How about if I drive so you can talk to your mom?" Hawk suggested. When everyone was settled—Justin in front, Amanda and Selby in the back seat—Hawk pulled smoothly into the exit lane.

Justin twisted around in his seat, continuing his monologue. "And I got everything else you said to buy, plus some other things, too. Let's see...the potty seat, safety plugs for the electrical outlets...um, and the youth chair...it fits under the kitchen table just great. Sara helped me with your shopping list. She came up for the weekend; I put her in the blue guest room. Hope that was okay."

Selby smiled and nodded, too tired to say she preferred that to Sara sleeping in his room. It was good to have Justin talking to her as he used to. Whatever had been bothering him about her seemed to be gone. That was good. She couldn't bear to lose Justin, too.

"Sara picked out a neat set of dishes with Winnie The Pooh on them. There's a plate, a bowl and a cup. And I found my old Tommy Tippy mug; Amanda can use it, too. Then I bought a huge teddy bear and a Brio train!"

"A train?"

"Yeah! It's made from really smooth wood, wheels, tracks, bridges and all. It's Swedish or German or something. It's really safe, the clerk said. It was expensive but it'll last for generations. What was funny, the clerk kept trying to sell Sara and me cribs and highchairs and stuff, like we were buying for our baby!"

Hawk and Selby laughed, understanding how people jumped to conclusions.

"Sara picked out some books and a puzzle with really big pieces. She's into educational toys. Then Adelina came to restock our freezer and I asked her to make lots of cookies—that was okay, wasn't it?"

Selby nodded sleepily, lulled by his happy chatter.

184

"Adelina said she had a small wicker rocking chair that her kids used when they were little and that Amanda could have it. Rio painted it white. We put it in the pink room. It looks great with the bear in it. The bear's bigger than Amanda!"

The child had fallen asleep by the time they arrived at LillyHill. Hawk put the car in the garage and helped Justin with the bags. "See you tomorrow. Call if you need anything."

Selby smiled and lifted a hand in farewell as he softly closed the door.

Amanda was awake again, looking around the kitchen, lower lip out, ready to cry. "Uncle J, how about getting your niece some juice? I'd like some, too, please." Selby said. "I get so dehydrated flying." She sat down in a kitchen chair and perched Amanda on the edge of the table in front of her. "And bring a few Cheerios in her bowl, too. No milk. Maybe a snack before we go to bed will help."

While the baby daintily ate the tiny pieces of dry cereal, mother and son looked at each other, each waiting for the other to open the subject of Mike.

"How...how did Mike...look?" Justin said, staring at the tabletop.

What was he really asking? she wondered. This certainly wasn't the time she wanted to go into details, yet he needed to begin closure, too. "It was okay. Unreal. I had his things shipped. You and Steve will...want to...go through them. I know it's going to be very difficult." She paused, waiting for another question. None came. "Are you still okay with Mike being buried with Rhonda in Virginia?"

"Yeah. I thought about it a lot. Sometimes I thought he should be closer to us, but it's okay." Justin's chin quivered ever so slightly. "I know I'd want...to be near...Sara...if anything like that...."

Selby reached out and laid her hand on his arm. "I'm glad Sara could help you with all the shopping I asked you to do. She's a lovely young woman. I'd like to get better acquainted. Maybe that will help all of us get through losing Mike and Rhonda."

"Yeah. What about the funeral?" Their conversation was interrupted by the small bowl of cereal landing on the floor with a clatter. "Glad the Pooh dishes are plastic," Justin laughed. "Man! It's going to be weird with a little kid around here!"

"You're right. I'm afraid I haven't given the ramifications much thought. I've been operating strictly on instinct. There's been just too much this week."

CHAPTER THIRTY

Everything seemed to go wrong the next morning. Selby had tucked Amanda into bed with her the night before so the child wouldn't be frightened in a strange place. The baby wakened with a messy diaper, a temperature and a snotty nose. Carla had warned Selby that whatever progress Rhonda had made in potty training seemed to have been forgotten. Selby wondered what kind of bug Amanda might have picked up on the plane. Of course she had nothing but adult remedies in the medicine chest.

Afraid to leave the baby alone while she showered, Selby took Amanda into the shower with her. This seemed to be a great solution, until she got soap in Amanda's eyes during the shampoo. Selby made a mental note to buy baby shampoo, baby Tylenol and more disposable training pants. Breakfast included spilled juice and an upturned bowl of oatmeal. Selby managed to drink a cup of coffee before another diaper had to be changed. "Amanda, we've both got jet lag and squiffy tummies," Selby told her granddaughter. "But we'll feel better in a couple of days. How about a nap on the couch?"

At last, Amanda fell asleep on the black leather couch in the family room. Selby sat at the dining table with a pile of mail accumulated over the last ten days. Bills, notes of condolence, catalogs, vineyard and winery newsletters—the pile seemed endless. The knock on the kitchen door made her jump.

"Hawk! Come in," she whispered, putting her finger to her lips. "I just got her to sleep."

He sat quietly at the table with her, whispering, "How are things going?"

"It's not been an auspicious beginning. I'd forgotten about the 'terrible twos'; add jet lag and you've got a really nasty child." She smiled as she said this, but Hawk could see that it was the truth. "Coffee?" she whispered.

"Half a cup. I have to get some parts to repair the crusher/stemmer. Can I get you anything while I'm out?"

"Yes, please. Baby Tylenol and more disposable training pants would be a great help. She's got a temperature and an upset tummy."

Whispering quietly with one eye on the sleeping child, they finished their

186

coffee while Hawk told Selby the status of the vineyard and winery. "We can cancel our participation in the Labor Day Wine Festival if things are too hectic around here."

"No. Let's keep things as normal as possible. I probably won't be as much help to you because I'll have to keep an eye on Amanda, but I think we should stick to our marketing plan."

"Okay." He stood, indicating with a motion of his head that he wanted her to step outside. Taking her arm and quietly closing the door, he rested his hands on her shoulders and looked soberly into her pale face. Speaking low, he said, "There's something I found out while you were gone and you should know...."

"Oh, no! Not more bad news...."

"I hope it's not bad news. I think it's good news: I'm in love with you."

"I beg your pardon?"

Before another word could be said, the telephone rang. Selby jerked away quickly dashing for the phone before it wakened Amanda. But it was too late. The child let out a loud screech, sat up and began to sob.

"Hello?"

"Hi, darling. It's Liam. How are things going? Is that the baby crying?"

"Yes...."

"I hope the phone didn't wake her up."

"No. Well, yes, but it's okay." She watched Hawk as he went over to the couch and scooped up Amanda, blanket and all, patting her back and swaying slowly, making soft hushing sounds.

"How are you doing? I'm sure it was a tough week. I'm so sorry about Mike and Rhonda. I can't imagine...." He paused, at a loss for words. "I'd like to take you out to dinner tonight. You can tell me all about it then. I can't imagine how hard it must have been. I've missed you so much. I need to see you. What time shall I come by?"

"Um, I can't do that. I don't have a sitter, and even if I did, it's too soon to leave Amanda with a stranger. She's having a rough time today, a temperature...."

"Oh." There was a long silence. This wasn't quite what Liam had planned. A velvet ring box from Tiffany's sat on his desk by the telephone. Even when Justin had told him that Selby was bringing her grandchild to LillyHill, he hadn't thought about how it might impact their relationship. "Well, then...why don't I bring some Chinese food? About seven?"

"I'm really tired...jet lag, you know."

"I won't stay long. I have to see you. It's been hell without you. Please."

"Okay. Bye." Selby hung up, not waiting to hear Liam's good-bye. She had been abrupt, even rude, she thought. Oh, well. She hadn't been listening all that closely to what Liam had been saying anyway. Did she imagine it, or did Hawk say he was in love with her?

She walked over to Hawk, who was carefully laying the sleeping child down on the couch. He placed his finger on his lips, signaling quiet, escorting her out the kitchen door again, unplugging the phone as he went by.

Folding her into his arms, he said, "As I was saying before we were so rudely interrupted, I love you."

Selby burst into tears. "But that's impossible!"

"Why?" He tightened his arms around her, crooning to her just as he had done with Amanda, hushing and rocking her gently.

"I didn't have a clue...that you..." she sobbed, searching the pocket of her shorts for a tissue. "I look a mess today and my ears are still ringing from the flight and I have a fussy baby in the house and Liam's coming over tonight."

Leaning away from her, Hawk asked, "Liam? Tonight?"

"I told him no but he said he was coming anyway with Chinese food."

Hawk began wiping away her tears with a dusty blue bandanna he'd found in his jeans pocket. It left muddy streaks on her face. "Are you in love with Liam?"

"No," she wailed. "He's a good friend, but I don't want to get married and travel around in his motor home."

"You don't have to do anything you don't want to do."

"I know that...." She pulled away, took the bandanna out of his hand and blew her nose, a great hearty honk. "Can we talk about this later?"

He chuckled and said, "You bet we'll talk about it. Look, I've got to get the parts for the crusher/stemmer or we won't be able to process grapes this fall. I'll drop off the diapers and aspirin as soon as I get back."

"No, not aspirin, it...."

"I know...."

Then he kissed her deeply, tenderly. "Get yourself together, woman. You're a mess."

CHAPTER THIRTY-ONE

Watching him drive away, she sighed, thinking he was the only man who could tell her she looked like hell and make it sound romantic.

Selby was light-headed for the rest of the day. She'd found herself reading the same letter of condolence two or three times. Nothing seemed to sink into her jet-lagged brain. The only thing that seemed real was the feel of Hawk's arms around her. When Amanda woke up an hour later, Selby plugged the phone back in. It rang immediately.

"Selby! I've been frantic. I couldn't get through. I thought something had happened at LillyHill again."

"Fiona? Where are you?"

"In Vancouver. We got back from the Continent on Monday. It's time for me to come home...er, back."

"Yes, anytime you're ready."

"My flight gets in at noon tomorrow. I'll be on Alaska Airlines."

"I'll pick you up. What's your flight number?"

"Flight 211."

"It'll be good to see you again. And I have a surprise for you. I'll show it to you tomorrow when I pick you up. Good-bye." Wow! Is Fiona going to be surprised when she sees Amanda.

Hawk sent Rio to the house with the diapers and the Baby Tylenol. First, he wanted to give Selby time to feel better and sort out his declaration of love. Second, Rio had been asking about the baby; the errand gave him a chance to be one of the first to see the newest member of the LillyHill family.

Rio said, "She's so little—and pretty, too." He was squatting down, eye-to-eye with Amanda who was clinging to Selby's leg, appraising this new face. Rio understood fussy babies; his younger brothers and sisters had gone through the same thing, he told Selby, adding, "My sisters can baby-sit for you."

"Wonderful! How old are they?"

"Well, Carmina is...let's see...Cristina is.... I'm sorry, I can't remember.

But they're in high school."

"Ask them to call me."

"I'll tell them if I can remember. You know I don't remember things very well."

"That's okay. I can call them. I really appreciate your suggestion. Oh, and thank you for painting the rocking chair. It's really cute. I haven't introduced her to her own room yet. She doesn't feel very well right now."

Later in the afternoon, Selby and Amanda took another shower together, making themselves presentable for the rest of the day. The Tylenol had dropped Amanda's temperature. She ate most of her supper. She was spooning in her banana pudding when Justin arrived. "Liam sent me home early so I could help you. He said you sounded a bit frazzled this morning when he called. He's really anxious to see you."

"Yes. I wasn't very gracious when he called," Selby said, as she tidied up the kitchen and rinsed out the baby food jars for recycling. "He's coming at seven o'clock with Chinese food. I'm sure he's bringing enough for you, too."

"No, Mom. I'll make myself scarce." He was smiling as if he were in on a surprise.

"That's not necessary. Oh, by the way, Fiona is coming home tomorrow. I'm going to pick her up at noon."

"Wonder what she'll think of Amanda?"

"That's the sixty-four-thousand-dollar question!"

By the time Liam arrived, Amanda was ready for bed and Selby looked and felt a little more like her old self, but she would have been happier to spend the evening alone. She stood at the front door with Amanda in her arms watching Liam carry in three large white paper sacks filled with cartons of Chinese food.

"There must be enough for an army!" Selby said with a smile. "I told Justin to stay for dinner, but he said he had other plans."

Liam kissed her on the cheek. "Smart young man, that son of yours. So, there's Amanda. Hi, Amanda."

Amanda turned away, burying her face in Selby's neck. "She's not feeling well—jet lag and a bug of some kind. I'll put her to bed and meet you in the dining room. The table is set and the tea is ready."

Amanda had no intention of staying in bed. It took four tries to get her settled. Selby had pulled out the lower trundle of the bed in the pink room so that if Amanda fell out of bed, she wouldn't have far to fall. The child repeatedly got out of bed and stood at the top of the now-gated stairs, screaming. It was a toss-up between Selby and Amanda as to who was more exhausted by the time sleep came to the child. At last, Selby tiptoed down the stairs and into the dining room, where Liam had eaten most of his dinner alone. "Let's sit out on the front porch. I think I can still hear her if she cries, but she should be exhausted by now. I know I am!"

"How long will Amanda be with you?" he said, taking her hand in both of his, stroking her ring finger.

Selby thought about the question for a moment. "You know, I've not thought it through yet. There's really no other place for her to go. I'm afraid her other grandmother isn't capable of caring for a lively two-year-old, and my guess is that her grandfather would put her in a boarding school as soon as she was old enough. I don't even know if they want the responsibility. Anyway, I couldn't bear to have anyone else take care of her. So, I guess I'm the logical choice."

Liam stared across the landscape, now patterned in dark shadows touched by the red-gold of the sunset. His marriage proposal to Selby had not included a new, young family. He was ready to work less, travel more. The ring box seemed to burn a hole in his pocket. "What about us?"

Selby nodded solemnly. "It does make a difference, doesn't it?"

Liam wondered if she was thinking that she would marry him now because she'd need to provide a traditional family for Amanda. The thought of being with Selby all the time warmed him. However, the thought of raising a small child at this stage in his life did not thrill him. But he could do it, if that's what Selby wanted.

Finally, she spoke. "Until Mike and Rhonda's death, I was concerned only about what I wanted from life. My options seemed limitless with the resources available to me. It was a wonderfully selfish daydream; I was quite content imagining what I could do, where I could go." She pulled his hand to her cheek. "Then you came along and gave me an option that had never crossed my mind—marrying again. It sounded wonderful to be loved and cared for again, yet...I've been enjoying my freedom—to do whatever I want, whenever I want." She released his hand, stood and leaned her head into the front hallway, listening for Amanda. Hearing nothing, she continued. "With Amanda here—whether it's only for a short time or for...forever—I can't honestly think of marriage now." She returned to her place beside him on the top step of the verandah, afraid to look at his face. "How do you feel about all this?"

Liam sorted through a variety of responses: One: It doesn't alter my feelings for you; you need me more than ever now. Two: Perhaps we should wait awhile before we decide anything. Three: Raising a baby wasn't on my agenda when I proposed; I rescind the offer. Instead, he reached for the ring box, took her hand and folded her fingers around the gift. "You may not be ready to marry now, but there's no reason why we can't be engaged. Open it."

Selby stared at the box with dismay, her mind turning to mush.

"I wanted you to have a ring from Tiffany's, that's why I hoped you'd fly East with me, meet the family, and get engaged there. Then you could have selected your own ring." He paused, waiting for her to speak. "Open it. I hope you like it. It's different, not a traditional diamond engagement ring."

Tears welled in Selby's eyes. Liam was so sweet, thoughtful. How could she hurt him? "I can't." Did she mean "I can't hurt you" or "I can't put the ring on"? Selby simply didn't know.

"Here, let me. Sometimes the springs are strong on these little boxes."

"No, that's not...." She stared down at the open box, the ring nestled in white satin. It was a cluster of opals, sapphires and rubies—beautiful and unique, verging on the gaudy.

"I'm...stunned." Please God, make the baby cry or the telephone ring or....

"Put it on."

"No...."

"Here, let me help you" He paused and looked at her. "No?"

"I can't...I don't want to make any important decisions now. Mentally and physically I'm a mess." Yes, a mess was what she was. Hawk had it right. "I'm sure you understand how the loss of a loved one can make any decision more difficult than it should be. I really value you as a friend and you're going to make a wonderful husband for...." She couldn't say "for someone else," even if that's what she meant.

"Damn! How could I be so thoughtless? You've been so strong about your loss that I forget how recent it's been. Even though we talked on the phone about it, it's different now that you're home. Of course you can't decide now. I was only thinking of myself. I'm so sorry." He put his arms around her, drawing her to him. "God, I love you so much. It's just that sometimes I feel that we don't have as many years to be together as I want."

"No, you're very thoughtful; it's just...me...tonight. Emotionally, I'm overloaded." Fragments of thoughts ricochet through her mind. Go home, Liam.

Please disappear!

"Tell you what: I'm going home now. You get a good night's sleep and I'll call you tomorrow. Okay?

"Yes. Thank you. Fiona's coming home tomorrow, so...." God, I can't even finish sentences tonight. I just want to cry, to sleep, to be in Hawk's arms.

She tried to avoid Liam's kiss good-night, but he persisted. She felt nothing but relief that he would be gone in a few moments. How in the world did she let this relationship get so far down the road toward commitment when she probably never had any intention of marrying again? "Good night, Liam. You are a dear, dear friend."

The next morning, Selby waited until Justin had gone to work before she came downstairs. She more or less hid in her room until she heard his car go down the hill. If he knew about the ring, he'd wonder why she wasn't wearing it. Being engaged to Liam wasn't a topic she cared to discuss with anyone today.

Amanda seemed on the road to recovery from whatever had upset her system. Selby dressed her up in a pale pink frilly dress, chatting about how they would go shopping and buy all kinds of pretty clothes one day. She wanted Fiona to be impressed with her beautiful grandchild. Now, if Amanda would just behave herself and not get into a "terrible twos" snit, but that might be asking too much, Selby told herself. Just hope for the best.

At the Alaska Airlines arrival gate, Selby and Amanda stayed to one side, letting other families meet their friends and loved ones. Amanda was standing on a plastic chair, stomping her feet, enjoying the noise her white Mary Janes made on the hard seat. At last, Selby saw Fiona, head up, looking eagerly through the crowd. She was wearing a light blue and white striped seersucker pants suit, and had a new carry-on bag slung over her shoulder. She was the picture of a seasoned traveler, Selby thought.

"Fiona! Over here."

"Well, who do we have here?" Fiona said, after greeting Selby.

"My granddaughter, Amanda, the newest member of the LillyHill family. I'll explain on the drive home. But first, I want to hear about your trip."

Later, she told Fiona of Mike and Rhonda's death and of bringing Amanda to LillyHill. "It's going to be very strange having a child at LillyHill. Do you think you can handle a busy little person running about the house?" When Fiona didn't come up with a quick answer, Selby teasingly said, "At least you know you can always take another trip if things get too crazy around here! Come on. I'll give you the two-dollar tour of the house."

Fiona seemed pleased with her newly decorated suite, yet Selby noticed a certain reticence as the older woman followed her around the house. Fiona said all the proper things about the house and the decorations, but Selby could tell that it hurt her to see it altered. The living room was the most changed, with its new color scheme of pistachio and white with accents of pale aqua and lavender.

"It looks very nice. Thank you for restoring Lilly's antiques for my room. That means so much to me." Fiona's eyes filled with tears. "I guess I'm a bit tired. If you don't mind, I'll go to my room and lie down."

"Sounds like a good idea. I may have a nap, too, if I can get Amanda down for hers. She's not in a routine yet. We'll have tea when you come down." The gods were with Selby that day. She'd found a convenient parking spot in the airport short-term parking garage, Fiona's luggage was part of the first batch on the carousel, and Amanda was willing to go down for a nap. Selby stretched out on her own bed; she needed quiet time to think how she could let Liam down easily and explain it all to Justin. Then there was the matter of Hawk's declaration. Did she hear him correctly? He was such a tease. No, he wouldn't do that to her. Maybe he'd feel differently later; he might have been trying to make her feel better. And if it were true, what then? It certainly would put their relationship on another level. Could they explore their new relationship with Amanda, Justin and Fiona around? Perhaps they'd be able to approach their feelings intellectually for once. They always seemed to fall into bed without thinking.

Her thoughts were interrupted by the telephone. It was Steve, back from a two-week trip. "Can you come for dinner tonight?"

"Yeah."

"Bring Chris, too, of course."

"Not this time. I just want to see you and Justin."

"I understand. You can meet your niece, too."

"Oh, yeah. I forgot. Is she cute?"

"Of course! You have a darling niece. Fiona is back now, too, but we'll have some private time after dinner. Come anytime you can; we'll eat about seven-thirty. I'll throw some steaks on the grill."

Later that afternoon, Selby fixed tea and a sandwich for Fiona, who had declined to have a late dinner with the family. The women talked about the house and Fiona's trip, and watched Amanda struggle with her spoon as she ate supper. Their talked drifted to loss of loved ones: parents, Frank and Lilly, Mike and Rhonda. When Hawk tapped at the back door, he found the two women with red eyes and a box of tissues on the table.

"Did I come at a bad time?"

"Heavens, no. Come in," Selby said.

"I just wanted to welcome Fiona home," he said, kissing her lightly on the cheek. "You look great! Travel agrees with you."

"Well...thank you," she said with a blush. "I did have a very good time. Annie and I got along splendidly. Oh, I have a gift for you. I'll be right back."

As soon as Fiona was out of the room, Hawk bent over Selby and gave her a quick kiss, then pulled up a chair and began talking to Amanda across the table. She held out a half-eaten Arrowroot biscuit, which he took, pretended to eat and then handed it back to her. The child giggled and continued the game until the cookie was gone and her fingers were a sticky mess.

"Here we are," Fiona said, handling simply-wrapped packages to Selby and Hawk. With murmurs of appreciation, they tore off the paper.

"How lovely!" exclaimed Selby. "Thank you."

"I found those handkerchiefs in Brugges; it's the most beautiful town in Belgium. They make lots of lace there. And chocolate."

Hawk's gift was a book featuring photographs of France's wine country. "Oh, Fiona. This is great. Thank you." He reached over and squeezed her hand. "Now, tell me all about your trip."

"I'll get Miss Messy cleaned up while you two talk. Sometimes I think she absorbs more through her skin than she gets in her mouth. I've ordered a book on early childhood development. I hope it will suggest I only serve her fish sticks and canned green beans! They would make her easier to clean up than this spaghetti."

The pleasant afternoon ended when a cloud fell over the happy foursome as Justin walked in. His barely pleasant greeting to Fiona was balanced by his scowl at Hawk. Selby felt obliged to give some kind of explanation. "Sorry about my grumpy son; I think he is cross with me."

"I'd better go," Hawk said. "Good to have you back, Fiona, we'll talk more about your trip later. Thanks again for the book."

"I'll walk out with you," Selby said. "Amanda could use a romp on the lawn."

Watching the child explore the bordering flowerbeds, Hawk said, "When can we get together?"

"Soon, I hope. Steve's coming for dinner. The boys need to begin closure.

Rio said his sisters baby-sit; as soon as I am comfortable with them, we'll go riding...or something." She smiled up at him. "Did I hear you correctly the other day?"

"You did."

"Perhaps you could elaborate on this epiphany you had."

Their conversation was interrupted when Justin banged the back door and joined them. Ignoring Hawk, he stooped down beside Amanda. "Hey, pretty girl. Whatcha' doin'?"

Hawk gave Selby a slow smile, looking deeply into her eyes. "You'll think epiphany when I see you," he chuckled. "I need to lock up the winery now. See you soon."

"Soon."

"What was all that about?" Justin said, turning his attention to his mother.

"I will not tolerate rudeness in our home. Hawk is welcome here anytime. He came to see Fiona, to welcome her back."

"What did you say to Liam last night?"

"Believe it or not, that's none of your business. Now if you'll excuse me, I'll start dinner. I told Steve we'd eat at seven-thirty."

While Selby prepared fresh vegetables for a green salad, Amanda and Justin sat at the kitchen table working on a child-sized jigsaw puzzle. They looked up on hearing the throaty sound of Steve's pickup truck. "'Dat?" said Amanda, looking up from her task.

Sweeping the child up onto his shoulders, Justin said, "I'll show you 'dat'; it's your Uncle Steve."

Selby followed them to the front door, watching her two sons fuss over their niece, who responded with smiles and giggles at being the center of attention. Giving Selby a quick hug, Steve said, "Hey, she's cute! What's it like having a little kid around?"

"Let's just say I've forgotten as much as I've remembered about having a two-year-old. We're working out the rough spots."

"Do you have to do all the bottle and diaper stuff?"

"Not really. She used a bottle on the flight home to ease eardrum pressure on take-off and landing. I haven't offered her one since. We still use diapers at bedtime, but soon we'll be done with those, too. And speaking of bedtime, I'd better get her ready. We'll eat once she's gone down. Why don't you guys set the table in the kitchen and open the bottle of Cabernet on the counter."

Alone in the kitchen, the brothers felt the tension of their fight in the pizza parlor parking lot some weeks ago. They hadn't seen or talked to one another since then. Silently, they performed the assignment Selby had given them. At last, Steve held out his hand to Justin. "Truce?"

"Yeah, truce," smiled Justin, taking his hand. "I think you might be right. I don't know."

They looked up as Selby entered the kitchen, Amanda in tow with a well-loved stuffed animal that might have been a puppy at one time. "You guys can grill the steaks while we have our nightly going-to-bed ritual. It includes a reading of *Goodnight Moon* and three or four choruses of 'You Are My Lovely Duck' while rocking in the little chair."

"God! I remember you singing that to me," Justin said with a smile. He began to sing it to Amanda, who shrieked and ran around the kitchen table, delighted at the game.

"Don't get her all charged up or I'll never get her settled. Say good night to your uncles." After tucking Amanda into bed, Selby ran lightly up the stairs to Fiona's room and tapped on the door, entering at the housekeeper's response. "Are you sure you wouldn't like something to eat before you go to bed?"

"No, I'm fine, thank you. Would you like to share these chocolates with your sons? Have they ever had Belgian chocolate?"

"How nice! I doubt if they have. These look wonderful. Thank you. I didn't have time to plan dessert. I'd forgotten how much time a youngster can take up. I suppose I'm being overly protective with Amanda now, not wanting her to get hurt or feel alone."

Fiona's response was a non-committal nod, saying, "I should be rested by tomorrow and be able to help around the house again, if that's what you'd like."

"Of course. That would be lovely. You do just what feels comfortable. Good night." Selby smiled to herself. Fiona's help would be welcomed. Maybe things would work out.

Returning to the kitchen, she felt something in the air between her sons. They seemed to have lost the easy teasing that had marked so much of their lives. It was probably Mike's death, she thought. "Looks like you did a great job on the steaks. And you've even tossed the salad. You guys will make great husbands one day." She stopped, realizing that the kidding remark was inappropriate for Steve and Chris. "Well...you know what I mean. Look what Fiona sent down for dessert. Belgian chocolates."

Lingering over coffee, wine and chocolates, the conversation turned to

Mike. Steve spoke first. "I should have known when Mike died; twins are supposed to know that kind of stuff."

"But you and Mike aren't identical. I'm glad you aren't. Can you imagine what that would have been like for Amanda when she saw you?"

Both men nodded, letting silence fill the room. Then Justin smiled and said, "Remember how Mike collected GI Joe stuff when he was little? I wanted to play with it so badly, but he wouldn't let me. But I'd sneak into his stuff when he was at school."

"Yeah, but he knew," laughed Steve. "He'd tell me how he was going to pound you, but he never did. He liked his little brother a lot. Hey, do you remember the time we all went swimming at Rooster Rock and wandered into the nude beach and Mike....?"

Selby sat back in her chair, letting them reminisce about their childhood with Mike. The healing had begun.

Liam's phone call was expected, so Selby took it in her office while her sons thumbed through the family album downstairs.

"How are the boys doing?" Liam asked.

"Fine, I think. They're looking at old photographs now. I'm glad you called so that I could leave them alone together." There was a long period of silence, neither Liam nor Selby knowing what to say next, how to open the subject of the engagement ring. "Justin asked me what I said or did to you last night. Was he aware of the ring?"

"Yes. I'm sorry. I shouldn't have told him; I was just too...."

"I understand. He's been playing Cupid for us for months. He has good taste in men. He just wants the best for me."

"So you think I'm the best?"

"Of course I do. But...not now."

"Probably never?"

"Oh, Liam. This is no way to discuss something so...sensitive."

"You're right." More silence. "I think I understand...that you think of me only as...a friend...that you don't feel the same as I do about you."

"I don't want to hurt you. You are such a dear person. The timing is all wrong for us."

"Will you still...see me?"

"Of course. Your friendship is important. But wait until things settle down. We've got the Labor Day wine-tasting event coming up this weekend. Then I have to find a pediatrician for Amanda, get her used to a baby-sitter, get

Fiona used to Amanda." Selby sighed deeply. "There's so much to do."

"I never expected a two-year-old to come between us. I thought it would be another man." More silence, then, "I love you."

"Good night, Liam."

Selby quietly hung up the phone, her lips quivering and tears filling her eyes. I don't want to hurt anyone, she thought. Everyone just leave me the hell alone until I get a handle on things.

CHAPTER THIRTY-TWO

The Labor Day weekend was perfect for those who liked bright sun, hot temperatures and crowds of people. Wine tasters lined up to buy stemware with the LillyHill logo, T-shirts and posters. They sampled everything that was offered and ate until Selby was concerned that the food would run out. She did what she could to help, while still keeping Amanda on her meal and nap schedule. Selby felt stability was the key to a happy transition to a new home and family.

She found Fiona sitting under a tree in the shade, talking with several neighbors who had stopped by to support LillyHill Winery's first large-scale tasting event. Lawn chairs drawn up into a semi-circle provided the ideal spot for Selby to leave Amanda. After greeting the visitors, she said, "Would anyone like to read Amanda a story while I help with the food table?" Smiles and nods, arms reaching out to the child, who ignored them all to climb into Fiona's lap.

"Guess we know who she likes best," someone said. Fiona beamed, and settled Amanda and the book on her lap as if this were a regular event, even though it was the first time Amanda had made such an overture.

Returning to the winery building, Selby quickly re-supplied the buffet table with a variety of cheeses, crackers, and table grapes, as well as tiny bunches of wine grapes, and thin slices of French bread. Looking up, she saw Hawk coming toward her. "Could I see you for a moment?" he asked with a solemn look.

"Of course. What's the matter?" she said, allowing him to hustle her into the office. He locked the door behind him and took her in his arms. She melted into the embrace, waves of desire cascading through her body.

"That's what's the matter."

"Oh, yes. But, don't you think...." He interrupted her with more deep, passionate kisses.

"That's what I think." Both of them were breathing hard, pupils dilated, faces flushed. "If I could, I'd make all these people disappear—right now!" He kissed her again, pulling up her T-shirt, sliding his hand inside her shorts and cupping her buttock in his hands, pressing her into his obvious desire. Releasing her, he said, "I don't suppose we....?"

"Absolutely not!" she laughed. "We need to get back to work."

Holding her away from him, he looked at her intently. "You don't believe I'm in love with you. You think I'm just a horny bastard."

"I've never said that," she said in a shocked at his accusation.

"If you expect me to court you with candy and flowers, like Liam does, that's not my style."

"I'm glad you don't. That would make me uncomfortable." She loved looking at him, to see herself through his eyes. "What is your style?"

"To tell it like it is."

"That works for me." She reached up and touched his face, tracing his strong jaw line, feeling the late afternoon stubble on his chin.

After kissing her tenderly once more, Hawk left the office, while Selby slipped into the washroom next to the office. The mirror reflected the face of a very happy woman. Bright-eyed and a bit flushed, she splashed cool water on her face and combed her hair. Before exiting, she made sure her T-shirt was tucked tidily into her shorts.

Several days later, Selby pushed the rewind button on the VCR and asked Elaine what she thought of the videotape.

"It's great! If the Elliots don't appreciate it, they aren't human. Amanda is quite a little star. I loved the scene of her rocking in the chair with her bear. What was she singing to it?"

"'You Are My Lovey Duck'—a silly thing I made up for the boys when they were babies. I sing to her each night as we rock. Justin still remembers it as part of his bedtime ritual. More coffee?"

"Please," Elaine said, reaching for another Belgian chocolate. "These are wonderful! I hope Fiona brought back a lifetime supply. You know, she looks great—more relaxed, even healthier."

"She's stopped smoking—thank God! And gained ten pounds. It makes her look less severe. She seems to be comfortable with what's been done to the house and she's taken up her old duties around the house. She also suggested that she do the laundry. She doesn't seem to mind Amanda too much, but it's probably too soon to tell. Amanda and I have spent a lot of time out in the garden. Liam brought her a set of little plastic garden tools.

When the rains start, and we're all cooped up for days, things may be different."

"Do the boys—guess I should say 'uncles'—like her?"

"Yes. They take comfort that Mike is a part of her, although they keep trying to see a resemblance and it's not there. She really looks like her mother with the dark hair and eyes. I think I told you that a woman at the airport thought Hawk was her father. I've wondered if there is a little Creole in Amanda's background. Grandmother Gloria may be a Southern belle, but who knows what's in the mix?"

"What does Liam think of Amanda?"

"I don't know for sure, but I don't think raising a youngster is what he has in mind. Anyway, I've too many other things on my plate right now to worry about him. I think we parted on good terms. Foremost is raising Amanda and making sure that the Elliots don't try to take her away from me. That's why I'm making an effort to keep them informed, be a part of her family. I'm considering adopting her."

"Really? I suppose that does make sense. But have you thought it through? How old will you be when she is, say, sixteen?"

"Nearly sixty. You're saying I couldn't handle a sixteen-year-old when I'm approaching my dotage?" Both women laughed, but then the conversation turned serious again.

"I know that I'm going to tire more quickly—that's obvious to me now. But I've taken steps to make sure that I don't get tired and grouchy. Carmina and Cristina Aznar, Robert and Adelina's teenage daughters, will help. One or the other of them will come after school each day from about three o'clock for two or three hours. That will give me time to take care of winery and board business each day, shop or whatever. On weekends they'll be available, too, although we haven't set up any type of schedule."

"I'm glad you realize that you're in the honeymoon period of raising her. You know it's going to be much more confining and difficult at times. You've just committed yourself to at least another fifteen or twenty years of motherhood."

"I know! This is the fun part. But, oh, she has stolen my heart! She smiles and those rows of tiny white teeth are just precious. I want to count each one! And she feels and smells so wonderful after her bath."

"You're definitely smitten. Think you'll feel that way when she turns thirteen-going-on-thirty?" The women laughed and made disparaging sounds.

"You're right, of course. The teen years will be the hard ones. I hope I can keep up with the times—not be rigid when it comes to fashion statements and dating. I don't think anyone has a clue to the twenty-first century teenager!"

"What about a male role model, other than Justin and Steve?"

"Why don't you just ask me how she and Hawk get along?" Again they laughed. "He's wonderful with her. I really didn't expect that, but he baby-sat his sister's kids when he lived close to them in California. Amanda took to him the night we arrived."

"And?"

A huge smile lit up Selby's face. "He told me he's in love with me."

"Get outta here!"

Selby described the day of the declaration. "What's frustrating is that we haven't had a moment to ourselves to talk about it. The tempo of the vineyard has picked up and I've had my hands full with everything. After Justin goes back to school Sunday, Hawk and I will try to find time to talk."

"Talk. Right."

"Oh, you're a terrible person! No, really. Amanda comes first; and, I'm in the middle of letting Liam down gently."

"You should write a soap opera about all that's happened to you!"

"What shall I call it? *All My Problems? As the Winery Turns?*"

"How about *One Grandchild to Raise?*"

"*The Old and the Restless?*"

"*Days of Our Dotage?*"

The friends were mopping tears of laughter from their cheeks when Justin came in. "Hi, there, you crazy ladies. What's so funny?"

"I told your mom she should write a soap opera based on what's happened to her the last two years. We were just trying out some titles."

"Let me know when you've got it figured out so I can avoid it," he laughed. "In the meantime, I'm going to start packing for school. I leave this weekend."

"That's what your mom said. I'm sure Amanda will miss you. How do you like having a niece?"

"She's great. I'm going to bring Sara up to see her as soon as we can get our schedules coordinated. See ya." Justin grabbed a chocolate and banged his way out to the garage and up to his quarters.

"He seems to be in a good mood," Elaine said.

"Yes. Much better than he was before you and I went to San Francisco. I think I know some of the problem. Liam raised his expectations about our relationship; you know how Justin's been playing Cupid since spring. He was bent out of shape when I declined to accept Liam's engagement ring. Justin also seems to resent Hawk."

"Is he aware....?"

"I don't see how, but who knows?

"I've got to go. It's been great seeing you. Good luck adopting Amanda. If you need a character reference or anything, just let me know." Selby walked Elaine to her car. They embraced and talked of when they could see each other again.

Selby was washing Amanda's face and combing her hair after her nap when Fiona peeked into the bathroom. "I didn't show you what I bought myself on the trip. Would you like to see my new thimbles?"

"I'd love to! We'll be right up."

Fiona's cherished collection of thimbles had been damaged or lost in the fire. The small lump of gold, a discolored ceramic thimble and a bent silver thimble were all that remained. "At each place we visited, I searched for a thimble that would remind me of the trip. Annie was so good at allowing me lots of time to look. She likes to shop, too, so it worked out well. These three are from Canada. This one's from Vancouver and this from Victoria; this one's from the Butchart Gardens," she said, handing them to Selby.

Murmuring appreciative sounds, Selby carefully examined each thimble, showing them to Amanda, slipping them on the child's fingertips. "These are lovely, Fiona."

"Now this one is from Brugge, Belgium; this one from Paris—in fact, I found two there. And these three are from London, Cornwall and Brighton. I found this one in an antique shop in Cambridge."

Amanda's fingertips were covered with the delicate thimbles. She was completely absorbed in keeping them on, fussing when one would fall off. "Okay, Amanda, time to give these back to Fiona." As Selby tried to retrieve the thimbles, Amanda screamed, pulling her hands away, sending the thimbles flying about the room. "Oh, oh. That's not the way we do things. Help me pick them up. Be careful now."

Fiona gasped and tried to snatch up the thimbles as they bounced and rolled across the floor. "Oh, my! Naughty girl! Bad, bad, girl!"

"We'll get them. No harm done. Let's see, one, two, three...is that all of them?"

"No; the one from Victoria is missing."

It was then Selby noticed Amanda sitting quietly with her mouth pursed. "Spit it out, Amanda. Thimbles go on fingers, not in mouths." The child shook her head violently, then suddenly looked wild-eyed and began making a strange strangling sound.

"Oh, my God, she's choking!" Selby said, turning the child upside down and giving her a solid thump in the middle of her back. The thimble flew out of Amanda's mouth and the child let out a great gasping cry.

"Naughty girl," Fiona said as she scrambled after the thimble. "Fiona won't let you see her pretty things ever again!" She began wiping each thimble with her handkerchief, placing them on the glass shelf.

"I'm sorry, Fiona, but that's just kids. Come on, Amanda, stop your crying. You're okay. Grandma had to give you a thump. This is a good lesson about putting things in your mouth that don't belong there." She held the child close and rocked side to side. "Shush, now. Let's go down stairs." Turning to look at Fiona, who was arranging her collection, Selby noticed the woman's down-turned mouth and tight jaw. "Are they okay?" Fiona nodded.

"Good. I'm really sorry. Come down and I'll fix tea."

Fiona did not answer. She was mentally justifying all she had ever thought about children. This just proved her point. Now she would have to think about living here. Could she stand it? Where would she go? Did she want to leave?

CHAPTER THIRTY-THREE

Dear Gloria and Richard,

Enclosed is a video tape of Amanda at LillyHill. I want you to have a picture of her environment and see how she has adjusted to her new surroundings. As you will see, she's quite a ham and willing to pose the minute I get the Camcorder out. One of the biggest surprises to me is her interest in the horses. No fear at all! There is a cute shot of her feeding carrots to our mare, Zephyr, a Tennessee Walker; you know how big they are. If Amanda continues her interest, I'll see about getting her a pony and lessons when she is five.

She is sleeping well in her trundle bed (you'll see video of her room) and the pediatrician says she is healthy and above average in verbal and motor skills. As for eating, right now she won't eat anything green. So she's not getting her spinach, peas and string beans. She won't even eat lime Jell-O. However, anything red or yellow is okay with her. Fortunately, this includes spaghetti, pizza and strawberry Jell-O. I suppose next week she'll only eat white foods!

I'm compiling a scrapbook for her with pictures of her mother and dad, and her uncles. I hope you'll send me pictures of yourselves to include in the keepsake and anything else that will help her to know and remember her background.

Do try to fly out to Oregon as soon as you can. There is room for you at LillyHill and I'd love to have you visit.

Sincerely,
Selby Browning

After a hearty Sunday morning breakfast, Justin packed his gear in the Explorer and prepared to return to the university for his junior year. "Well, Mom. This is it. You're on your own again. Think you can handle Amanda?" Justin smiled.

"Yes, but only if you and Sara will come for a visit soon. I'd like to thank her personally for helping to get LillyHill ready for Amanda. Anyway, it sounds like she might be in the running to be my daughter-in-law. Right?"

"Too soon to know yet, but, yeah, she's special. Steve likes her, too. And she likes Chris."

It sounded strange to Selby to think of Chris as part of the family. She must make an effort to get better acquainted with him, she thought.

"Do you have everything? The cookies from the freezer?" Embracing him, she said, "Have a safe trip. Call me once in a while and try to get back for the harvest barbecue."

"I will. And...be nice to Liam. I know, I know. You guys aren't going to get married right now. Just be nice to him, okay?

"Of course I will. I don't want to hurt him. He's a fine man. Just not the man for me at this time. Now go. Love ya."

"Love ya. Bye, Amanda."

She and Amanda watched the Explorer go down the hill and past the winery office. Hawk and Rio came out of the office as he passed, waving as he went by. Hawk would probably come up tonight; maybe then they could finally talk about their feelings for each other. Her thoughts were interrupted as the child tugged at her hand, wanting her to see something she'd found in the grass. "That's a toadstool, Amanda. Let me tell you about them. First, *never* put one in your mouth!"

Fiona watched grandmother and granddaughter playing in the yard. The housekeeper's feelings toward the child had eased a bit. There was no question that the child should never come into her room again. As for the rest of the house, it would be harder if Lilly's nice things were still there. She couldn't stand sticky fingerprints on the antiques or broken things, but now that everything was different, it was Selby's property that would get dirty and broken, not Lilly's. With the earnings from her annuity, she could travel as often as she liked, Fiona thought. Maybe invite Annie to visit LillyHill. Yes! That was a good idea. If Selby wouldn't let Annie use the blue guest room, Fiona's bed was big enough for two. With that happy plan in mind, she went outside to see what was so interesting in the grass.

At eight o'clock Hawk called to see if Selby wanted company. "Of course. Come up. It seems very quiet around here with Justin gone. Amanda's asleep and Fiona said she was going to watch a re-run episode of 'Upstairs, Downstairs.' Have you had dinner? How about coffee, then? I'll even drag out the Belgian chocolates I hid from Justin."

Selby had just zipped up her yellow silk jumpsuit when the doorbell rang. If he remembered that she'd worn this outfit when she verbally attacked Adrianna, maybe he'd have second thoughts about loving a woman with a penchant for breaking things when she was angry.

"Hi, pretty lady," he said, kissing her lightly when she opened the door for him.

"Hi, yourself. Let's sit in the living room. I'll bring the coffee."

She found him relaxed in one of the generous overstuffed chairs upholstered in a subtle pastel print. He looked content—legs stretched out, ankles crossed and hands folded on his stomach. After handing him a mug of coffee, Selby curled up across from him on the pale pistachio sofa and waited for him to speak.

"What are you doing way over there?"

"I thought we were going to talk." She had tried to keep a straight face, but a broad grin betrayed her.

"Okay. If you insist," he laughed. "Walt called today. Said he'd like to come for a visit."

"Wonderful! He can stay here, if you'd like. Are you glad your father's coming?"

"Yeah. It'll be good to see him again. I told him harvest would be in a couple of weeks and I'd put him to work if he comes then. He'll let me know when; he needs to decide·whether he'll drive up or fly."

"How do you know when it's time to harvest?"

"Test for sugar content. I'll probably do that tomorrow."

"How?"

"Come down mid-morning and see. Did I tell you we sold twenty-three cases of wine and two-hundred fourteen single bottles during the tasting festival? I think that's good for our first public event." The conversation continued on vineyard and winery matters. Selby offered him chocolates, which he refused, and soon found herself sitting on the floor at his feet. "This is more like it," he said, stroking her hair. "My lap would be even better."

Staying on the floor, she leaned her head on his knee, saying, "Tell me what you want from life."

"That's easy: a small, exemplary vineyard, good friends...and you."

Hearing "and you" sent a surge of happiness through her body. However, she pushed her desire for him to the back of her mind and said, "You'll want to marry again and have children, won't you? I'm not a candidate for that."

"Why not?"

Here it was again: the issue of age. "I'm too....pregnancy isn't on my to-do list," she laughed.

"What do *you* want from life? Don't shake your head at me. I answered the question, so can you."

Taking a few moments to prioritize her wants, which were many and complicated, she finally said, "I want to bring Amanda to young womanhood without bad things happening to her, to see her on a solid path to happiness and success. I want to see Justin and Steve successful in business and in their personal relationships. I want LillyHill to be, as you say, an exemplary winery."

"But what do you want just for you?"

She looked up at him. Now was the time to tell him how she felt, if she could possibly put her emotional attachment to him in words. Every nerve seemed on fire. Her heart threatened to burst from her chest. She took a sip of cold coffee to moisten her dry throat. "I want a close, loving relationship that is intellectually and sexually satisfying. It would have to be based on mutual trust and a commitment that was agreeable to both parties. Whatever it was, it would have to be civilized." She smiled, trying to verbalize a most important part of her ideal relationship. "What I'm trying to say now is: love me, love my grandchild. No relationship will work for me if she isn't in the mix...and the home environment must be...warm and...gentle. I'm going to adopt her. Amanda's best interests will come first, then mine...and then the man in my life."

"You really lay it out, don't you?"

"You asked."

"You don't think that I could raise Amanda as my own? That she couldn't be the family you think I need to have?"

She searched his face, wanting to see if he meant that. "That's a long-time commitment, as far as I'm concerned. She's lost her parents once; I don't want her to lose someone else she might learn to love, to depend on being there."

"I understand."

"Do you? What if we became her family and you decided after a few years that you wanted a child of your own, that I was too...."

"You say 'old' and I'll leave right now, walk right out of here. That's the one thing about you that drives me nuts! Forget age. Forget wrinkles, false teeth and gray hair. Everyone gets them!" They both smiled at his vehemence.

"Get up here on my lap, woman."

"I can't think straight when I'm in your arms."

"What's to think about? You're crazy about me."

"You egotistical...."

He knelt on the floor, taking her in his arms, kissing her playfully, enjoying her half-hearted struggle, gently pushing her flat on the floor and stretching out beside her.

"Vile villain, do not take this pure maiden...."

"I'll pure maiden you...." He stopped, looking up as the stairway light came on. "Damn, it's Mrs. Danvers."

Giggling, they righted themselves. Selby called out, "Fiona, would you like some coffee?"

As Fiona reached the bottom of the staircase, she peeped into the living room, seeing Hawk and Selby sitting primly on the sofa, and said, "Please. I was hoping that there might be some left. Good evening, Paul. It's good to see you. I've been watching 'Masterpiece Theatre.'"

This brought the evening to a close, much to the disappointment and amusement of both Selby and Hawk. Walking him to the verandah, Selby said, "It's probably just as well. Both of us have lots to think about."

"You're right. But one of these days, woman...." He folded her into his arms, tenderly kissing her. They were oblivious to a stunned Fiona who just happened to come back down stairs for a chocolate to go with her coffee.

CHAPTER THIRTY-FOUR

The next morning, Selby woke to the sound of gunshots. She leapt from bed and ran to her window, then in to check on Amanda, who was still sleeping. Dashing out into the hall, Selby saw Fiona coming down from her upstairs suite. Seeing Selby's concerned look, Fiona said, "Those are bird cannons. Each year they set up those noisy things to scare off the flocks of starlings."

"Wow! It sounded like World War III had started. I wish Hawk had warned me. I'm getting too old for that kind of wake-up call."

Fiona gave Selby a questioning look and said, "I'll start the coffee."

"Thanks. I'll take a quick shower before...too late. Good morning, Amanda."

At breakfast, Selby felt Fiona's eye on her no matter what she was doing—fixing Amanda's cereal, making toast, pouring coffee. After sitting down, Selby said, "Hawk's father, Walt, is coming for a visit. We don't know exactly when, but soon. I've suggested he stay here."

"That would be lovely," Fiona said. "Did you say that you had met him when you were in California?"

"Yes. He's a very interesting man, very knowledgeable about wine. I think you'll enjoy him." She sipped her coffee, still feeling as if Fiona were trying to peer into her soul. "You know, Annie might like to visit you. Invite her to LillyHill whenever you wish. The guest room is there; we might as well use it."

"Oh, what a lovely idea," Fiona said, as if she hadn't already thought about it. "Perhaps in October?"

"Good timing. I hope to have Justin, Sara, Steve and Chris here for Thanksgiving. I want Amanda to begin to experience family traditions. We'll have to pencil guest visits on the calendar so we don't get too many things happening at once."

The telephone rang and Selby left the table to answer it. While she listened to the business call, she was aware of the table conversation that was getting louder and louder.

"Use your spoon, Amanda. Don't pick the bananas out of your cereal with your fingers."

"No."

"It's not nice to eat cereal with your fingers. Use your spoon!"

"NO!"

"Here, let me feed you."

"NO! NO! NO!"

Selby hung up and turned to see her two charges glaring at each another, two strong wills refusing to give in. "Looks like breakfast is over, Amanda. Drink your milk and we'll go see Hawk." Turning she said, "Lighten up a bit, Fiona. She's still a little kid."

The long gravel driveway down to the winery office had proved to be a barrier to quick visits when Amanda was with Selby. She solved the problem by purchasing a Red Flyer wagon. That way, Selby got her exercise and Amanda didn't get tired walking. They both enjoyed using the wagon. It had crossed Selby's mind to get in the wagon with Amanda and coast down the hill, but visualizing the results of a wreck at the bottom changed her mind.

They found Hawk in the bottling room with a small batch of crushed grapes and a variety of strange-looking instruments. He smiled at them as they entered the room. "Just in time. I'm measuring the sugar content. We hope for twenty percent or more," he said, holding the refractometer to the light. "Pushing twenty-one. We pick in two weeks, unless the wasps or an early rain beats us to the crop."

"I get the impression that the crop is good?"

"Yes, but I'll check the sugar content in each field. Rio's out picking grapes and labeling each batch."

"How's Rio doing? He seems to be functioning quite well lately."

"He is. Even Robert noticed. As you know, it takes Rio longer to learn things, to remember them, but he's made remarkable progress this summer. Why?"

"Oh, I was just thinking. I'll tell you later when I have things clear in my mind. By the way, I called Levy this morning and he's starting to draw up the adoption papers. We're on our way to being a legal family." She smiled down at Amanda who was engrossed with a bin of discarded corks, then watched as Hawk stooped down to help the child with something she was attempting to do. She smiled, seeing the two of them play together. Hawk wasn't just putting on an act, she felt sure; he had a knack with children.

"The bird cannons were a rousing alarm this morning. Fiona explained what they were for. Are starlings really that much of a problem?"

"You've seen the flocks swooping around; they're beginning to band into even larger flocks now. They can do a lot of damage to the crop. The cannons run on compressed gas, so you don't need to be concerned about gunpowder." Standing up, Hawk continued. "You can begin getting the pre-harvest barbecue organized. I've already contracted for the migrant crew, but need to give them a definite date. The way it's been done in the past, the barbecue was held the day before harvest. The crew and neighbors who will help are invited. It's a time for getting organized, as well as fun and showing LillyHill's appreciation."

"How long will it take the crew to harvest?"

"They'll work maybe six hours in the morning, then go on to the next vineyard. We can't process all the grapes at once. Then they'll come back again the next day—sometimes in the morning, sometimes in the afternoon—and work the fields that they missed. Once this begins, you won't see much of me." He smiled down at her and then at Amanda, still busy on the floor. Selby melted into his arms. He said, "I'd like to wake you up one morning, and it wouldn't be with a bird cannon."

"You are really bad," she whispered, staying within the circle of his arms. "Fiona was acting strangely this morning. Do you think she saw us last night?"

"What if she did? I'm beginning to think that we're the worst-kept secret at LillyHill." They both laughed, turning their attention to Amanda, who was pulling at their pants legs and jabbering about something.

While collecting grapes from each field for the testing, Rio decided to take a break and read the comic he had stashed in his hip pocket. He loved reading comics. But because of his short-term memory loss, if he stopped in the middle of a story and began again the next day, he'd lost the thread of the plot. Today, he decided that he'd read this comic from start to finish. Settling down in the shade, his back to one of the trellis supports, he opened up the brightly illustrated adventure: *Vega Man Vs Cryptokiller.*

This field, next to the county road, was the most mature, its vines thick and strong, its leaf canopy dense with leaves and heavy with fruit. A large white sedan cruised slowly past the field, then back again. The flickering of the light-colored car caught Rio's attention. He loved cars. In spite of his short-term memory problem, he was able to name and describe a wide variety of vehicles. He was getting better all the time at remembering. Perhaps his interest in memorizing car models was helping his overall performance. At least that's what his dad had told him.

The third time the sedan cruised by, it slowed to a stop, then pulled ahead again, parking close the shallow ditch that separated LillyHill property from the county road.

Rio tried to return to his comic book, but his curiosity got the best of him. He watched a pair of feet shod in tennis shoes climb into the dry ditch and up the other side, next to the vines. The person walked to the end of the row and began making his way between the first and second row. Stopping now, the walker put a red can on the ground and unscrewed the lid. Rio moved quietly to his hands and knees, peering under the vines; next, he stood and peered over them. Someone was doing something to the vines. It was then he noticed the smell of gasoline.

"Hey! What are you doing?" he shouted.

Whoever it was dropped the can, splashing the liquid over the ground. Rio gave chase. By the time he ran the length of the row and over three rows, the intruder was back in the car and had sped away. Rio's heart was beating rapidly as he retrieved the red gasoline can and sprinted back to the office to find Hawk, shouting as he ran.

Hawk heard Rio's shouts and stepped outside.

"What's the matter? " Selby asked, catching up with him.

"It's Rio. Sounds like he's run into a wasp's nest. Here he comes."

Waving the red can above his head, Rio dashed up the office yard. "Someone was putting gas on the vines! Look. I got the can. They drove away in a white Lincoln Towncar!"

Hawk and Selby looked at each other. They knew someone who owned a white Towncar.

"Are you sure about the kind of car, Rio?"

"Yes, Hawk. I saw it. Were they going to burn the grapes?"

"Come on in the office while I call the sheriff."

"I'd better take Amanda back to the house. Keep me posted. Okay?" This was too weird, Selby thought. Could it have been Estelle? If it were, she had gone over the edge. Perhaps she should call Levy, alert him to their suspicions.

The next two weeks were a blur of activity. Hawk and Robert were buried in pre-harvest and crushing preparations. Even though they knew the routine, there was still a tension in the air—listening to weather reports, equipment failures, finding and destroying wasp nests. Selby had to read drafts of legal papers for Amanda's adoption, and materials from the Reed-Steiner &

Company. There was a quick trip to the pediatrician for a rash Amanda had developed. It was nothing but a grandmother's overreaction.

The mysterious visitor to the vineyard had been Estelle. And she had gone over the edge. The Jacob's attorneys arranged for charges to be dropped if Estelle took a long rest. Since no damage had been done, and Estelle would be supervised by her psychiatrist and family, there was no point in making an issue of the event. However, Rio was the hero of the summer and glowed under the praise and attention he received for being so clever.

The barbecue for fifty or more people took up much of Selby's concentration. There were invitations to be mailed or phoned, trestle tables built and set up, and the purchase of paper plates, napkins and plastic dinnerware. Selby arranged for a caterer who specialized in barbecues to bring his large gas grill and cook four dozen chickens. The local distributor dropped off cases of soft drinks and a refrigerated keg of beer with a tap and twelve dozen beer cups. Adelina, Selby and Fiona made gallons of potato salad and cole slaw. Some of the invited neighbors would bring rolls, pies and cakes.

Walt arrived the day before the barbecue, having decided to drive to Oregon. Fiona readied the guest room and arranged bouquets of flowers throughout the house. Selby was amused by Fiona's enthusiasm, but realized that this is what the former housekeeper was comfortable doing. She was back in her element. She happily peeled and minced a pound of shallots for the shallot and sun-dried tomato tart which Selby had selected for one of the appetizers. The jalapeno and dry jack cheese wontons would be served with guacamole. The first course would be a chilled zucchini soup, followed by a roast beef tenderloin, marinated in minced garlic, soy sauce and a touch of fresh ginger root. A mushroom-barley casserole, fresh green beans and Fiona's peach pie completed the menu.

Amanda ate her supper early and played contentedly with her train in the corner of the dining room while the adults enjoyed their dinner. Over coffee and the last sips of wine, Walt, Hawk and Selby chatted while Fiona cleared the table. She had been pleased to be included in the dinner, but insisted that it was her job to clean up.

Walt said, "That was a magnificent meal, Selby. I think I'll propose to you. What do you think, Hawk?"

"I think you should stay out of my territory."

"Really?"

Selby's heart gave an uneven thump. Were these men starting their father-and-son one-upmanship routine again? It had been such a pleasant evening. Walt's only gaffe was mentioning Hawk's haircut, but that was smoothed over without a problem. But this.... Putting on an exaggerated Southern drawl, Selby said, "Gentlemen, gentlemen. You'll have to get in line. I'm just swamped with proposals. I have to decide what to do with Rhett and Ashley at the moment."

"And Liam," added Hawk with a twinkle in his eye.

"Oh, so the lady has a suitor?" Walt said with interest.

Selby took control of the potentially dangerous conversational trend. "This lady is busy with her granddaughter and the business at the moment. Now go sit outside while I put Amanda to bed. And behave yourselves! I'll be down after a reading of *Good Night Moon* and several choruses of whatever song she requests."

Amanda was still shy around Walt, but she happily hugged Hawk goodnight, then held Selby's hand as they walked up the stairs to bed.

"The little girl seems to like you."

"We get along fine. When I met Selby at the airport on her return from Frankfurt, one of the passengers mistook me for Amanda's father. I guess we do have the same coloring."

"Are you and Selby....?"

"That's up to her. She's aware of my feelings for her."

Walt nodded and stared out into the evening shadows. "I almost stepped in it, didn't I? Sorry. I hope it works out for you. She's a fine woman."

When Selby came down from tucking Amanda in bed, she was tense in anticipation of what she might find. Would father and son be at each other again? But they were calmly discussing aspects of the imminent harvest. All seemed well. Selby sighed with relief, reaching out for Hawk's hand, giving it a warm squeeze. The three of them watched the stars come out, and, when it became too cool to sit outside, they retired—Walt to the blue guest room, Hawk to his quarters over the tackroom, and Selby to her lonely king-sized bed. The pale light from the moon touched the simply-framed print of mother and child. How prophetic her selection of that particular watercolor had been.

CHAPTER THIRTY-FIVE

Barbecue day dawned muggy and overcast. No rain was predicted for several days, but there was concern. If the rains came early, the grapes would mildew, spoiling the crop. Breakfast was a quick affair, with Walt off to find Hawk and see what he could do either in harvest preparation or for the barbecue at noon. Selby, Fiona and Adelina were putting the finishing touches to the salads; Amanda pretended she, too, was making salad with the plastic bowls and wooden spoons Selby gave her from the kitchen cupboard. By eleven o'clock the caterer had set up his large gas grill near the winery building and began to cook the chicken halves. Neighbors arrived and set up lawn chairs; some had brought small folding tables. Everyone seemed to know what was expected. By the time the contracted harvest crew arrived, the first batch of chicken was done and the picnic began.

Selby invited Steve and Chris but had not received a response. She guessed they were on the road and probably wouldn't be able to attend. Justin said he didn't know for sure if he could come, but he would try. She dressed Amanda in new light blue and white striped overalls and a pink T-shirt. A pink ribbon held the child's dark hair in a miniature ponytail.

"Let me put some sunscreen on your nose," Selby said, gently smearing it all over Amanda's face. "There now. You look so pretty. I think you're ready for the picnic. Help me get dressed, okay?" Selby slipped into tan chino pants, a pastel plaid camp shirt and her cowboy boots. She was less interested in making a fashion statement than making sure that the barbecue went well.

"Hoo, hoo," Fiona called from the hall. "I'm ready."

"Great. Walt packed the ice chests with the salads and took them down the hill. Adelina took care of everything else. "You look like you're ready for a picnic, Fiona."

She was wearing the blue jogging suit and athletic shoes Selby had bought her after the fire. She had a broad-brimmed raffia hat perched squarely on her head. "I feel quite festive today," she laughed, reaching for Amanda's hand as they walked down the stairs. "I wish Lilly and Frank knew the barbecue was still being held. Perhaps they do."

A table placed in the shade of the winery building was reserved for the host family. Selby fixed a plate of food for Amanda and turned her over to Carmina, then left to circulate among her guests. To her delight, Steve and Chris arrived. She hugged Steve, saying to Chris, "Okay if I give you a hug, too?"

"Of course," Chris laughed. "This looks like fun. I haven't been to anything like this since I was a little kid." He removed his sunglasses and tucked them in the breast pocket of his shirt. "We used to have a family reunion each year around Labor Day. There must have been a hundred of us."

It seemed to Selby this was the first time she'd seen him without his dark glasses and the first time he'd said more that one or two words to her. His eyes were a pale blue, ringed with long light lashes to match his blonde hair. With his fitted shirt and tight jeans, he looked like a model from *GQ* magazine. Perhaps he had been as nervous as she when they first met months ago. "I'm so glad you could come. I was afraid that you'd be on the road."

"I guess I didn't tell you," Steve said. "Chris isn't driving anymore. He's gone back to school this fall."

Selby looked at the two young men, confused, waiting for one of them to explain.

"Chris needs an MBA for when we have our own business. He's the brains of the outfit."

"Oh, I see. Wonderful," Selby said, not much wiser than before. "You have your bachelor's degree already?"

"Yes. A BA in Communications from UCLA. But I needed to make some money to pay off my loans before I racked up more debt on the Master's. Driving truck was the best way for me to do it. I'm enrolled at Portland State University full-time. I wait tables at Perfidia at night."

Unconsciously, Selby's mind jumped to her notion of a swishy gay waiter; however, it no longer fit, now that she was getting to know Chris. "Good for you! Do you miss the traveling?"

"Yes and no. It's always hard to go back to school at first, but I'm enjoying the classes. I miss the photography opportunities of being on the road. Life's just a trade-off."

"I didn't know you were interest in photography."

Steve said, "There's a lot you don't know about Chris. He's quite an artist when it comes to photography."

Selby turned her attention to Steve. "Well, what does this change do to your schedule?"

"He makes me do more stuff around the condo so that he can study," Steve laughed. "I drive the same amount of time; just got back last night, so I'm kinda wasted today."

"Where have you been?"

"Omaha, Dallas, then LA and back to Portland."

"Well, relax, and eat lots. The beer's over there. You guys can sit with Amanda, if you don't mind sticky fingers. She's over at the table with Fiona." She watched them walk away.

"Yeah. She needs to meet Uncle Chris," Steve said.

Hawk was talking with the harvest crew leader, a burly man, toasted and wrinkled from his years in the sun. The crew—a mixture of migrant workers and local people—was sitting to one side, enjoying the food, talking among themselves. She could hear snatches of Spanish and much laughter from the group. Selby considered joining Hawk, but saw Liam arrive. She was surprised to see him and a bit apprehensive. Walking over to him, she accepted a light kiss on the cheek and said, "Hi, there. Glad you could come. As you see, we have quite an eclectic group. Have you been to this event before?"

"No. I didn't know the Steiners. Justin seemed to think I should come. I hope that's okay."

"Of course!"

"How are things going? With Amanda, I mean?"

"The formal adoption process has been started. I don't want anyone to try to take her away. You might say that I'm completely smitten with her! But I suppose all grandmothers are that way."

"Not all. My grandmother didn't care much for kids. She was very authoritarian. Her rigid attitude made our mother spoil us even more when we got home from those dreadful visits to Grandmother Walsh's house." He looked tenderly at her, then said, "I can't stay long; hope you'll excuse me if I eat and run. I just wanted to see you."

"Of course. I'm glad you came. Why don't you sit over there with Fiona? The man next to her is Hawk's father, Walt Kestrel. He drove up from the Napa Valley to see where good wine is grown."

He put a hand on her arm as if he wanted to say something more, then changed his mind. "Maybe I'll see you before I leave."

"Of course," she smiled. Next, she checked with the caterer to make sure everything was running smoothly. Once satisfied, she retrieved Amanda from the care of Carmina. "Your turn to eat, Carmina. I'll take Amanda around to meet some of the neighbors. Oh, here come Justin and Sara. I didn't expect to see them."

"Mom!" Justin waved, his other arm possessively around Sara's shoulders.

"This is wonderful, but what classes are you two cutting?"

"Hello, Mrs. Browning."

"Welcome to LillyHill, Sara. I'm so glad you could come."

"Sara didn't have any classes today and I just cut a lab. I can make it up next week." Justin picked up Amanda and swung her around, making her giggle. "Amanda, this is Sara."

"Ooh, she's darling! Hi, Amanda." Sara knelt on the ground, smiling at the child who was overcome with shyness again. "Look what I have, Amanda," she said, pulling a bottle of bubbles from her jacket pocket. "Now watch." The ice was broken; Amanda and Sara became instant friends. They were the center of attention as the bubbles floated about the scene.

"We're starved!" Justin said. "Come on, let's eat."

"There's room at the table with Fiona, if you like. Hawk's dad is there and so is Liam."

"Hawk's dad? What's he doing here?"

"Visiting. Sara, would you like to freshen up? There's a washroom next to the office."

"Thanks, Mrs. Browning," Sara said. "I'd like to get this bubble goo off my hands before I eat." She handed Amanda the bottle of bubbles, telling her to be sure to hold it upright so it wouldn't spill.

"Aren't you going to eat with Liam?"

"Soon. I want to introduce Amanda to some of the neighbors right now. You and Sara get something to eat; I'll see you later."

"But...."

"Scoot. Be sure to introduce Sara to everyone. She's a darling!"

Selby saw Hawk talking to Chris and Steve near the buffet table and then was waylaid by the owners of Leaning Tree Vineyards. They fussed over Amanda when Selby introduced them. "We're so glad you kept the barbecue tradition. It's about the last time growers can be social for the next month or so with harvest, crushing and all. We know it must be a lot of trouble."

"Not at all. I didn't do all that much. Everyone seems to know what to do. It's great how the neighbors bring such wonderful desserts."

Amanda slipped away from Selby and ran to Hawk, who was walking toward them. The plastic jar of bubbles spilled, and Amanda burst into tears. Stooping down, Hawk dried her tears, then picked her up and perched her high on his shoulders. "Midge, Jack. How are you?" he said, shaking hands with them.

Justin and Liam were watching Selby, Amanda and Hawk talking with friends and neighbors, moving smoothly from group to group. "Liam, don't give up on Mom. I'm sure she likes you."

"I know she likes me, but she has already chosen who will help her raise Amanda."

"But...."

"Its okay, Justin. I'm not anxious to raise a youngster at this time in my life, but if that's what your mother had wanted, I would have done the best I could with Amanda. Look at the three of them. They already look like a family. Did you see how Hawk handled the spilled bubble situation? He's a natural. I doubt if he's aware how difficult it can be to raise children."

"But...."

"If you really think about it, your Mom chose Hawk long before she brought Amanda home."

Justin sat stunned at hearing what he didn't want to hear. "Sara, what do you think?"

"Gee. I don't know. I've barely met your mother and Hawk. She does look happy," Sara said thoughtfully. Then softly in Justin's ear she said, "And he's gorgeous!"

While Liam was explaining the facts of life to Justin, Walt and Fiona were watching Selby, Hawk and Amanda, too. "Can I get you a beer, Fiona?"

"Oh, no thank you, Walt." As he stood up, she reconsidered. "Well, maybe just a half of one. I do like beer. Lilly and I used to share a bottle of beer once in a while on a hot day."

Returning with the foaming cups, he said, tipping his head in the direction of his son, "Hawk is good with little kids. He used to have a great time with his sister's children when they were little. Let's see...they must be ten and thirteen by now."

"He seems to have so much patience with Amanda; she minds him, too," Fiona said, sipping her beer. "I imagine he'll have children of his own one day."

"Well, probably not," Walt said, with a sad look. "He had a terrible case of the mumps when he was about fourteen. The doctor said he'd probably not be...."

"Oh, dear!" Fiona said, not wanting to hear any intimate details.

"I hope it works out between Selby and Hawk. I think they're crazy about each other."

"Oh, dear!" said Fiona again, taking a swallow of beer. This was getting embarrassing. But perhaps Walt was correct. After all, she did see them kissing. What if Hawk and Selby got married? Would she still be welcomed at LillyHill? Oh, dear! Life was getting so complicated. She gulped the last of her beer and stifled a belch.

"More beer, Fiona?"

"Well, just a half."

Amanda's nap time was fast approaching. She had her cheek on the top of Hawk's head, her eyelids heavy. "Looks like I need to have Carmina take Amanda up to the house for her nap," Selby said to Hawk.

"Fine," Hawk said, taking Amanda from her perch atop his shoulders. "The barbecue should be over about three o'clock. How about a ride then? The horses need to be worked before we get busy the next couple of weeks."

"Sounds good. Let's ride over to your property. There are a couple of ideas I'd like to bounce off you."

The remaining friends and family gathered at the picnic table, saying good- bye to Justin and Sara, who had to drive back to the university that afternoon. Liam slipped away quietly after asking Fiona to thank Selby for her hospitality. Steve took Selby by the arm and led her to one side. "In a week or so, Chris and I may have a business plan to show you. Okay?"

"Definitely. Make it two weeks and call to set up a time. I want to be sure that nothing interrupts us. Thanks for coming today. Have a safe trip whenever and wherever you go." Selby watched Steve and Chris leave, her heart lighter than it had been in a long time. She returned to the table where people were saying their good-byes.

"Carmina, will you please take Amanda up to the house for her nap?"

"I'll drive them up," Fiona said. "I've had enough picnic."

Selby handed Fiona the keys to the Mercedes, thinking, You've had enough beer, too, seeing several empty cups at her place at the table. Instead, she said, "Carmina wants to pull Amanda home in the wagon. But I'd appreciate it if you would take the car up the hill; Hawk and I are going to exercise the horses."

Leaving the barbecue clean-up to Robert, Adelina, Rio and the caterer, Hawk and Selby brushed and saddled Zephyr and Tucker. "Did you ever have a chance to eat?" she asked Hawk.

"About as much as you did. Invite me for leftovers tonight."

"It's a deal." They mounted and walked the horses up the hill past the house, down the draw and eastward to Hawk's property line. "You know," Selby began, "it would be simple to cut a road from LillyHill to your place. A DC 10 and a load of gravel would do it."

Laughing, Hawk said, "What do you know about building roads? Are you talking about a bulldozer or an airplane?"

"A Caterpillar tractor, you know—the things with the big blades."

"I think you mean a Cat D8. Good try." He was smiling broadly, enjoying her gaffe. "You're right, of course. It wouldn't be all that difficult and then we could easily move equipment between the two vineyards."

"It would save time, too, not having to go around the long way on the road to reach your house and land."

"Why do you want to make it easier for me to get from here to there?"

"Not so fast. I need some other information." Zephyr lunged up the other side of the draw, making Selby pay closer attention to riding. When they reached the top of the hill, she continued. "Do you think Rio is improving? I mean his memory, his general work habits?"

"Yeah. He does seem to be functioning better. Why?"

"Perhaps we should hire him full-time and have him live at the vineyard. He'd care for the horses, serve as security and take on more vineyard duties. I'm sure we could find enough work to make it a full-time job."

"And where would he live?"

"In your quarters." They pulled their horses up side-by-side and sat looking at each other. Hawk touched Tucker with his heels and walked the gelding around in a circle, reining in again beside Selby, facing the opposite direction. The maneuver seemed to give Hawk time to think about what he heard her say and to interpret what she really meant.

"You're throwing me out?"

"In a sense. You do have options, though." Her voice was thin and soft.

"And they are to live in my dilapidated farmhouse or....?" He raised his eyebrows, waiting patiently for her to get to the point.

"Or come live at LillyHill." Her eyes had a wide, frightened look.

A smile crept across his face. "Is that a proposal or a proposition?"

"I'm not sure." Selby looked away, listening to the thud of her heartbeat. A breeze lifted the hair around her face but did not cool her burning cheeks.

When she looked at him again, his grin was in full bloom. "What are the conditions?"

"Well, you know the situation," she said, with a nonchalant shrug. "A grandmother with a temper, a two-year-old child, and a Housekeeper from

Hell. Add a son who thinks I should marry the man he picked out, a gay truck-driving son and his lover, and forty acres of vineyard to run. Not your traditional family."

"Doesn't sound too bad," Hawk said, rubbing his chin with his thumb. "You're a pretty good cook. Walt thinks so, at least. But you're high maintenance; seems like I've had to take you to the emergency room quite often." They both smiled at this, sitting quietly, waiting for the other person to speak. Hawk gazed toward the west, watching the sun sink into the clouds forming along the Coast Range. Selby looked to the east across the rolling valley hills, once again seeing the agricultural plaid of vineyards, farms and fields she loved.

Hawk continued. "You'd have to put up with Walt's criticism of me. I know that bothers you, but that's just his way. I'm learning not to take it so seriously."

She nodded, asking, "How do you feel about becoming an instant parent?"

"Instant parent," he said softly. "You don't know...I've never told you...that...well, I probably will never be able to have children of my own. Mumps at the wrong time of life."

Selby's soft, sympathetic sound was lost in the breeze as Hawk spoke again. "I'll have to admit I've coveted Amanda at times...wishing she were mine. Are you saying that you want me to help raise her? To be more than Grandma's friend?"

"Yes. It's obvious that she adores you."

He smiled broadly, pleased at Selby's generous offer. "She's a handful, just like her grandmother."

"It doesn't—wouldn't—bother you that..."

"Stop right there." Hawk's smile was gone. "No, it doesn't bother me a bit. I love you. I don't care if you are a grandmother. You don't look like one and certainly don't act like one." He reached out to her, but the horses moved apart, seeking new patches of grass. Dismounting, he held Zephyr's reins as Selby slid from her saddle to the ground.

Embracing her, he kissed her tenderly. "What else do you have to offer?" he asked with an insinuating smile that showed the tip of his tongue.

"Well, I suppose I could share my king-sized bed with you. It's been very lonely lately."

"That sounds fair." He placed his hand on her cheek, running his thumb gently over her lips. "There is one condition, however," he said. "I want a long-term contract."

"Sounds good to me. What do you have in mind?"

"A Christmas wedding at LillyHill with all the weird friends and family we seem to have accumulated the past few months. And you haven't even met my best Navy buddy. Or my sister and her family." Hawk raised his eyebrows at her. "What strange friends and relatives do you have hidden away?"

"That's for me to know and you to find out," she smiled. They held each other gently, all the tension and bantering gone for the moment. "I think we're good together, don't you?"

"We're perfect."

EPILOGUE

Fifteen years later, on a late summer evening, Hawk and Selby relax on the verandah, listening to the rural sounds that softly fill the air. The bark of a dog is answered from an opposite hill. Crickets chirp, then hush as some winged thing silently swoops on the hunt.

This is the first time they have really been alone at LillyHill. Their "Bon Voyage Party" guests are gone, as is Bobbie after cleaning up the party debris. Amanda and three of her friends are off to Hawaii for two weeks before college starts. She will be a freshman at Stanford in the fall. Grandpa Richard and his new wife, Sybil—who is half his age—are the chaperones for this post-graduation gift. Gloria's four attempts at drying out at a rehab clinic failed. Her alcohol-weakened body finally gave up to pneumonia.

Fiona died at the age of seventy-two, after filling in the roll of traditional grandmother or great- aunt for Amanda. Their bonding had been slow and troublesome the first two years, but after that, the love that developed was deep and abiding.

Steve and Chris have a fleet of over one hundred transport units. After Chris finished his MBA, he became CEO of the fledgling company, which flourishes under his strong business acumen. Steve drove eighteen-wheelers until his back gave out. Now he just hangs around their trucks and the drivers, regaling them with stories about how it used to be when he and his dad drove.

Justin did not marry beautiful, brown-eyed Sara and set up his own landscape architecture business. Instead, he married Liam's youngest daughter, who is three years older, and manages the Walsh family landscaping and nursery business. They have three children. Liam married his long-time bookkeeper. They travel extensively through North America and Mexico in their upscale motorhome. The couple remains good friends with Hawk and Selby, seeing them each year at the annual grape harvest barbecue.

The Aznar family continues to serve LillyHill in various capacities. As the children grew and their children came along, there is always a member of the family to help in the vineyard and in the house. Rio became restless and wandered off with a group of migrant workers. The last the family heard, he is someplace in Texas.

LillyHill wines continue to hold a strong market share. The more experimental wines, under the Kestrel label, receive mixed reviews, but are still sampled with anticipation.

Hawk and Selby are holding hands. "This has been another vintage year for us, hasn't it?" Selby says, more to herself than Hawk.

"We've had fifteen vintage years as far as I'm concerned."

"I guess our relationship has been rather like the wine we grow."

"How so?" he asks, releasing her hand and placing his arm around her shoulders.

"Well, it started out with smoke and oak...."

Hawk chucked, saying, "With hints of rose petals and crushed pepper."

"We are very complex...."

"Well-rounded and aging like last year's Pinot Noir."

"With a long lingering finish?"

"A long, creamy finish...."

Selby cuddles up to Hawk and says, "I like a long, creamy finish."